ROUTLEDGE LIBRARY EDITIONS:
AUTOBIOGRAPHY

Volume 3

NARCISSUS AND THE INVENTION OF PERSONAL HISTORY

NARCISSUS AND THE INVENTION OF PERSONAL HISTORY

KENNETH J. KNOESPEL

Routledge
Taylor & Francis Group
LONDON AND NEW YORK

First published in 1985

This edition first published in 2016
by Routledge
2 Park Square, Milton Park, Abingdon, Oxon OX14 4RN

and by Routledge
711 Third Avenue, New York, NY 10017

Routledge is an imprint of the Taylor & Francis Group, an informa business

British Library Cataloguing in Publication Data
A catalogue record for this book is available from the British Library

ISBN: 978-1-138-93641-6 (Set)
ISBN: 978-1-315-67463-6 (Set) (ebk)
ISBN: 978-1-138-93990-5 (Volume 3) (hbk)
ISBN: 978-1-138-94202-8 (Volume 3) (pbk)
ISBN: 978-1-315-67380-6 (Volume 3) (ebk)

Publisher's Note
The publisher has gone to great lengths to ensure the quality of this reprint but points out that some imperfections in the original copies may be apparent.

Disclaimer
The publisher has made every effort to trace copyright holders and would welcome correspondence from those they have been unable to trace.

Narcissus

AND THE

INVENTION OF PERSONAL HISTORY

by

Kenneth J. Knoespel

GARLAND PUBLISHING, INC.
NEW YORK & LONDON
1985

Library of Congress Cataloging in Publication Data

Knoespel, Kenneth Jacob, 1947–
Narcissus and the invention of personal history.

(Garland publications in comparative literature)
Bibliography: p.
Includes index.
1. Ovid, 43 B.C.–17 or 18. Metamorphoses.
2. Ovid, 43 B.C.–17 or 18—Influence.
3. Narcissus (Greek mythology)—in literature.
4. Literature, Medieval—History and criticism.
5. Guillaume, de Lorris, fl. 1230. Roman de la Rose.
I. Title. II. Series.
PA6519.M9K58 1985 873'.01 84-48362
ISBN 0-8240-6713-4 (alk. paper)

The volumes in this series are printed on
acid-free, 250-year-life paper.

Printed in the United States of America

For

AMY *and* LINNEA

Contents

Introduction

This is a book about Echo and Narcissus and their reception in the Middle Ages. Unlike other work on Ovid's fable it is neither a theme study or a specialized discussion of the fable's meaning in the courtly love lyric. Rather it takes a different tack by looking at the way Ovid's fable encourages the invention of narrative strategies that would explain and finally transcend Narcissus' experience. For the Middle Ages as for Ovid's audience the story of Narcissus related an event that was understood as literally impossible. Together with the masterful narrative the very improbability of the story helps account for its popularity. The strange event is not simply retold but invites readers to wonder if it might happen and even more often to ask what is meant by the puzzling tale of deception and death and invent narratives that would establish its meaning.

For practical reasons I begin with the classical setting of the text. In order to understand how later texts use the fable it is necessary to have a detailed idea of the Latin story within its setting in the *Metamorphoses*. Study of the Latin fable does something more as well by reminding us that Ovid's narrative is not isolated but actually part of an account of Theban history. Awareness of this historical setting permits one to understand even more the shift that occurs when the fable is taken out of its setting and relocated by means of the Christian commentaries and mythographic handbooks. While I am interested in considering the allegorical significance medieval commentators found in Narcissus, I am even more concerned with how they control Ovid's text. The limits placed on the fable by the commentaries allow us to appreciate even more that narrative expansion of the fable in twelfth and thirteenth-century poetry. One text in particular occupies my attention in the final part of the study—the *Roman de la Rose*—because it is shaped by a thorough amplification of Ovid's fable involving narrative detail, physical allegory, and criticism of idealized notions of love. The *Roman* provides the most elaborate assembly of material from Ovid's text, commentaries, and early poetry. Here we see in detail how the fable works as a narrative encouraging the invention of a story that would at once use and transcend Narcissus in the creation of another history. The *Roman* does not simply criticize Narcissus but becomes a demonstration of how the fable could be used in descriptions of personal maturation.

Several ideas return frequently in the text and must be mentioned here. Implicit in my discussion is an interest in the ways fable is used as a means for knowledge. Here I am thinking not simply of moral knowledge but knowledge of physical nature as well. In both Ovid and the Middle Ages Narcissus and Echo must be thought of as a collection of physical information about visual and aural phenomena. The fable is not simply an example of the deceptive nature of such phenomena but provides a means for their study. For this reason the fable becomes a vehicle for *scientia*. The scientific nature of the fable helps account for the elaboration of the physical allegory of vision in the *Roman de la Rose*. The study reminds us that literature was part of an evolving scientific ideology. This was encouraged by medieval practice. Virgil and Ovid were carefully studied not only because they provided linguistic models but because they simultaneously supplied guidance in the comprehension of the physical universe. We must work hard to overcome the exclusive moral-theological frame given medieval literature by the nineteenth century.

While this study looks at a particular fable in detail it naturally raises questions about the study of the *Metamorphoses* as well. Several critical assumptions must be mentioned here. To think of the *Metamorphoses* as a source for later literature risks making the study of Ovid's work superficial. While Ovid's importance for literature is widely acknowledged it sometimes seems that the citation of references or the suggestion of an allusion is sufficient in itself. This is only a beginning. Because source studies often implicitly regard Ovid's work as a quarry for ornamentation rather than a text that can affect narrative at deeper levels, they only direct one to the surface of the fable under consideration. This is even more apparent when we remind ourselves how thoroughly medieval students learned to think of Ovid's fables not simply as plots but as a means of thinking about language itself.

Studies weighted with allegorical readings must also be approached with caution. The presence of an Ovidian fable does not mean that its meaning must automatically be sought in a commentary or even worse that one must search mythographic handbooks until an interpretation is found that seems to explain the use of fable. Such habits have especially been encouraged by modern iconographic studies. While the attention given to Ovidian commentary by art historians has influenced literary scholarship enormously, it has also drawn attention away from Ovid. Today we must look more carefully at Ovid's own texts rather than be swayed too quickly by iconographic or allegorical research. We cannot simply decode Ovidian references in poetry with a spectrum of allegorical possibilities. We must learn to anticipate ways that Ovid's Latin provides syntactical and narrative models. What has happened, of course, is that we are moving from a predominantly iconographic approach to Ovid to one that is increasingly rhetorical. Literary scholarship gains more by approaching Ovid's text not as a gallery of names filled with hidden meaning but as a collection of narratives that may structure other texts and provide psychological components illustrative of human experience. This is nowhere better seen than in the medieval reception of Echo and Narcissus.

While this study is eclectic it is fundamentally concerned with historical not theoretical scholarship. While I do not hesitate to look for structures in Ovid's version of early Theban history, consideration of their meaning takes me to Varro rather than Lévi-Strauss. While I write about the importance of language in the fable, my study takes me closer to Cicero than Derrida. This does not mean that either Lévi-Strauss or Derrida have been scorned. It means rather that orientation is sought within historical rather than theoretical terrain.

Reference to modern theory raises an even more obvious question. One cannot help but be aware of the psychoanalytic meaning the fable has generated and the bearing it has had on literary theory and analysis. In the course of my work people have often assumed that I was a minister to the wedding of Ovid and Lacan. This is not the case. To say this, however, does not mean that the study avoids psychology. On the contrary, I frequently consider the psychological questions raised by the fable. When I do so, however, it is from the vantage point of earlier theories of epistemology and faculty psychology. In part the study may be considered an inquiry into the psychological significance of Echo and Narcissus before Freud and Kohut. For this reason my work is accompanied by an implicit assumption that the study of the fable in medieval commentary and literature allows me to approach psychological ideas of an earlier period as well. Medieval, not modern, psychological theory provides the background for this study.

While each of the chapters may be read separately as essays,they are intended to complement each other. This will be particularly evident in the attention given to Echo in each chapter and in the discussion devoted to the part the fable plays in the generation of narrative.

Before turning to the first chapter, I would acknowledge some of the silent histories that play upon the text before the reader. This project was begun at the University of Chicago where it was guided by Michael Murrin, Paolo Cherchi, John Wallace, and Winthrop Wetherbee. Each contributed not only to my training in medieval and renaissance studies but to the meaning and pleasure of my work in Hyde Park. A one-year appointment as a Visiting Assistant Professor in the English Department at Chicago gave me the special fortune of thinking about Ovid with Ralph Johnson and Janel Mueller as well. The book was written in the English Department of the Georgia Institute of Technology where my work in the Program in Literature and Science has engendered even more theoretical attention to the function of fable and narrative in the assimilation of scientific discovery. For his special support and counsel in the preparation of this monograph I thank A. D. Van Nostrand.

The generosity of the Committee on Comparative Studies in Literature, University of Chicago, the Humanities Division of the University of Chicago, the Whiting Foundation, New York, and the Georgia Tech Foundation has also supported my work financially at different stages and I gratefully thank each institution.

Friends and colleagues, those who create the communities in which one lives and thinks, have also shaped this work. I would especially remember Michael Srigley, Alan Nagel, Tom and Patricia Jobe, Camilla Nillus, Elias Crim, and Stephen Kerce. I especially want to thank my friend Paul Gehl who read each chapter critically and who shared with me his knowledge and reverence for medieval Latin tradition.

Sharing all these histories with me have been those who are closest and it is to them I dedicate this book.

Kenneth J. Knoespel
Georgia Institute of Technology
November 20, 1984

Narcissus and the Invention of Personal History

CHAPTER ONE

The Language of Thebes

The story of Narcissus (*Met.* 3:339–512)[1] receives almost constant attention, yet its study is marked by curious limitations.[2] Classicists examine the episode in detail but have only begun to ask how the story fits into the narrative and thematic structure of Book III.[3] Textual, rather than narrative criticism, continues to dominate the study of the text.[4] Medieval and renaissance scholars, drawn to the moral function given the story in later periods, or interested in the imitation of the story in vernacular literature, look to Ovid as an *auctor* who permits access to other texts.[5] Literary theorists play Ovid against himself to find contradictions about reading and writing[6] and modernists from numerous disciplines probe the text to further their own commentary on narcissism.[7] That Narcissus can be perceived in such a manner is not surprising considering the ambiguous position of the *Metamorphoses* in literary study. Is it a mythological handbook, a collection of stories, or universal history?[8] More often than not it continues to be read as a dictionary of mythological figures where the apparently fixed authority of each may be consulted. The work remains what a famous edition in the fifteenth century called *The Bible of the Poets*.[9]

As classicists seek sources for Narcissus, as literary historians treat Narcissus as a source, and as theoreticians find Narcissus a source for psychological data, Ovid's own creation slips away. It is revealing that the most extensive thematic study of Narcissus devotes only a few pages to Ovid's text.[10] This points to a critical assumption that is seldom identified. By designating a text as a source, scholarship conveys an idea that it carries authority and stability and that its meaning is self-evident. The opposite is more correct. Texts called sources are often the ones that have the least hermeneutic stability. The history of their reception in later literature points in this direction.

Reception of the Narcissus story raises additional questions. Frequently reference to Narcissus does not mean reference to Ovid's text at all but reference to a general version or even interpretation of the story. The manipulation of the story in the Middle Ages and Renaissance through moral allegory determined perception of the fable. Today discussion of Narcissus continues to be shaped but now by the new allegories provided by psychoanalytic theory both in popular and more specialized forms.[11] If people think about Narcissus at all it is usually in an interpretive context. Few ever look at Ovid's story and challenge the abbreviated form of the fable which so often distorts Ovid's creation.

If the Narcissus text is infrequently studied by itself, it is even less often regarded in its narrative context. The fragmentation of the *Metamorphoses* started by medieval commentary and continued by nineteenth-century *Quellenforschung* has made it unusual to ask what relation the story has to Ovid's book of Theban stories.[12] Only recently have critics like Brooks Otis begun to consider how the story functions in its larger context.[13] It is even rarer that the larger chronological structure of the *Metamorphoses* is taken seriously and that we are reminded that Ovid's narrative approaches history.[14]

This essay emphasizes the importance of returning to Ovid's own text through commentary on the Narcissus episode and discussion of its function in Book III. Its approach is historical. This does not mean that psychology or problems of writing and speech raised by recent theoretical discussion are ignored. Historical study actually expands the importance of perception in the fable by showing the meticulous manner in which the carefully ordered narrative ironically conveys the instability of meaning. The question of meaning raised by the story is not restricted to the episode itself. By placing the story in its larger narrative setting we see that it articulates the problem of meaning in early Theban history and finally in history itself. This discussion is divided into three parts. Mythic and genealogical matter relevant to the episode comes first and is followed by close study of the narrative. Questions about the fable and history, though anticipated throughout, come last.

Myth and Genealogy

The mythical significance of the narcissus flower preceded its personification.[15] This is evident from the criticism of the story found in Pausanias and from the presence of the narcissus flower in the cyclical myths of Hera and Dionysus.[16] In the Hymn to Demeter, Persephone gathers narcissus flowers before she is seized and drawn into the underworld by Pluto.[17] The association of the flower and death in this myth is furthered by Greek funerary use of the flower.[18] Such custom, in turn, corresponds with the soporific or death-like effect attributed to the flower medicinally.[19] In antiquity the name of the flower in Greek itself conveyed its physical effect and its symbolic association with death.[20] An etymological link between the Greek words narcissus and narcotic was observed as early as Pliny.[21] The death-like qualities associated with the flower stand behind Strabo's report, in his first century A.D. guidebook, that Narcissus' monument was a place of silence.[22]

Greek poetry also associated the flower with Dionysus because of its beauty and probably because of the physical effect it could have on the body. In Sophocles' *Oedipus at Colonus*, a narcissus flower appears in a grove sacred to Dionysus.[23] The connection with Dionysus appears in later works as well. In Nonnus' work the *Dionysiaca*, from the fifth century A.D., the flower is special to Dionysus.[24]

The personification of the narcissus flower probably developed from folk stories. Two stories, mentioned in classical literature, deserve special attention. Conon, a contemporary of Ovid, tells that Narcissus caused the suicide of a certain Ameinias because he refused to love him.[25] When Narcissus looked into a spring he became "in a strange way his own lover." Later Narcissus, who believes he has been justly punished, kills himself. Pausanias' version, already mentioned above, is especially notable because it shows the effects of euhemeristic criticism.[26] After discounting the possibility that a person could actually fall in love with his own reflection, Pausanias tells a more reasonable version. After the death of his twin sister, Narcissus thinks he sees her image in a pool and drowns while trying to reach the figure in the water. In comparison with Ovid's developed narrative, these stories appear more like folktales or legends.[27] Tracking the Narcissus story within the matrix of Greek myth and legend calls attention to the distinction that must be made between myth and narrative in regard to Ovid's text. While Ovid alludes to cyclical myths such as Persephone in the story, it is for narrative not mythic considerations. The story that Ovid shapes around Narcissus is far more important than the underlying mythic ground.

The distinction between myth and narrative raises questions about Ovid's knowledge of mythography and its relation to his work. Although it appears as if the story of Narcissus in the *Metamorphoses* is Ovid's invention, we do not know for certain. His method of composition suggests that he probably knew other versions such as Conon's. Numerous handbooks and guides were available in Augustan Rome and textual criticism has shown that Ovid used some of them.[28] Because the stories of Echo and Narcissus play with the relation between reflected sound and light, the attention such phenomena receive in earlier poetic philosophy such as Lucretius may also play a limited role in Ovid's creation.[29] While there is no single version of Narcissus that is comparable to Ovid's story, Apollodorus' *Library* provides insight into Ovid's composition of the Theban material in Book III and his invention of Narcissus. Although we cannot say that Ovid knew the *Library*, as a work from the first century B.C. it gives us a glimpse of the kind of handbooks to which he had access.

In contrast to Apollodorus who follows the orthodox version of Cadmus and his offspring, Ovid rearranges family history by mixing children and grandchildren.[30] For example, the story of Actaeon, a grandson of Cadmus, comes before Semele, a daughter. This is not an oversight. By drawing the stories of Semele and Pentheus together, Ovid shapes a more dramatic relation between the violent origin of Bacchus (conceived through the annihilating intercourse of Zeus and Semele) and Bacchus' own subsequent destruction of Pentheus. The stories of Semele and Pentheus, however, are not simply juxtaposed. They are linked by the story of Narcissus. To regard the Narcissus episode as a digressive link does not diminish its importance. The realization that it does not appear in traditional accounts of Thebes gives special importance to its placement in Book III. In part the story solves a problem of time. If Semele and Pentheus were side by side the reader would move too quickly from the god's birth to his manifestation as a young man.

But there are more strategic reasons for such a link as well. The story establishes the reputation of Tiresias and gives authority to the warning he gives Pentheus about the young Bacchus. At the same time that it functions as narrative digression, it works rhetorically as an exemplum. Significantly, it works as a very special kind of exemplum, for instead of affirming something that is already known it becomes a vehicle for new knowledge about Tiresias and psychology. At the very beginning of the story we learn that what we are about to hear will make known "a new genus of insanity" (genus novitasque furoris, 350). The revelatory function of the episode, underscored by the text itself, is extremely important. By referring to a new category of thought at the beginning of the story, Ovid invites his auditors to substantiate its presence in his subsequent description. As we will see further on, what initially appears as a narrative digression becomes not only an exemplum but even a diagnostic commentary on the course of Theban history. At this point it is sufficient to emphasize the strategic location of the Narcissus episode, for such an awareness prepares us for the detailed explication of the episode to which we now turn.

Narrative

To facilitate analysis of the story, I have divided it into several parts: l) prologue, 339–58; 2) Echo, 359–69; 3) Echo and Narcissus, 370–401; 4) retribution and description of the pool, 402–12; 5) deception at pool, 413–31; 6) narrator's intervention, 432–36; 7) complaint, 437–73; 8) dissolution, 474–503; 9) conclusion, 504–10. Each will be considered in turn.

Prologue

Ovid's narrative evolves through a series of puzzles introduced in the prologue.[31] One involves Narcissus' origin, another an ironic reversal of the famous Delphic injunction to know thyself, and yet another the amplification and playful synthesis of details concerned with light and sound. By posing and then resolving such puzzles, Ovid displays remarkable synthetic ingenuity. Part of the fascination the story holds comes from these puzzle-like characteristics which the reader reexperiences each time he hears or reads the story.

The genealogy Ovid invents for Narcissus separates Narcissus from Cadmus' relatives and anticipates his own water-generated transformation into a flower. His mother, Liriope, is a nymph whose name Ovid has created from the Greek word lily, λείριον, the plant family to which the narcissus flower belongs.[32] His father is the river Cephisus and his rape of Liriope (which suggests the effects of a swollen river on its flowering banks) anticipates the importance of water as a deceptive agent throughout the story. Thus genealogy not only helps create a natural setting; it connects human genealogy with natural history and physics.

Ovid reverses the traditional authority of the Delphic oracle in Tiresias' prophecy about Narcissus' future. In contrast to the oracle (also of Theban origin) Narcissus will grow old only if he does not know himself—"si se non noverit" (348). Actually the subsequent narrative becomes a formal test and proof of Tiresias' ability. The reader need not wait, however, to the end of the story for such confirmation. By abbreviating the plot in the prologue, Ovid celebrates the seer's perspicacity and generates further interest in the story. Although Tiresias' words long appear *vana* (349) they are substantiated: "exitus illam/resque probat letique genus novitasque furoris" (350). [But what befell proved its truth—the event, the manner of his death, the strangeness of his infatuation.] In addition to the revelatory aspect of the episode conveyed in these lines, the discovery of this new kind of madness is amplified through its association with the ironic reversal of the Delphic oracle.

The prologue also graphically introduces the reader to the physical phenomena accompanying the story. When Narcissus was sixteen years old he attracted both young men and women but was so hardened with pride (*dura superbia*, 354) that they could not touch him.

> multi illum iuvenes, multae cupiere puellae;
> sed (fuit in tenera tam dura superbia forma)
> nulli illum iuvenes, nullae tetigere puellae. (353–55)

> [Many youths and many maidens desired him; but there was such hard pride in his slender body that no youth, no maiden, touched him.]

In Latin the lines are syntactically arranged to represent the idea they express. By partially mirroring line 355 in line 353 Ovid places before his audience the reflection of images so important in the story. But here too the differences are as important as the suggested reflection. *Nulli*, *nullae* negate *multi*, *multae* suggesting the vacuous nature of the reflected image and the placement of *superbia* between *cupiere* and *tetigere* suggests the frustration of desire. Several lines later he also anticipates the subsequent importance given to the reflection of sound.

> adspicit hunc trepidos agitantem in retia cervos
> vocalis nymphe, quae nec reticere loquenti
> nec prius ipsa loqui didicit, resonabilis Echo. (356–58)

> [Once as he was driving the frightened deer into his nets, a vociferous nymph, resounding Echo, who could neither keep quiet when others spoke nor speak until others had spoken, saw him.]

Vocalis and *resonabilis* not only call attention to Echo's speech but are arranged syntactically to graphically depict the phenomenon.

Echo

In the description of Echo Ovid explored the relation between speech and retribution. Echo has lost her capacity for normal speech because she kept Juno from interrupting Jove's sexual play with the nymphs (364–65). While the nymphs were under Jove in a sexual embrace, Echo would detain the goddess with talk so the nymphs could escape.

> cum deprendere posset
> sub Iove saepe suo nymphas in monte iacentis,

illa deam longo prudens sermone tenebat,
dum fugerent nymphae. (362–65)

[for often when she might have surprised the nymphs making love with Jove on the mountain-sides, Echo would cunningly engage the goddess in long conversation until the nymphs had escaped.]

Prudens, the adjective Ovid used to describe Echo's linguistic ability, emphasizes the skill with which she could wield her speech before she was punished and anticipates the skill she will need to manipulate her voice after it is altered. The characterization of her speech as drawn out, *longo sermone* (364), indicates how she could use speech as a barrier to keep the listener from action. It also anticipates the way her new speech can be used to detain Narcissus.

When Juno realizes she has been tricked, the punishment she gives corresponds to the manner in which she has been tricked.

postquam hoc Saturnia sensit,
"huius" ait "linguae, qua sum delusa, potestas
parva tibi dabitur vocisque brevissimus usus." (365–67)

[When Saturnia realized this, she said to her: "That tongue of yours, by which I have been tricked, will have its power curtailed and enjoy the briefest use of speech."]

While Echo was previously able to deceive Juno by engaging in lengthy conversation, she is now given only the most limited use of speech. But punishment does more than simply curtail Echo's ability for extended discourse. It also transforms her into the opposite of what she was before—a listener, capable only of reiterating what has already been said. Her ears rather than her tongue become her most crucial organ of communication.

Echo and Narcissus

The consequences of Echo's handicap are evident when she meets Narcissus for the first time. Unable to attract Narcissus to herself through amatory speech of her own, she must wait for him to speak. Their exchange—which provided a model for much "echo" poetry in the Renaissance—may be abbreviated to make their interplay even more obvious.[33]

Narcissus: ecquis adest?
Echo: adest!
Narcissus: Veni!
Echo: Veni!

Narcissus:	Quid me fugis?
Echo:	Quid me fugis?
Narcissus:	Huc coeamus!
Echo:	coeamus!
Narcissus:	Manus conplexibus aufer! ante emoriar quam sit tibi copia nostri!
Echo:	sit tibi copia nostri! (379–92)

[Narcissus:	Is anyone here?
Echo:	here!
Narcissus:	Come!
Echo:	Come!
Narcissus:	Why do you run from me?
Echo:	Why do you run from me?
Narcissus:	Here let us meet!
Echo:	Let us meet!
Narcissus:	Hands off! Embrace me not! May I die before I give you power o'er me!
Echo:	I give you power o'er me!]

Each gives the other's words different interpretation. *Coire* (387), the verb Narcissus uses to call Echo from the woods, means something different for each. For Narcissus it means simply 'come together'; for Echo it suggests that her desire for Narcissus will be fulfilled by sexual intercourse. The word *copia* also generates different meanings. While the word means copiousness, fullness, abundance, and certainly applies to speech, it also conveys a sexual meaning. While Narcissus will not share his sexual abundance with Echo, he gives her his verbal abundance without knowing it. The irony of these lines becomes stronger when considered with the parting exchange between them at the end of the story. Echo repeats Narcissus' final words showing that his earlier declaration, "'ante' ait 'emoriar, quam sit tibi copia nostri'" (391) are fulfilled. Only in death does Echo gain the *copia* of Narcissus by quite literally having the final word.

The initial success of Echo's speech is determined by Narcissus' ignorance. Echo is able to live only as long as she is misunderstood. Narcissus' inability to understand that he hears his own words certainly anticipates the difficulty he has in comprehending his own image.

What emerges from Ovid's account of Echo is the power of speech and the ability of Ovid's own written language to control that speech. Even though Echo is handicapped by Juno's punishment, her handicap paradoxically emphasizes the adaptability of speech. Ultimately it is the power of the written language, Ovid's own narrative, that emerges from the description of

Echo's language. By inventing a handicap for Echo, Ovid is able to overcome that handicap and make her speech intelligible through the manipulation of his own words.

Retribution and Description of the Pool

Narcissus is punished because he has deceived those attracted to him. When a young man Narcissus has held in contempt (*aliquis despectus*, 404) prays that he may love himself the way he has loved others (405), the landscape itself becomes the answer to the prayer and a place of retribution. The pool becomes a visual trap.

> fons erat inlimis, nitidis argenteus undis,
> quem neque pastores neque pastae monte capellae
> contigerant aliudve pecus, quem nulla volucris
> nec fera turbarat nec lapsus ab arbore ramus;
> gramen erat circa, quod proximus umor alebat,
> silvaque sole locum passura tepescere nullo. (407–12)

> [There was a clear pool with silvery bright water, to which no shepherd ever came, or she-goats feeding on the mountain-side, or any other cattle; which neither bird nor wild animal nor falling branch ever disturbed. Grass grew all around its edge, fed by the water, and a shady grove that would never let the sun to warm the spot.]

This is not the peaceful and abundant landscape of the *locus amoenus*.[34] It is a sterile setting that corresponds to the isolation of Narcissus. Many elements of the traditional pastoral scene are conspicuously absent. Here no shepherds ever come; here there are no female goats (a detail that emphasizes sexual isolation), no cattle, no birds, no boughs or raindrops to disturb the tranquillity of the pool. Instead the pool dominates the setting and attracts Narcissus. Described as *argenteus* (407) it appears as a silver mirror similar to those used in antiquity. The word *inlimis* (407) (related to *limis*: sidelong, askew, aslant, askance) even suggests the pool is a place where one cannot see straight.[35] The absence of sun and warmth further corresponds to the frigidity of the figure that enters this place.

Deception at Pool

Although Narcissus appears attracted to the pool because he is tired from hunting, there is a more profound affinity between the person and the place. As he approaches the pool, Ovid tells us, he is drawn to the water and the appearance of the place: "faciemque loci fontemque secutus," (414). Here the use of *facies* not only denotes appearance but hints at the face he is about to discover. As the water quenches his physical thirst it carries into his body an even more intense desire.

> dumque sitim sedare cupit, sitis altera crevit,
> dumque bibit, visae conreptus imagine formae
> spem sine corpore amat, corpus putat esse, quod unda est. (415–17)
>
> [While he tries to quench his thirst another thirst rises within him, and while he drinks he is overwhelmed by the form he sees. He loves an unsubstantial hope and believes that a body which is only water.]

Narcissus quite literally drinks from the image before him and is poisoned. Hearing his own voice return from the woods, he is described as someone *deceptus imagine vocis* (385). Here, *visae conreptus imagine formae* (416) does more than recall and amplify the earlier line. He is no longer simply deceived but seized by a reflection on the water's surface or a shadow which in Latin is associated with death.[36] Here Ovid probably alluded to the mythological association of the narcissus flower with Persephone.[37] There is no extended comparison, however. Ovid was attracted to the settings of such Greek stories for their potential in depicting subtle mental changes, not their ritual meaning.

Gradually the evolving narrative intensifies the confusion within Narcissus. Earlier when he was deceived by the rebounding image of his voice, Ovid described him as astonished, *stupet* (381). Now after he is seized by his reflection, Ovid emphasized his astonishment with a word of his own invention, *adstupet* (418). The addition of the preposition *ad* (meaning toward or near to) intensifies the meaning of *stupere* and indicates even more active involvement. His experience renders him senseless and he appears suspended as if he were a beautiful marble statue. By comparing Narcissus to a statue ("ut e Pario formatum marmore signum," 419), Ovid at once reminds us of Narcissus' remarkable beauty and his numbness. The comparison also depicts Narcissus' growing alienation from himself because as he looks into the water he becomes a spectator viewing his own image as an abstracted form.

> spectat humi positus geminum, sua lumina, sidus
> et dignos Baccho, dignos et Apolline crines
> inpubesque genas et eburnea colla decusque
> oris et in niveo mixtum candore ruborem
> cunctaque miratur, quibus est mirabilis ipse. (420–24)
>
> [Lying on the ground, he gazes at his eyes, twin stars, and his hair worthy of Bacchus, worthy of Apollo; at his smooth cheeks, his ivory neck, the

> splendor of his face, the blush mingled with snowy white: all things he admires for which he is himself admired.]

The reference to Bacchus is hardly coincidental. Besides appearing in a sequence of stories that include the mother and first victim of Bacchus, it points to the Dionysian setting of the narcissus flower.[38] The description of the statue is developed with great care as well. The blush that tinges the snowy white surface (it may literally describe a vein of different color in the marble) hints at the first sign of emotion in Narcissus. The eyes in particular are given special attention.

The equation of the eyes to stars suggests the radiant nature of vision appropriate for an extramission theory.[39] This is also suggested by the rational explanation given by the narrator for Narcissus' confusion. Narcissus, we learn, perceives the shadow of a rebounding image ("ista repercussae, quam cernis, imaginis umbra est:" 434). The word *repercussa* suggests the presence of an active ray repelled by the water and sent back to the eye. Although we cannot say that Ovid adhered strictly to an extramission theory, the very problem he portrayed argues for its serious consideration.

The relation between reflected sound and light, commonly associated in epistemological discussions in antiquity, lends itself to Ovid's ingenious narrative play with Echo and Narcissus. Here we may emphasize how ideas of reflection are also inherent in the psychological experience on which Ovid based his story. In antiquity the process of falling in love was conceived as an attraction to an image of the self seen in the retina of the beloved. In other words, falling in love with another was portrayed as falling in love with a reflection of oneself. Plato's *Phaedrus* offers a good account of this process. Contrary to impressions sometimes furthered by medievalists, Narcissus does not first become a means for analyzing love psychology in the Middle Ages. Such psychological matter is distinctly present in Ovid's story. It is simply treated differently here than it is within the later Platonic-Christian setting. Unlike Plato, and later Plotinus, Ovid did not use love psychology for the idealization of beauty but rather for further invention.[40] The importance attributed to vision in ancient love psychology and love's dependence on reflection offered Ovid a setting for a wonderful joke and remarkable pathos. The person whose beauty traps others, traps himself. Ovid was successful because the story suggests that if his audience took their ideas about vision and love seriously they would have to admit, at least for a moment, that someone could be entrapped by his own vision. For an audience that at least in part adhered to an extramission theory of vision, this optics of retribution would have been even more convincing.

Because Narcissus does not comprehend the phenomenon of reflection, he provokes himself into greater excitement and confusion. Syntax, shifting verb tense, and word play, all contribute to Ovid's depiction of visual provocation and entrapment.

> se cupit inprudens et, qui probat, ipse probatur,
> dumque petit, petitur pariterque accendit et ardet. (425–26)
>
> [Unwittingly he desires himself; he who he praises is himself and while he seeks, is sought; equally he kindles love and burns with love.]

Inprudens, related to *providere*, tells us of one who desires himself because he has no foresight. With imperfect vision the distinction between subject and object is obscured. The alternating active and passive verb forms effectively convey this. For a moment Ovid even appears to confuse the reader by making him uncertain whether the source of passion is Narcissus or the image. As earlier in the text we are quickly reminded that Narcissus is the author of his own confusion.

> inrita fallaci quotiens dedit oscula fonti!
> in mediis quotiens visum captantia collum
> bracchia mersit aquis nec se deprendit in illis! (427–29)
>
> [How often he gives encouraging kisses to the deceptive pool! How often he plunges his arms into the water trying to embrace the neck he sees unable to clasp himself in them!]

The kisses which are given in vain also incite. Even the syntax conveys the futility of plunging his arms into the water to grasp the reflected image. Falling between *visum* and *collum*, *captantia* (428) suggests the expectant arms thrust vainly into the water. The lines that end the section are really a simple recapitulation of the error already displayed in so many ways.

> quid videat, nescit, sed quod videt, uritur illo
> atque oculos idem, qui decipit, incitat error. (430–31)
>
> [What he sees he does not recognize; but what he sees he burns for, and the same delusion mocks and allures his eyes.]

The eyes of Narcissus have driven him into error.

Narrator's Intervention

The sudden sound of a voice addressing Narcissus reminds us once more of Ovid's sophisticated linguistic play.

credule, quid frustra simulacra fugacia captas?
quod petis, est nusquam; quod amas, avertere, perdes.
ista repercussae, quam cernis, imaginis umbra est:
nil habet ista sui: tecum venitque manetque
tecum discedet, si tu discedere possis. (432–36)

[O foolish boy, why vainly try to hold a fleeting image? What you seek is nowhere; turn away and you will lose what you desire. What you see is the shadow of a reflected image; it has no substance of its own. With you it comes, with you it stays, and it will go with you, if you can go.]

The intervention is remarkable because it follows a long period of silence. Up to this point description, not conversation, has dominated the narrative. Now the sudden presence of a voice makes us aware of this silence and urges us to listen with greater care. These lines do much more than stress the danger confronting Narcissus. They recreate a situation analogous to the one Narcissus finds himself in. As the narrator seeks to communicate with the figure he has brought to life on the page before him the separation between fiction and reality breaks down as it has for Narcissus. That the narrator does this while delivering a pseudo-scientific commentary on optics is wonderfully ironic.

A great part of the story's fascination lies in Ovid's ability to subtly translate Narcissus' unique psychological experience into others which are universally shared. Ovid provided access to Narcissus through commonly experienced physical phenomena, emotions based on love, and shared experience of narrative. Only Narcissus was so deceived in self-love, but has not everyone momentarily identified with a figure in a narrative and thus for an instant broken a boundary between reality and fantasy which commonly guides our sanity?

Complaint

Unable to extricate himself from his shadowy surroundings, Narcissus more and more becomes part of them.

non illum Cereris, non illum cura quietis
abstrahere inde potest, sed opaca fusus in herba
spectat inexpleto mendacem lumine formam
perque oculos perit ipse suos (437–40)

[No thought of food or rest can draw him from the spot; but, stretched on the shaded grass, he gazes on that false image with eyes that cannot look their fill and through his own eyes perishes.]

His lack of appetite (portrayed as a lack of interest in Ceres as a metonomy for food) is a symptom of his intense preoccupation. Indeed rather than consuming food, Narcissus consumes himself. The reference to Ceres again invites us to compare Narcissus with Persephone. This time, however, the reference is decidedly more humorous: just as Ceres could not remove Persephone from the realm of shadows, a grumbling stomach cannot draw Narcissus from his shadow.

When we first see Narcissus we learn of his *dura superbia* and his marble-like form. Now Narcissus becomes increasingly like the water in which he sees his image. *Fusus* (438) suggests that he is not simply outstretched in the grass but actually spread or poured out as a liquid. The more he peers into the watery pool the closer he comes to the landscape which finally absorbs him.

When Narcissus begins to speak his speech is a playful adaptation of a lover's complaint. As we follow the speech, however, it begins to function as an instrument for humor, irony, and finally self-discovery.

> paulumque levatus,
> ad circumstantes tendens sua bracchia silvas
> "ecquis, io silvae, crudelius" inquit "amavit?
> scitis enim et multis latebra opportuna fuistis.
> ecquem, cum vestrae tot agantur saecula vitae,
> qui sic tabuerit, longo meministis in aevo?
> et placet et video, sed, quod videoque placetque,
> non tamen invenio: tantus tenet error amantem!
> quoque magis doleam, nec nos mare separat ingens
> nec via nec montes nec clausis moenia portis:
> exigua prohibemur aqua!" (440–50)

> [Raising himself a little, and stretching his arms to the trees, he cries: "Did anyone, O ye woods, ever love more cruelly than I? You know, for you have been the convenient haunts of many lovers. Do you in the ages past, for your life is one of centuries, remember anyone who has been so consumed by suffering? What I see pleases me but what I see I cannot find: so far I am deluded by my love. And to make me suffer even more, no mighty ocean separates us, no long road, no mountain ranges, no city walls with close-shut gates; by a thin barrier of water we are kept apart.]

The address to the trees, the short rhetorical questions accentuating the misery of the lover, the natural and man-made barriers that obstruct human passions—all recall the lover's complaint expected in pastoral poetry. Here, however, the grandeur of the complaint collapses into a thin barrier of water and an emphasis on his unique experience. Read as an interjection by the narrator, the comment "tantus tenet error amantem!" (447) even undercuts the apparently serious complaint.

But Narcissus' speech is also more than a terribly ironic lover's complaint. It is an argument through which Narcissus discovers himself. Such dialectic is not unusual within pastoral poetry; Virgil's Second Eclogue is an example and the *Heroides* demonstrates Ovid's own adaptation of the form. What is special about Narcissus' complaint is the way Ovid can convincingly review what we already know but now through a more restricted perspective.

> quiquis es, huc exi! quid me, puer unice, fallis
> quove petitus abis? certe nec forma nec aetas
> est mea, quam fugias, et amarunt me quoque nymphae.
> spem mihi nescio quam vultu promittis amico,
> cumque ego porrexi tibi bracchia, porrigis ultro;
> cum risi, adrides; lacrimas quoque saepe notavi
> me lacrimante tuas; nutu quoque signa remittis
> et, quantum motu formosi suspicor oris,
> verba refers aures non pervenientia nostras.
> iste ego sum! sensi; nec mea fallit imago: (454–63)

> [Whoever you are, come out! O peerless youth why do you elude me? Where do you go when I try to reach you? Surely it is not my body or age that you avoid; even the nymphs have loved me. You give me hope with your friendly face and when I have stretched out my arms to you, you stretch yours too. When I have smiled, you smile back; and when I cry, I have often seen tears on your cheeks. You answer my gestures with your nod; and, I suspect from the movement of your beautiful lips that you answer my words as well, but the words do not reach my ears. I am he! I know it; my image no longer deceives me.]

The argument develops inductively from the question Narcissus has posed: "quid me, puer unice, fallis/quove petitus abis?" (454–55). Seeking an answer, he begins to list reasons for believing the figure is attracted to him. Visual evidence argues that the form seeks Narcissus. But then suddenly while describing the mouth, he realizes that the words do not reach his ears and that he is watching the visual image of his own speech. Paradoxically, through speech the absence of speech is discovered.

The intersection between vision and speech that takes place here is an elaboration of the phenomenological questions already raised by Echo and Narcissus. If we think of Ovid's narrative as shaping a puzzle-like configuration in which the erratic qualities of both sound and light are manipulated through different figures, the moment of self-recognition is the very center of the puzzle. What makes us so easily drawn into it are the faculties of vision, hearing, and speech, on which our existence depends and which are called into play when we read or listen to the text.[41] That Ovid is aware of this is shown by the narrator's intervention. The interaction between Echo and Narcissus, and between Narcissus and the image before him, is effective because we know how sound and light complement each other in the function of human faculties. Sound, usually as speech, functions as a corrective to the error that may accompany vision. Sound, however, though it may correct through speech or through its materialization in writing, may also obstruct and lead to error. In contrast to vision, which is subjective and restricted to the present, speech and writing can be objective and function as a mediator with the past and future. By discovering his own voice, Narcissus releases himself from the present. In the complaint that follows self-discovery, it is significant that he compares himself to past lovers. Speech and writing, not vision, create communities of men and place them in time.

The psychological matter contained in the story gives it a universal quality which in part accounts for its popularity. Its appeal, however, comes even more from the abnormal experience it portrays. We are drawn into the story because of Narcissus' confusion and because his confusion makes him transgress a boundary between love ordained by society and self-love which is taboo. Could such transgression ever take place? The story works effectively because such a question is possible. There is no profound philosophical truth in Ovid's text as such. There is only an intricate story that tempts us to look for truth.

The complaint also fulfills Tiresias' prophecy and seals Narcissus' fate.

> uror amore mei, flammas moveoque feroque.
> quid faciam? roger, anne rogem? quid deinde rogabo?
> quod cupio mecum est: inopem me copia fecit.
> o utinam a nostro secedere corpore possem!
> votum in amante novum: vellem, quod amamus, abesset!—
> iamque dolor vires adimit, nec tempora vitae
> longa meae superant, primoque exstinguor in aevo.
> nec mihi mors gravis est, posituro morte dolores:
> hic, qui diligitur, vellem diuturnior esset!
> nunc duo concordes anima moriemur in una. (464–73)

> [I burn with love for myself; I both kindle the flames and suffer them. What shall I do? Shall I be wooed or woo? Why woo at all? What I desire, I have; the very abundance of all I have makes me impoverished. Oh, that I might be parted from my own body! and, strange prayer for a lover, I wish that what I love were absent from me! And now grief is sapping my strength; but a brief space of life remains to me and I am cut off in my

> life's prime. Death is nothing to me, for in death I shall leave my troubles; I would he that is loved might live longer; but as it is, we two shall die together in one breath.]

When Narcissus was born, his mother asked if he would live to an old age (347). Here Narcissus answers the question himself: "nec tempora vitae/ longa meae superant, primoque exstinguor in aevo" (469–70). The reason for his early death is found in the paradox "inopem me copia fecit" (466). The line fits with his earlier renunciation of Echo: "'ante' ait 'emoriar quam sit tibi copia nostri'" (391) and shows him fulfilling his own self-prophecy. The line is ironic as well for at the same time that it shows him able to formulate a reason for his dissolution, it reveals that he is still unable to fathom giving himself to any other. Indeed no matter how great his self-knowledge he would not be able to separate himself from his image because such knowledge would continue to fulfill Tiresias' prophecy. On one level he is quite simply a victim of narrative. As a figure in a story subordinated to another story he can never extricate himself from the plot. No matter how great his knowledge it will never extend beyond his own story.

Dissolution

When Narcissus has finished speaking he again turns to the reflection of his own face to seek comfort. But this time Ovid describes him explicitly as being disturbed and unable to reason. He is *male sanus* (474), literally insane. His tears display his disturbed condition. When they drop into the pool they agitate both the image and the one who depends on it. Even more they establish a physical relationship between the two forms. The similes Ovid used show that Narcissus is quite literally being consumed or melting away. Unable to touch his image he desires to feed his miserable passion through his eyes (479). By comparing his body to ripened fruit, Ovid suggested that the food which feeds this passion is Narcissus himself. When he beats himself in grief and sees the bruises on his own body appear in the water his dissolution intensifies. Like wax exposed to heat, or frost to the sun, he is slowly altered. In both cases the similes point to his fluidity. Finally, enfeebled by love, so emptied by having given himself to the image in the water, he himself is transformed into liquid: "sic attenuatus amore/liquitur" (489–90). The form once loved by Echo literally flows away and is absorbed by the earth. As Echo repeats his final words, Ovid describes him as slowly seeping into the earth: "ille caput viridi fessum submisit in herba" (502). Narcissus does not become a flower abruptly; he is liquified. The description is far more natural than we think for it fits nicely with the account of his crying. His death becomes synonymous with his dissolving in tears.

CONCLUSION

Even at the very end Ovid made a playful distinction between the physical Narcissus and his image by providing two conclusions. In the first, Narcissus is received into the internal realm and continues to gaze at his image in the Stygian pool. Here too there is considerable irony for being in Hades means that Narcissus has become an *umbra*. In effect Ovid suggested that Narcissus—even as an *umbra*—continues looking at his *umbra*. The second conclusion, of course, tells of the dissolution of his body into the earth and reappearance as a flower to which he gives his name.

Prehistory

At the beginning of this study I showed how the Narcissus episode connects the stories of Semele and Pentheus. Subsequent discussion has considered some of the intricacies of this digression. It remains for us to consider the story in the broader context of Theban history.

The argument that there is no order in the *Metamorphoses* other than a superficial chronology has for the most part been abandoned.[42] Today, because of Brooks Otis's book, discussion tends to center on thematic order.[43] Although Otis has been criticized in numerous ways,[44] he has without question encouraged more serious study of Ovid's poem. Unfortunately much of this study does not include historical consideration of the work.

Preliminary work toward historical interpretation, however, has most carefully been put forward in a book largely ignored in English-speaking countries.[45] In *Struktur und Einheit*, Walter Ludwig suggests that the chronology of the *Metamorphoses* is not superficial but is in itself comparable to ancient models. Rather than approaching the work by the assessment of themes alone, he shows how the work may be divided into three major periods that relate to periods used by ancient historians. These periods—cosmological, mythical, and historical—correspond, for example, to divisions found in *De gente populi romani* by the Roman scholar Varro.[46]

The value of Ludwig's discussion is seen if we look more closely at the implications found in the mythical period. Ancient historians agreed that myths went back to a period before recorded history. They did not agree, however, on the meaning this material had for history. Some avoided it because they thought it impossible to order.[47] Others found order and sought parallels between mythical and historical matter.[48] What was difficult for the historian could offer a special challenge for the poet. Exactly because prehistory was unordered it permitted freedom to invent order. Greek poets showed how the *spatium mythicum* could become a special domain for the poet. Yet for them this realm usually remained separated chronologically from their own period. For Ovid, however, prehistory became connected with the present through a "carmen perpetuum" and is a place where invention may actually be a means of interpreting history.

The *Metamorphoses* is not simply a mythological handbook or a collection of stories but may also be considered as a unique attempt to write a continuous universal history using *fabulae*. One purpose of this universal history would have been to create, through interlocking *fabulae*, an account of Roman evolution from the beginning of time. Further study of the *Metamorphoses* may well show that the stories we find in the work do not exist as separate vignettes but actually are part of a larger account of the rhythmic evolution of the Greek city-state up to the emergence of Rome.[49]

The implications this vast undertaking has for the study of the Narcissus episode cannot be ignored. Ovid actually contributed to prehistory by the addition of Narcissus to the Theban material. Even more important is whether Ovid conveyed a particular attitude toward history through the reassembly of Theban genealogy. Specifically, does the story of Narcissus contribute to an interpretation of Theban history?

The story of Narcissus surely does more than add a digression to the Theban matter in Book III. By contributing to the book's special pastoral atmosphere, the story furthers our sense of remote antiquity. That the ancient past could be evoked by the portrayal of rural landscapes is obvious from the *Aeneid* and much other Augustan poetry. We need only look at the *Fasti* to find examples in the work of Ovid. What is noteworthy about the pastoral settings in Book III is their lack of tranquillity. Although they may at first suggest great peace, they actually become loci for violence.

When we survey the stories in Book III, we find that violation is a prerequisite to the foundation of Thebes and continues to accompany the Thebans. The land Cadmus comes to is virgin. The heifer that guides him and that gives her name to the land, Boeotia, has never felt the plow (10–11). When the martial dragon that lives in an ancient forest untouched by an axe (28) is disturbed, he destroys the Cadmeans. Later the destruction of the dragon is reason for the transformation of Cadmus and Harmonia into snakes (4: 572–73). Actaeon wanders into a remote vale and by accident penetrates Gargaphia, the sacred grove of Diana (156). For his error he is turned into a stag and destroyed. Tiresias interrupts snakes mating in a green forest (324) and becomes a woman. Pentheus violates the sacred rites of Cithaeron (702) and is destroyed.

The disruption of the Boeotian landscape is an expression of the tension between obedience and disobedience also found in the book. Although violation underlies Cadmus' actions and becomes explicit in the actions of his followers, Cadmus himself is able to found Thebes only because of his obedience to the gods. Actually the stories develop from Cadmus' obedience to Pentheus' disobedience. This development is also a movement from *ratio* to *furor*, and is manifest in the text as the difference between Pallas and Bacchus. Filled with *pietas* Cadmus is aided by Pallas (101–03), the goddess of wisdom, who tells him to sow the teeth of the recently slain dragon. In contrast to Cadmus, Pentheus is a *contemptor deorum* (514) and scorns Bacchus, the god of madness and frenzy. Unlike Cadmus who vanquished the dragon of Mars, Pentheus urges his followers to be more dragon-like (543–46). A book that begins with coherence unravels into incoherence.

The disruption in these stories may be explained mythographically by the appearance of Bacchus. His very Boeotian origin gives Ovid substantial reason for portraying disorder in Book III. The mythographic tradition stresses the madness Bacchus brought to his aunts, uncles, and cousins. What Ovid adds, however, accounts for this disorder in a way that goes beyond Bacchus. Order and disorder are portrayed as a manifestation of speech and the emergence of disorder is portrayed as a drift into incoherence. Throughout the book figures who threaten the gods are tricked by language or plagued by impediments to their speech. Speech, which is often the cause for the gods' revenge, is also the very faculty disrupted by retribution. Actaeon loses his speech because Diana fears she will be violated by his speaking of her. Semele is tricked by Juno's speech because Semele has placed excessive faith in her beauty. Pentheus refuses to listen to the warning of Tiresias and has no patience for Acoestes' twisted parable (692–93). Later he himself is not heard.

Just as the Narcissus story is unique within the Theban narrative, it is unique as a thematic expression of the faculties that cause violation. By portraying a new kind of passion, *novitas furoris* (350), Narcissus amplifies the disorientation pervading the entire pastoral sequence of Book III.

While we identify speech as an instrument of violation in Theban history, we need to stress the irony which underlies Ovid's historiography. As we saw in our discussion of Echo, the hierarchy that Ovid presented between the mortals and gods is actually a convenient fiction that permitted him to manifest his own control over language as an author. The traditional division between gods and mortals, between sublime and mundane, is levelled by the very speech that violates. The gods, like mortals, are vulnerable to harm inflicted by speech. It is this vulnerability to speech on the part of gods and mortals alike that creates much of the humor in the *Metamorphoses*. Yet, at the same time some of this comic element is diffused by the pathetic description of transformation that often includes the gradually increasing incoherence that accompanies the mutation of speech organs. Traditional hierarchy is gone but psychological intensity that comes from the description of incoherence takes its place. Indeed, this intensity does not stem from the portrayal of incoherence as much as from the resilient nature of speech—the adaptability of language. There is a sense in which the *Metamorphoses* is a history of speech like Joyce's *Ulysses*. Ovid delighted in altering voices or removing them altogether, often only to invent new ways for the figures to communicate their dilemma.

Ovid's manipulation of language, seen throughout this discussion, displays his rhetorical skill. Through this ability, Ovid's Theban figures receive psychological identity which allows them to live. It is wrong, however, to view Ovid's rhetoric only as a way to achieve an immediate effect and as lacking any larger purpose. As I have suggested, it is appropriate to view his depiction of Theban difficulties with speech within the dimension of history. Speech, as Cicero and others showed, could draw men together or bring chaos to their cities.[50] Ovid, however, is not Cicero, and the *gravitas* with which Cicero's own words trace the power of language on men is absent in Ovid. Instead, Ovid uses language to evoke an idea of speech as a necessary but chronically disruptive agent in history.

Ovid's emphasis on speech is also an ironic commentary on the material he inherited. This would have been even more apparent to Ovid's audience, which was more adept in mythography than we are. It is likely that they would have been even more immediately aware that speech, as well as Bacchus, is the real agent of change in Thebes. Ovid's emphasis on speech creates an unexpected intimacy with history. We may even wonder if Ovid's audience found irony in the recognition that Cadmus, as the man who tradition declared had taught the Greeks the use of letters, had sons and daughters plagued by problems with speech.[51] Not only did Cadmus found a troubled city; he gave his offspring a way of telling their troubles as well.

Narcissus is not found in earlier accounts of Thebes for the simple reason that he is not related to Cadmus. By including the Boeotian story of Narcissus in his account of Cadmean misfortune, Ovid succeeded in rewriting Theban history as it had been known traditionally. In part Narcissus functions as a digression to create an illusion of narrative time. But the story, so vividly related, also complements the pastoral and prehistoric atmosphere in Book III. For poets and teachers that came later Ovid not only invented a story, he discovered an event they could assimilate in their own histories.

CHAPTER TWO

Medieval Ovidian Commentary

Narcissus' place in Theban history was determined by Ovid's manipulation of traditional genealogy. Medieval commentary transposed the fable into a different framework, the new order of Christian history. Boeotia was no longer a geographical province visited by young men on the grand tour as in Ovid's time, but a remote location imagined in the course of learning Latin grammar and rhetoric and used for mapping human weakness. The fables which told of man's early history with irony and humor became instead tools for understanding the human spirit. While Ovid playfully showed us the limitations of language, language at the point of losing control, the commentaries considered that language—theirs as well as Ovid's—was a way to bring order and control. Ovid's skeptical tone was redirected. Rather than questioning the possibility of rational communication, the commentaries assumed that meaning was not only possible but had to be shared. Instead of mistrusting reason, the commentaries mistrusted the body. The problem of Thebes was no longer one of *ratio* and *furor*. Instead the city of Cadmus became a setting for Christian conflict between reason and sin, godliness and ungodliness, and, in regard to Narcissus in particular, a place to consider the struggle between the glory of God and the empty glory of the earth.

The five commentaries examined here belong to three different periods. The anonymous *Narrationes*, from the late classical period, comprises the earliest known commentary on the *Metamorphoses*. Because it was known in some form to all subsequent commentators, the work gives orientation essential to Ovid's early reception. The philosophical renaissance of the twelfth and thirteenth centuries provides ground for the *Allegoriae* of Arnulf of Orleans and the *Integumenta Ovidii* by John of Garland. These two related commentaries, regarded as authorities on Ovid's major poem at least until the fourteenth century, take us close to the interpretive methods taught in the rapidly developing schools. The two moralizations considered last, the

French *Ovide moralisé* and Pierre Bersuire's *Ovidius moralizatus*, come from the fourteenth century and demonstrate the growing interest in the application of Ovid's poem beyond the medieval schoolroom.

The commentaries, as well as what they tell us about Narcissus, occupy my attention for a simple reason. To be fully assessed, readings of individual fables must be placed in their larger interpretive context. The limited attention given the commentaries adds impetus for broader discussion as well. Although they are cited, they seldom become the subject of study themselves.[1] Until only recently even the chronology of these commentaries was uncertain.[2] Their significance has been even more difficult to determine. Earlier in the century E. K. Rand concluded that early commentary was moral and helped transform Ovid into a Christian theologian.[3] Recently Paule Demats and others have shown that Ovidian commentary is more intricate and sophisticated.[4] As we will see, while some of the earliest commentary was moral, it was also closely associated with philosophy. Before Ovid became a source of Biblical moralization he became an *auctor* who permitted his students to come closer to nature.

The early popularity of the Narcissus fable did not arise from the study of the *Metamorphoses* alone but depended on the separation of the fable from the larger work and its circulation in other versions. Its appearance as a decorative motif and its possible use in the pantomime repertoire in the Roman theater,[5] or its use as an exemplum in works by Plotinus[6] and Clement of Alexandria,[7] cannot depend on Ovid's text alone. Such varied application of the fable shows that in the late classical period the stories included in the *Metamorphoses* were not regarded as Ovid's inventions but as material belonging to a common heritage. For this reason the *Metamorphoses* must initially be regarded as an encyclopedic compendium.

Handbooks and mythographies from the late classical period indicate that this fabulous reservoir could be arranged differently. Hyginus, for example, includes Narcissus in his *Fabulae*,[8] while Fulgentius excludes the story from his *Mythologiae*.[9] These two works actually suggest different ways of dealing with mythographic material. Arranged according to psychological abstractions which may be traced to Hesiod,[10] Fulgentius' work stands behind a long tradition of commentary that includes Alberic of London's thirteenth-century treatise (also known as the Third Vatican Mythographer),[11] Natales Comes' *Mythologiae*, and even later handbooks such as H. J. Rose's *Greek Mythology*. Hyginus' *Fabulae*, on the other hand, organized according to principles of ancient history, may be related to the genealogical structure of the *Metamorphoses* and its Greek ancestors such as Apollodorus.[12] For the Latin West it is above all the *Metamorphoses* and its commentaries that make up this tradition. The texts considered here are part of this later tradition and lead in the Renaissance to intensified study of Ovid's major work as poetry as well as a mythographic encyclopedia arranged according to a schema of universal history.

Narrationes

The anonymous *Narrationes*, wrongly attributed to Lactantius in the Renaissance, is the earliest known commentary on the *Metamorphoses*. Although the earliest remaining version of the work comes from the ninth century, the renaissance editor Victor Giselinus refers to even earlier manuscripts which are now lost.[13] Brooks Otis has suggested a fifth-century origin.[14] Today the *Narrationes* is either ignored or viewed as little more than Latin prose versions of Ovid's fables, even though D. A. Slater and Brooks Otis showed this was not the case years ago.[15] D. C. Allen's remark that the *Narrationes* "was unknown to the Middle Ages" is a good example of the uncertainty that still surrounds the work.[16] Actually texts of the *Narrationes* appear with such regularity in the earliest manuscripts of the *Metamorphoses* that they were used earlier in the present century to establish the stemma of Ovid's work. They are cited in the two earliest Vatican Mythographies and are known by later commentators.[17] In the Renaissance they appear in major editions of the *Metamorphoses* as the prose *argumenta* that precede the actual text of the fable and for this reason can easily be overlooked by modern readers who assume they are simple prose summaries added by a renaissance editor.[18]

Although no *accessus* or introduction to the *Narrationes* remains, the glosses provide important information on the early study of Ovid's text. Set off in the margin or designated by rubrication within the text, the glosses would have functioned as a finding aid. In contrast to handbooks such as Hyginus, Fulgentius, and the Vatican Mythographies, which are relatively short and accessible, the *Metamorphoses*, with its verse moving without break from one fable to the next, would have been difficult to consult. The early addition of these glosses to Ovid's work may in part be explained by the need to facilitate access to the poem and even make Ovid's compilation appear more like handbooks such as Fulgentius' *Mythologiae*.

The glosses supplied more than a simple finding aid, however. As their title indicates they are *narrationes*, or an ordered prose rendition of fables written in verse. By retelling the fables in prose the author shows that he assumes rudimentary comprehension is a function of prose, not poetry. This pedagogical assumption stands behind the use of the *Narrationes* in later printed editions of the *Metamorphoses* as well and may even be compared to the prose reduction of a poetic text still used in *explication de texte*. By transforming *fabulae* into *narrationes* the author also shows that he finds value in the study of fable. This simple observation is important for it suggests that the work may be related to Macrobius' early defense of the fable as *narratio fabulosa*.[19] Although the glosses do not share Macrobius' interest in the selected use of fable in philosophical discourse they do demonstrate a belief in the potential value of all fables. For this reason the glosses anticipate the defense of the *narratio fabulosa* developed by William of Conches in the twelfth century.[20]

While the prose *Narrationes* aid the comprehension of fables, they are not a substitute for Ovid's verse. Instead, they provide an *expositio* from which to return to the poetic text.[21] As an *expositio* the prose version of the fable provides an abbreviated text useful in untangling Ovidian syntax. But at the same time that the prose gloss helps the student construe Ovid's Latin, it also controls the meaning emerging from the text. This is especially evident in what is left out of the prose account. Abbreviation deters the reader from straying among the sexual or pagan details of the fable. The gloss functions as a filter separating the valuable detail from the matter judged extraneous or potentially misleading.

The glosses of Echo and Narcissus appear fifth and sixth in the series of nine glosses devoted to Book III. To make them easier to consult we will look at them together.[22]

> Liriope Nympha ex amne Cephiso procreavit Narcissum, cui Teresias, Everi filius, omnia prospera responsọ pollicitus est, si pulchritundinis suae nullam habuisset notitiam. Hunc igitur Echo eum diligeret neque ullam viam potiendi inveniret, cura et sollicitudine iuvenis, quem extremis vocibus persequebatur fugientem, extabuit; eiusque reliquiae corporis in lapidem conversae sunt. quod ei incidit Iuonis ira, quia garrulitate sua eam saepe esset morata, ne Iuppiter in montibus persequens nymphas manifesto deprehendi posset. Fertur Echo, filia Iunonis, ob deformitatem montibus recondita, nequid eius praeter vocem inspici posset: quae tamen post obitum auditur.
>
> Narcissus autem supradictum ob nimiam crudelitatem, quam in Echo exhibuerat, Nemesis ultrix fastidientium in amorem sui impulit, ut non minore flamma ille exureretur. Qui cum ex assidua venatione fatigatus secundum fontem in opaco procubuisset et diutius ibi remoraretur, novissime extabuit, ita ut vita privaretur. Ex cuius reliquiis flos exstitit quem Naides Nymphae flentes casum fratris Narcissi nomine eius annotaverunt.
>
> [The nymph Liriope conceived Narcissus by the river Cephisus. Tiresias,

> the son of Everus, promised great prosperity to Narcissus if the boy did not pay any attention to his own beauty. Echo loved him but could find no way of possessing him. Because of her care and concern for the youth, who fled from her and whom she pursued to her last words, she perished. And what was left of her body was turned into stone. The anger of Juno was incited against Echo because she was often detained by Echo's speech. This prevented Jove, who was in the mountains chasing nymphs, from being captured red-handed. Echo, the daughter of Juno, is said to be hidden in the mountains because of her deformity so that nothing of her could be considered but her voice. Nonetheless, she is heard even after her death.]

> [Because of his great cruelty, mentioned above and revealed by Echo, Nemesis, avenger of those whom Narcissus loathed, caused him to love so that he was not inflamed by any lesser passion. Tired from continual hunting, Narcissus lay down in the shade near a fountain and remained there for a long time. He wasted away in a way not known before so that finally his life was lost. A flower grew from his remains which the Naiads, crying at the fate of their brother Narcissus, called by his name.]

Even though description, word play, and psychological detail are absent, the glosses are much more than simple summaries.

Genealogy is the primary interpretive method imposed on Ovid in the *Narrationes*. Genealogical information appears about Tiresias and Echo not found in Ovid. Tiresias is identified as the son of Everus; Echo is the daughter of Juno. The reference to Everus even indicates that Hyginus may have been consulted.[23] The identification of Echo as Juno's daughter shows that the author regards the fable as appropriate for physical interpretation or the identification of natural phenomena within fabulous matter. Juno or Hera was commonly associated with air and here Echo's physical dependence on her as a daughter emphasizes the relation between air and reflected sound. The repeated formulaic notation of ancestry shows that such a procedure was regarded as a means of bringing order just as it was in the genealogy of Apollodorus. In Book III, for example, Actaeon is "Aristaei et Autonoes filius"; Semele is "Cadmi et Harmoniae filia"; Pentheus is "Echionis et Agaves filius."[24] The presence of such genealogical information in Hyginus and Fulgentius shows that the author is following an established tradition. Ovid too worked with genealogy, as we saw in the first chapter. He was so familiar with family histories that he could imaginatively fasten and unfasten family bonds—manipulate genealogy—for his own poetic purpose. The *Narrationes* author, in contrast, works to maintain these bonds and regards genealogical structure as a form of knowledge.

The translation of Ovid's fable into prose also leads to other interpretations. In Ovid's text, Tiresias' prophecy is enigmatic and remains on the level of psychological abstraction. Narcissus will grow old *si se non noverit* (348). The question of what is meant by *nosse* creates tension that affects our engagement in the fable. The gloss, on the other hand, resolves Ovid's ambiguity by making Tiresias' prophecy specific. Narcissus will grow old if he does not pay attention to his own beauty. The emphasis on beauty corresponds to the stress on physical appearance also found in the exemplary use of Narcissus by Plotinus and Clement of Alexandria.

A distinctly Christian desire for specificity is also found in the vocabulary. Three words attract special attention: *diligere*, *amor sui*, and *privare*. The word choice simplifies the violent and charged words Ovid used to depict love and shows the gloss carries implicit moral significance.[25] A recent study of Latin and Greek words used to describe love in early Christianity suggests that the words *diligere* and *amor sui* can imply a distinction between love guided by reason and love dominated by emotion.[26] An example is found in Augustine's use of these two words in the well-known passage from *De civitate dei* (XIV:28) concerning two kinds of love.[27] While *diligere* does not convey a positive meaning by itself, it describes a love directed away from the self and thus a love with a potential for good. Ovid, who used both *amor sui* and *diligere* to describe Narcissus' love, made no such distinction. The author of the *Narrationes* does. *Diligere* indicates Echo's active love for Narcissus while *amor sui* designates Narcissus' love which is totally centered in himself. The use of *privare*, a word not used by Ovid, emphasizes even more the effect of Narcissus' love and shows that the author has drawn a moral from Narcissus' fate. In the gloss *privare* literally means to deprive or lose but it also suggests that Narcissus dies alienated or removed from others. Augustine's use of *privare* in his discussion of self-love in *De genesi ad litteram* (XI:15) ("sui amor privat sancta societate") indicates that the association of *amor sui* and *privare* in the *Narrationes* is not unique but fits early Christian accounts of self-love.[28]

The vocabulary, genealogical detail, and simplification of plot, show that the gloss is more than a prose translation. At the same time that it provides a version of the story that can help construe the grammatical structure of the text, it supplies a framework for interpretation.

The glosses provided a tool that was useful for a long time. Their inclusion in the first two Vatican Mythographies attests to the importance of the earlier work in the mythographic tradition which continued to develop parallel to Ovidian commentary.[29] They appear with such frequency in the first Vatican Mythography that we suspect the author has simply copied out *Narrationes* glosses suitable for his compendium. The absence of a gloss on Echo and Narcissus in Fulgentius may even be the reason for their presence in this early mythography. The second Vatican work (now generally attributed to Remigius of Auxerre) repeats entries from the first as well as adding others. It follows the first in joining the Narcissus and Echo glosses from the *Narrationes* into a single paragraph.

The ease with which glosses on the *Metamorphoses* could be included in other handbooks suggests that the simplified versions of Ovid's fables better represent contemporary understanding of Ovid's stories. It is likely that the Narcissus story was thought of according to its simplest plot structure, in glosses like those found in the *Narrationes*. Fable in its most rudimentary form was a simple narrative that could be expanded. For this reason a work like the *Narrationes* should not only be viewed as an abbreviated explication of fable or a narrative reduction of a larger work but as a promptbook for further elaboration.

The *Narrationes*' implicit identification of Ovid as a *mythographus* has considerable importance for the study of Ovid in the Middle Ages, for it helps explain why Ovid's other poetry receives attention before the *Metamorphoses*. In the early Middle Ages Ovid's major work was primarily seen as a work of scholarship in verse. It was not avoided because it dealt with pagan gods or sexual aberrations; these could be amply found in the *Ars amatoria* or the *Heroides*. It was approached with caution because it was viewed as a difficult work of scholarship. A means for making Ovid's major work accessible was first developed in the twelfth century and applied with such effect that the work became at once an encyclopedia and a philosophical work in verse.

Arnulf of Orleans

The *Allegoriae* on Ovid's *Metamorphoses* and the *accessus* that usually precedes it belong to a series of school texts on classical Latin authors undertaken by Arnulf of Orleans in the last quarter of the twelfth century.[30] Though his work includes a commentary on Lucan's *Pharsalia*, much of his study and teaching appear specifically devoted to Ovid.[31] Taken together his *accessus* and glosses on the *Ars amatoria*, *Remedia amoris*, *Fasti*, *Ex ponto*, *Tristia*, and the *Metamorphoses* represent a virtual Ovidian industry and what must be regarded as a substantial contribution to a century that Ludwig Traube called an *aetas Ovidiana*.[32] Since the *accessus* to the *Metamorphoses* provides the most elaborate indication of Arnulf's interpretive methods, I will consider it before the *Allegoriae*.

ACCESSUS

Although florilegia and imitations of the *Tristia* and the *Heroides* show that some of Ovid's poetry was rediscovered as early as the eleventh century, it is first with the formal *accessus* that we see the more methodological acceptance of Ovid into the school curriculum.[33] As the word indicates an *accessus* provides access to the study of a particular text. An *accessus* opened a work by reviewing the author's life—really an early example of biographical criticism—and by approaching the text itself with six standardized categories. These included a discussion of a work's 1) title, 2) subject, 3) use, 4) purpose, 5) the area of philosophy that supports the book, and 6) method. This format, which was widespread in twelfth and thirteenth-century commentaries on classical *auctores*, and which may be traced to Servius, appears in Arnulf's introduction to the *Metamorphoses*.[34]

The *accessus* to the *Metamorphoses* has special interest because it shows how effectively philosophical distinctions could order Ovid's elaborate collection of transformations, demonstrate its accessibility, and defend the continued study of the work as a register of natural phenomena. The philosophical discipline is especially evident in Arnulf's remarks on the poem's subject and intention. Logic provided an effective tool for simplifying a text filled with detail. After noting that Ovid's subject consists of transformation, Arnulf divides change into three broad logical categories: 1) natural transformations which involve the reformulation of matter (represented in the change of sperm into a child, or an egg into a chicken); 2) magical transformation which involves change in appearance but not in the innate spirit (Lycaon's transformation into a wolf and Io's into a heifer are identified as examples); 3) spiritual transformation which involves changes in the spirit but not in the body (such transformations specifically concern shifts between sanity and insanity and are illustrated by Agave and Autonoe, sisters who dismember Pentheus in a Dionysian rage).[35] The inclusion of sexual reproduction, not described in the poem, reminds us that Arnulf does not approach Ovid's text as self-contained but rather as a work useful in explaining fundamental principles in nature. The work is not simply a collection of plots, or a vehicle for moralizations, but also a storehouse of natural phenomena. The study of the *Metamorphoses* is also a study of physics.

The metaphoric vocabulary Arnulf uses to discuss natural transformation reflects the Platonic background behind Arnulf's attention to physical detail. Natural transformation involves the weaving or unweaving of elements.

> Naturalis est que fit per contexionem vel retexionem elementorum: per contexionem quando s. elementa coniunguntur ut de spermate fiat puer et de ovo pullus, per retexionem elementorum quando s. retexuntur et dissolvuntur elementa in quelibet corpora vel per ignem vel alio modo in pulverem redigendo (25).
>
> [Natural change pertains to the weaving and unweaving of elements. An example of such weaving is found in the conjugation of elements which create a child from sperm or a chicken from an egg. The unweaving of elements is found when elements are unwoven or dissolved into some kind of bodies either through fire or in some way by being ground into dust.]

Here the weaving together and taking apart of elements point to the generative and degenerative function of nature found in Chalcidius and his twelfth-century commentators and dramatically portrayed in works such as the *Cosmographia* by Bernard of Silvestris.[36] Arnulf's use of such philosophy remains limited, however, and certainly is not original. In contrast to Chartrian inquiry that gives special attention to primitive cosmology or the primordial chaos and the origin of the elements, Arnulf limits his observations to the sensible four-part elemental world.

Arnulf next sets up an even more logical schema for approaching transformation by using combinations of two abstractions—animate and inanimate bodies.

> Notandum est etiam quod mutatio fit de re animata ad rem animatam ut de Licaone homine in lupum, de animata in inanimatam ut de domo Baucidis in templum, de inanimata ad animatam ut de statua Pigmalionis in virginem. De animata ad inanimatam ut de dracone mutato in saxum. Mutatio igitur rerum est sua materia (25).
>
> [It must be understood that mutation may occur when something animate is transformed into something else which is animate as in Lycaon changed into a wolf; or something inanimate transformed into something animate as in Pygmalion's statue becoming a young girl; or something animate transformed into something inanimate as from a snake into a stone. Thus it is seen that the mutation of a thing takes place through its material nature.]

The use of such logical distinctions at the very beginning of a course on the *Metamorphoses* again reminds us that comprehension of *fabulae* did not intelligence in the heaven and profit by them, for the revolutions of our own simply concern grammar or the memorization of plots but involved knowing how to manipulate plot structure according to larger abstractions.

Particularly strategic application of logical categories is found in a gloss on the line that signaled Ovid's philosophical intent to the Middle Ages. The first line of the *Metamorphoses* initiates a physical account of genesis that could be accommodated to Christian ideas of nature only through careful interpretation.

> *Formas mutatas in nova corpora*, per naturam negatur hoc posse fieri quia res unius predicati nulla ratione efficitur res alterius predicati; sed sic legetur; quia forme qualitates sunt, corpora vero substancie, dummodo diceremus formas, mutari in corpora non posset fieri quia qualitates non mutantur in substanciam, sed fiat ipallage for. mu. in no. cor. idest corpora mutata in novas formas, quia circa corpora habent fieri diverse forme et cetere qualitates et actiones et passiones. Unde Aristotles: sola substancia susceptibilis est contrariorum secundum se (25–26).
>
> ['Forms changed into new bodies,' this statement is denied by nature because there is no reason for any object already predicated to affect another predicated object. Nevertheless the statement stands because 'form' refers to qualities and 'bodies' pertains to substance. Thus we say that it is not possible for 'forms' to be changed into 'bodies' because qualities are not changed into substance. Let 'forms changed into new bodies' rather refer to bodies changed into new forms because bodies may have a variety of forms, qualities, behaviors, and passions. For this reason Aristotle said: only the substance itself is susceptible to its own internal contradictions.]

The reference to Aristotle and the use of logical categories does not mean that Arnulf is approaching Ovid with tools taken directly from the study of the few Aristotelean works known at the time. The distinction made here could have been drawn from many works in the period.[37] The proto-Aristotelean distinctions together with the attention given to "the weaving and unweaving of elements" above all reflect Arnulf's relation to eclectic twelfth-century philosophy.

Discussion of the work's intention contains the single most important distinction made in the *accessus*. According to Arnulf Ovid's transformations would teach men about their erratic nature and urge modification and regulation of psychological instability. The argument, of course, is based on the assumption that a moral or pedagogical intent exists in the *Metamorphoses*. Lest a student fail to notice the moral significance of Ovid's work, Arnulf specifically calls attention to ethics in his comment on the kind of philosophy inherent in the poem.[38] The moral function of the work rests on an even more crucial distinction. Rather than representing actual physical alteration, Ovid's transformations pertain to human psychology.

> Intencio est de mutacione dicere, ut non intelligamus de mutacione que fit extrinsecus tantum in rebus corporeis bonis vel malis sed etiam de mutacione que fit intrisecus ut in anima, ut reducat nos ab errore ad cognitionem veri creatoris (25).
>
> [The purpose of the work is to discuss transformation so we may comprehend that transformation occurs not only externally in corporeal things, whether good or evil, but also occurs internally as in the mind. Knowledge of transformation would draw us away from error towards an awareness of our true creator.]

The importance of the observation cannot be overemphasized for it identifies not only an interpretive position in Arnulf's commentary but an assumption in subsequent commentary up through the Renaissance. The *Metamorphoses* displays *not* extrinsic or formal change but rather demonstrates changes in mental activity. Here for the first time we are invited to think of the *Metamorphoses* as a collection of psychological case histories. The importance of the logical distinction between extrinsic and intrinsic change or movement is further emphasized by the way Arnulf places it in a larger cosmological context.

> Duo sunt motus in anima unus rationalis alter irrationalis: rationalis est qui imitatur motum firmamenti, qui fit ab oriente in occidentem, et e contrario irrationalis est qui imitatur motum planetarum qui moventur contra firmamentum. Dedit enim deus anime rationem per quam reprimeret sensualitatem, sicut motus irrationalis VII planetarum per motum firmamenti reprimitur. Nos vero rationabilem motum more planetarum negligentes contra creatorem nostrum rapimur (25).
>
> [There are two kinds of motion in the mind, one rational and another irrational. Rational motion imitates the movement of the firmament which moves from east to west. Such movement is contrary to the irrational motion which imitates the movement of the planets which move contrary to the firmament. God gave man the power to reason so that he could rebuke his sensuality just as the irrational movement of the seven planets is rebuked by the movement of the firmament. But we, when we fail at rational motion, after the manner of the planets, are carried off away from our creator.]

Arnulf's ideas are related to Plato's observation in the *Timaeus* that "the god invented and gave us vision in order that we might observe the circuits of thought, which are akin to them, though ours be troubled and they are unperturbed."[39] It is even more directly related to William of Conches' gloss on the *Timaeus* passage.[40] More than a simple analogy stands behind the comparison between the mind and the movement of the heavens. The mind does not simply imitate the heavens but is permeated by the same principles. It is a microcosm linked inextricably to the macrocosm by bonds that only centuries later come to be replaced by natural law. The comparison reminds us too that for Arnulf the study of nature is intimately bound with the exploration of human psychology.

We must notice too that Arnulf's psychological argument also functions as a defense for the continued study of Ovid's fables. This is especially apparent if Arnulf's position is compared to Conrad of Hirsau's attack on Ovid's major work earlier in the century. Because they represented human deformation into stones, plants, beasts, and birds, and challenged scripture which said that man's form in God's image was perfect and not susceptible to change, the German doctor argued that the study of Ovid's transformations was dangerous.[41] The argument put forward by Arnulf countered such literal interpretation by stressing that any designated change refers to internal not external transformation.

A final remark on Ovid's intention shows that Arnulf's implicit defense of Ovid's fables stems from Platonic arguments that supported the use of such narratives in philosophical inquiry.

> Quod Ovidius videns vult nobis ostendere per *fabulosam narrationem* motum anime qui fit intrinsecus (25). (italics added)
>
> [Through fabulous narrative Ovid seeks to show us that motion of the mind which occurs internally.]

The reference to *fabulosa narratio* signals that the Macrobian argument for the philosophical potential in fabulous narrative stands behind Arnulf's explication of fable. In his commentary on the *Somnium Scipionis*, Macrobius distinguished between fables used for entertainment (fabula) and those suitable for education (fabula narratio).[42] This argument was known widely in the twelfth century and expanded by William of Conches to apply to all fables.[43] Arnulf's use of *fabulosae narrationes* confirms his interest in the sophisticated application of fable and his knowledge of the extra-Ovidian defense for such narratives.

As we look at the *accessus* we must notice that its comments are most significant for what they tell us about the study of Ovid in the classroom, not for their philosophical acumen. They are notes, not a theoretical discussion.

For this reason they help orient Ovidian research because they represent what anyone undertaking the study of the *Metamorphoses* in the late twelfth or early thirteenth century was expected to know.

Allegoriae

While the *accessus* provides an introduction to the study of the *Metamorphoses*, the *Allegoriae* established a vehicle for the more careful study of individual fables. Like the *Narrationes*, the *Allegoriae* should first be regarded as a pragmatic pedagogical device useful in guiding the formulation of sense and controlling evolving interpretation.[44]

Before looking at Arnulf's comments on Narcissus we must consider the interpretive categories underlying his investigation. At the beginning of each book he declares that he will explain fables allegorically, morally, and historically.[45] Allegory, as used here, denotes physical interpretation or the reduction of fables to an account of specific physical phenomena. The interpretation of Tiresias as the sexual force underlying the change of seasons (52) would be an example. Of course, interest in such physical interpretation corresponds to Arnulf's discussion of *materia* and natural transformation in the *accessus*.

Moral interpretation concerns lessons useful in regulating behavior and complements his earlier discussion of fable as representative of intrinsic or psychological change. That the ethical assumptions pervading the *accessus* also provide the dominant mode of interpretation in the *Allegoriae*, may be easily demonstrated with examples from Book III. Actaeon is a man who no longer wants to hunt and who is destroyed by his timidity (52). Semele is a woman who becomes lascivious because of drinking (52). Pentheus is seen as a man devoted to God and a man who struggles against the influence of wine on his countrymen (53). Because such interpretation is ultimately related to reason and the control of the senses, it really becomes a form of psychological analysis. This is characteristic of twelfth and and early thirteenth-century moralizations and distinguishes them from later moral commentaries related more directly to the Bible. We will have an opportunity to notice this even more below in the discussion of Bersuire.

Historical or euhemeristic interpretation, not touched upon in the *accessus*, discerns a specific historical event in certain fables which are also assumed to have a moral function. The incorporation of this interpretive mode shows that among its various functions the *Metamorphoses* continues to be approached as a text bearing historical impressions. For example, Arnulf views Cadmus as the historical founder of Thebes and also as the man who taught the Greek alphabet to the Phoenicians (51–52). By assigning Cadmus the role of an early teacher Arnulf demonstrates how the combination of letters can be a means for refuting falsehood and proclaiming truth. As a pedagogue instilled with the moral authority to teach, Cadmus is also an expression of the moral assumptions present in Arnulf's own profession as a teacher of grammar and rhetoric.

The gloss on Echo and Narcissus fits within the category of moral interpretation and quickly transforms the plot into a vehicle for abstraction that extends beyond a love story.

> Narcisus puer admodum pulcher multis placuit, et Echo. Quam quia contempsit, ea pre dolore latens mutata est in lapidem. Ipse postea videns umbram, sui captus amore, quia umbram obtinere non potuit, deficit pre dolore adeo quod in florem mutatus fuit. Re vera per Narcissum arroganciam accipere possumus, que multis placet si et illi placet arroganti. Per Echo hominis bonam famam, que arrogantem amaret et benedicendo extolleret nisi ipse se cunctis preferendo bonam famam contempneret. Quia igitur contempta fuit, latuit nichil boni dicendo de eo. Et mutata in lapidem dicitur quia in locis saxosis melius resonat echo quam alibi. Narcissus vero umbram suam dicitur amavisse quia excellenciam suam cunctis rebus pretulit. Unde deceptus deficiendo cum iam nullius haberetur momenti, mutatus est in florem id est in rem inutilem, quia cito evanuit ad modum floris.

> [Narcissus was an extremely beautiful boy who was pleasing to many, including Echo. Because he spurned her she was transformed into a stone through suffering. Narcissus, seeing his shadow, was captivated by love for himself and since he was not able to possess his shadow he perished through suffering and was even changed into a flower. Truly, by Narcissus we understand arrogance which is pleasing to many just as it is pleasing to those who are arrogant. By Echo we understand a person's good reputation, which loves the arrogant person and would extol that person through speech except that by preferring themselves to everything else, such persons scorn good reputation. Because Echo was spurned she said nothing good when speaking about him. It is said that she was changed into stone because an echo resounds in a stony place better than in others. It is said that Narcissus loved his shadow because he preferred his own excellence to all other things. Thus deceived and fading, since he was already considered worthless, he was changed into a flower, that is into something useless, because he vanished quickly like a flower.]

Arnulf has condensed the plot into three sentences and devoted the rest of the gloss to commentary. The commentary translates the plot into abstractions which subvert the desire to view the story as an account of an actual relationship. Arrogance and reputation replace Narcissus and Echo and together come to formulate a kind of moral equation. Just as Echo and Narcissus would complement each other, arrogance and reputation seem to belong together. But just as Echo and Narcissus frustrate each other's desires, so arrogance and reputation cancel each other's force.

The commentary does not simply correspond to the fable but fashions a parallel narrative which must be completed by the reader. Arnulf would have us think that it is logical for an arrogant person to be attracted to good things said about him. But beyond such a correlation Arnulf would also have us imagine arrogance so extreme that it would deny even reputation. Such arrogance not only destroys itself but even brings about the failure of reputation. The commentary transforms Ovid's story of desperate love into another narrative that would be concluded by the reader's own ability to apply the fable to his own experience. Arnulf does not really urge the reader to think about the fortune of Narcissus at all but would have him reason about the problematic nature of arrogance and reputation. In contrast to Ovid who explored the epistemological potential of the fable, Arnulf expands its ethical significance.

The ethical attention given the fable is most obvious through Echo's association with *bona fama*. At first the interpretation seems contradictory. How can a figure known for deception be associated with good reputation? To formulate an answer the reader must establish a synthesizing abstraction. Not only Echo but fame too deceives and remains virtually empty. Like visual reflection, *fama* is inherently untrustworthy and reflects whatever comes into its path. Both Echo and *fama* are promiscuous for they indiscriminately report anything—good or bad.

Naturally the correspondence between Echo and *bona fama* stems from their association with speech. Ovid's own text supplied Arnulf with ample detail for such an interpretation, for Echo's reputation as a talker is emphasized repeatedly. Her talk holds the attention of Juno and ultimately leads to her permanent reputation. Echo, the garrulous one, becomes a phenomenon of sound, an echo, the one who talks back. Though reputation is not specifically named in reference to Echo, Ovid gave his entire story to *Fama* (3.512) who in turn creates the reputation of Tiresias and amplifies the fate of Echo and Narcissus.[46]

To the twelfth-century reader Arnulf's gloss would have made Echo a manifestation of a figure familar to anyone who had studied Latin.[47] Virgil's personification of *Fama* in the *Aeneid* (4.173–96) was well known. Servius even suggests that Dido was ruined because she did not heed *Fama*.[48] Macrobius' argument on the futility of fame further indicates the kind of traditional authority behind Arnulf's reading.[49] And of course, for the danger inherent in earthly fame, the Bible itself supplied the final authority.

While the meaning given to Ovid's fable is not unexpected, the method used to attain this meaning deserves notice. Echo, *not* Narcissus, becomes the significant force behind Arnulf's interpretation. Once defined as *bona fama*, she effects the resolution of meaning. This is significant because it shows that a commentator like Arnulf does not invoke completely alien abstractions to engender meaning but will instead evoke them from the text if possible. Once the significant abstraction is drawn from a fable it supplies the conceptual framework with which to hermeneutically arrange the rest of the text. We will see further examples in the next commentary as well.

John of Garland

John of Garland's *Integumenta Ovidii*, composed in the last half of the thirteenth century, demonstrates how the phenomena assembled in Ovid's transformations expanded philosophical study.[50] While Arnulf shows how Ovid could be defended by philosophy and how individual fables had moral significance, John resolves fables into larger abstractions. The title and the cryptic philosophical matter accompanying the early glosses exemplify John's broader inquiry. Drawing upon twelfth-century Platonic matter which includes Arnulf's *accessus*, John's commentary represents an important rediscovery of transformation as a vital, ongoing force in creation. Since the work was written at a time when the Paris schools were turning to logic and away from the classical *auctores*, it must also be regarded as an animated defense of fables, not simply as vehicles for prosaic moral exempla, but as forms for abstract thought. The verse form of the *Integumenta*, which makes the text unique within Ovidian commentary, must also be seen as part of John's larger purpose. Composed in two hundred and sixty distichs, the work not only functioned as a pedagogical aid for the memorization of stories but signaled that they were intended for application and elaboration in other narratives. Looking at the work from our own vantage point we see that John fashioned an appreciated text. The *Integumenta* was included in a large number of manuscripts, usually interspersed with Arnulf's *Allegoriae*.[51] According to archival records, the commentary was present in a copy of the *Metamorphoses* chained to a lectern in the Sorbonne library at the end of the thirteenth century.[52] It was through the *Integumenta* and the *Allegoriae* that Dante studied Ovid's fables.[53]

The most obvious indication of John's philosophical interest is the title he gives his commentary. Although *Integumentum* was applied in diverse ways and cannot be strictly defined to fit all its usages, as Jeauneau has shown, certain features are generally recognized.[54] The term itself, which simply means a covering, came, especially in the twelfth century, to refer to the narrative surface of a fable which, when properly understood, could direct one to an underlying truth.[55] Although the term at times appears synonymous with allegory, it actually designates secular fable as a specific kind of narration. *Integumentum* thus is more specific than allegory, which continues to have broad application both in sacred and secular texts. As others have shown, *integumentum* shares much with Macrobius' early defense of *fabulosa narratio* as a narrative form suitable for use in philosophy.[56]

Rather than surveying twelfth-century use of *integumentum*, we may look at John's own explanation of the term in *Poetria Parisiana*.[57]

> Si narratio fuerit obscura, per fabulam appositam vel per appologum clarificetur, per Integumentum quod est veritas in specie fabule palliata.
>
> [If a whole narrative is obscure, it may be made plain by means of a suitable story or fable, through the device known as integument which is truth cloaked in the outward form of a story.]

The description reminds us that an integument cannot exist solely by itself but always has another more complicated narrative as referent. This is important for it shows that the study of integument requires the ability to discern relationships. It is important too that an integument is *not* an analytical explication of an obscure narrative but rather a narrative simplification of something more complex. In effect the figure functions as a philosophical exemplum which would give access to abstraction. Quite properly, the *integumentum* may be thought of as a kind of linguistic equation or framing device that permits the student to envision principles that otherwise might be cumbersome to recall or difficult to comprehend.

John's verses on Pentheus from the commentary provide an example of his own use of *integumentum*.[58]

> Auditum visumque notat tibi flebilis Ino,
>   Pars est Autonoe frontis imago prior.
> Est intellectus Semele, ratio per Agavem
>   Signatur, Pentheus est studiosus homo.
> Dilacerant et diminuunt auditus ocellus
>   Et ratio nec non cella suprema virum. (171–76)

> [Things heard and seen are brought to your attention by the weeping Ino. Autonoe stands for the imagination in the front of the head. Semele represents the intellect, Agave signifies reason. Pentheus is the learned man. Sounds and sights may disrupt and destroy, reason may be displaced as the brain's supreme component.]

In the fable of Pentheus' dismemberment by his family, John discovers a schema of faculty psychology.[59] Proper names brought together by the plot reveal themselves as a configuration of signs pertaining to the senses and reason. The distich form contributes to the process as well, for by knotting Ovid's text they ask the reader to untie its significance. Ino represents the visual and auditory data that enter the mind; Autonoe the *vis imaginativa* located in the cranium's center. Identified as *ratio*, Agave is an attribute of the intellect and also belongs to the central chamber or cell. The omission of memory, *vis memorativa*, usually included in such accounts, may even be intentional for its absence actively demonstrates its role. By drawing attention to the physical faculties involved in any action and their schematic relationship, the integument demonstrates the psycho-physiological framework which actually directs moral action. In effect the fable delineates the mechanism inherent in Arnulf's *motus intrinsicus* in greater detail. Fables not only describe psychological fluctuations between reason and irrationality but permit the comprehension of the psychological structure in which reason must operate.

John's gloss of the earliest portion of Ovid's creation account gives a substantial description of the philosophical assumptions behind his *integumenta*.

> Mundus ydealis fit mundus materialis
>   Constituens genesim principiique thesim.
> Ars et natura, typus et magus, a genitura
>   Mutant que pereunt, dant veneunt et emunt.
> Dicitur artificis mutatio quando recedit
>   A silva veteri flamma remota solo.
> Mutat natura generans dum defit in esse
>   Et genitum perdit res variare potens.
> Fit tipice, magice mutatio: vir leo factus
>   Est tipice, magice stat retro currit aqua. (9–18)

> [The ideal world becomes the material world, bringing forth the genesis and fount of all things. Art and Nature, Types and Magic—these give order to generation by accounting for transformation, dissolution, future events, and the setting forth of new things. It is said that the artful change takes place when the cosmic fire withdraws from *hyle*. It is said that nature's generation brings about change because being itself is transformed

> and that which is generated loses its generative power. By Types and Magic understand the following: The man who becomes a lion is an example of a type. Changing the direction of flowing water is an example of magic.]

One notices quickly that the riddling lines not only make up John's gloss of the early lines of the *Metamorphoses* but also function as his *accessus*. This is no coincidence. Where Arnulf applied categories (*natura, magica, spiritus*) to Ovid's transformations as useful external abstractions, John would have his reader understand that his categories (*ars, natura, typus, magus*) could be deduced from Ovid's work. More particularly he would have his audience notice that his distinctions describe moments of a creative process which originated in creation and which is still evolving. The perception of the active, dynamic quality of Ovid's work, which involves the reader in the transformations taking place both around and within him, is John's special contribution. The four categories not only order the text but engage the reader according to a larger cosmological schema. Considered together they comprise pairs representing the macrocosm and microcosm. *Ars* and *natura* describe the macrocosm; *typus* and *magus* the microcosm.

Man's potential for psychological development is signified in *typus*. It is significant that the change illustrated under this category is positive. To become a lion implies the generation of moral values, not their degeneration. This is different from Arnulf who used Lycaon as an example of degenerative mental (*spiritus*) change. Since *typus* is related to typology which perceives a preordered sequence in historical events, such change is also a manifestation of divine plan. We are not, I think, primarily intended to think of types in a Biblical context here.[60] Instead the study of fable provides a complementary secular vehicle for the comprehension of divine order. Just as the study of God's presence in history could be discerned through Biblical types, God's presence in nature could be known through the study of *integumenta*.[61] By signifying an array of natural change already known to God fables direct one to an understanding of principles always at work in nature and in man. Ultimately knowledge drawn from fabulous types would teach one about God's laws and draw one toward spiritual transformation.

While types represent psychological or spiritual change, *Magus* designates man's ability to work changes on nature. John's cryptic example of stopping water or making it flow upstream probably refers abstractly to man's power to manipulate elements rather than any specific engineering feat.

Ars and *natura* denote categories of change especially descriptive of the macrocosm. Procreation and death are within the sphere of *natura*. *Ars*, illustrated by the operation of the *flamma remota* on *silva*, refers to the divine animation of the primordial chaos. The inclusion of such an example shows John working in the setting of early Platonic discussions in which primordial chaos was named and sometimes personified as *silva* or *hyle*.[62] According to such discussions the initial act of creation involved the separation of basic elements from cruder matter. Here John's use of *flamma* pertains to the *ignis artifex* or divine presence which left its ordering imprint on *silva*.

For Arnulf the relation between the macrocosm and microcosm was evoked in his discussion of cosmic motion (*motus extrinsicus*) and the power it had to inform man's own psychological stability based on reason (*motus intrinsicus*). John's investigation urges an even more detailed realization of the intersection of the macrocosm and microcosm in regard to creation itself. Man is not utterly divorced from God's creative force but also has within him vestiges of divine ability. For man this creative power is manifest through his power to effect magical transformations in nature. The relation between the supernatural and natural, which informs the categories assigned to transformation, also stands behind John's strategic verses on Prometheus, the first fable in Ovid's work. Within the structure of the *Metamorphoses*, Prometheus marks Ovid's own demarcation between cosmological and human history. By locating his interpretive lesson just here, John emphasizes that man's role is to comprehend his place in the macrocosm.

> De terra figulum finxisse Promethea primo.
>   Fabula fert hominem. Res clamidata latet.
> Est sermo fictus tibi fabula vel quia celat,
>   Vel quia delectat, vel quod utrumque facit.
> Res est historia magnatibus ordine gesta
>   Scriptaque venturis commemoranda viris.
> Clauditur historico sermo velamine versus,
>   Ad populi mores allegoria tibi.
> Fabula voce tenus tibi palliat integumentum,
>   Clausa doctrine res tibi vera latet.
> Fabula clave patet, tua nam doctrina, Prometheu,
>   Informasse prius fertur in arte rudes.
> Celitus affirmas lucem rationis oriri
>   Celestesque plagas a ratione peti.   (53–66)

> [Prometheus was the first to fashion a small figure from earth. The fable conveys the origin of man. It holds something hidden. The language of the fable is false because it conceals or entertains or because it does both at once. History concerns the ordered actions of great men, written to remind coming generations of the past. These verses are covered with a

> cloak of historical writing and contain an allegory about the habits of men. Reader, an integument is cloaked with the voice of a fable, and the matter which is concealed hides a valuable lesson. With a key the fable is opened. For it is said, Prometheus, that by your teaching man was told how to make raw materials into an art. You maintain that the light of reason arises from a celestial source and you affirm that the celestial regions are sought by reason.]

In effect the verses provide a pedagogical test of the reader's interpretive skill. The lesson takes place in stages. First the student is given a condensed, literal version of the fable and reminded that behind the overtly false language of fable one may expect hidden meaning. One comprehends this meaning either through moral allegory which is related to history or through *integumenta* which pertain to *vera doctrina* or philosophical truth. The brief discussion suggests that the difference between allegory and *integumentum* is really a distinction between genre. Allegory appears appropriate to historical poems; *integumentum* applicable to shorter narratives such as fables. Having made these distinctions, John returns to Prometheus and hints that its integument teaches one first to think about man's own creative ability to transform raw matter into art and then to comprehend that this capacity is a manifestation of reason which comes from the heavens.

The fable points to the intersection of the microcosm and macrocosm. It is no coincidence that John uses an integument on human creativity to present a survey of interpretive procedure applied to the creation. Just as the integument is an object which begs to be opened up, so all creation is an object which asks to be given meaning through the agency of human reason. Interpretation reverses and also extends creation by once again making the material object ideal.

Knowledge of John's interpretive principles permits us to look with more precision at the distichs given Echo and Narcissus.

> Narcisus puer est cupidus quem gloria rerum
> Fallit que florent que velut umbra fluunt.
> Dicitur in silvis Echo regnare quod illic
> Aer inclusus verba referre solet. (163–66)

> [Narcissus was a greedy boy whom earthly glories deceived which bloom and flow away as shadows do. Echo is said to reign in the forest because the air enclosed there is accustomed to return words.]

As in the other *integumenta* the vocabulary supplies signs from which the fable can be given interpretive direction. This is especially true of the abbreviated rendition of Narcissus. *Puer*, *cupidus*, *fallere*, *florere*, *umbra*, *fluere*—each recalls a motif in the fable. Echo, however, is not treated in the same way, but retains a more abstract identity. To understand why we must once again look at earlier commentary.

In contrast to Arnulf, John separates *fama* or *gloria* from Echo and thereby stresses the physical source of Narcissus' deception. *Gloria rerum* conveys a negative meaning more directly than Arnulf's *bona fama*. As a result John's interpretation of Narcissus becomes a warning against being enveloped by the material world without any awareness of how ideas may provide guidance. But something even more significant occurs as a result of this shift. By distancing reputation from Echo, John is able to give special attention to the physical phenomena associated with Echo. Her hermeneutical significance in the fable initially depends on her appearance as a personification. Such personification, which supplies a logical basis for Ovid's etiological story, offered a convenient departure point for subsequent explication. Ovid's own rhetorical interest in providing origins for the natural world contributes substantially to his medieval reputation. The *integumentum* works with more than etymology, however. The reference to *aer* recalls Juno, the goddess traditionally associated with air. Within the context of Ovidian commentary this in turn recalls the reference in the *Narrationes* to Echo as the daughter of Juno. Thus the distich works both as a mechanism to as- of Juno. Thus the distich works both as a mechanism to associate fabulous figures and as a formula establishing sound's dependence on air.

We have already mentioned the references to faculty psychology that appear in John's gloss of Pentheus. Here we may observe how applicable such a schema is to Narcissus and Echo as well. The reference to *visus* and *auditus* in a gloss that follows Echo and Narcissus actually invites correlation between the fables. If Ino, Semele, and Agave represent the internal senses instrumental in psychological analysis, Echo and Narcissus provide examples of the potentially deceptive sensual phenomena to be analyzed and point to the care which is essential in attempting to derive moral meaning from physical or textbook phenomena. The empirical interest John shows in his physical interpretation of Echo certainly fits with his delineation of human psychology, and the reflection of light and sound is precisely the kind of phenomenon that the *intellectus* would be called upon to deal with. The complementary function of fables within commentaries suggested by their treatment of common psychological matter deserves more attention. We are accustomed to expect a synthesis of fable in poetry but still think of mythographic works as rigid taxonomic systems from which meaning can be drawn only on an individual basis. It is quite probable that many more interrelations than have been recognized exist in commentaries. The meaning given to a particular fable in a gloss may not only be applicable to another text but may actually help define detail present in other glosses. A more precise understanding of how such complementarity works in commentary may help us understand how fabulous matter is assembled in poetry.

When we look at the interpretations given to Echo and Narcissus by Arnulf and John, we see that it is Echo, not Narcissus, who attracts special attention. In the case of Arnulf it is specifically Echo who provides the abstraction used to interpret Narcissus. For Arnulf Echo is the *bona fama* which complements arrogance. For John Echo is more immediately distinguished as a transitory physical phenomenon that demonstrates the association between air and speech. What is significant is that in each commentary Echo provides important access to the meaning of the fable. Pentheus has already shown us how one fable could be used to elaborate another; Echo and Narcissus show how one fable could supply abstractions useful in initiating commentary on itself.

In the first chapter I mentioned how discussion of reflected light and sound occurs together in ancient philosophy. This correlation continues in twelfth and thirteenth-century philosophy. Such coupling of natural phenomena shows that there was an unchallenged assumption that knowledge of one could lead to better understanding of the other. The importance given to Echo does not mean that the physics of light which so pervades Ovid's description of Narcissus was ignored; rather it suggests that aural phenomena are a means for investigating vision. The reason for this is quite simple. Echo personifies not only reverberation but speech. For both John and Arnulf this figure signifies the manner in which one's own reason may be acknowledged through *verba* or *bona fama*. In both works speech testifies to one's moral condition. Echo reminds the reader that speech is always imperfect and always potentially deceptive. For this reason Echo also reminds the reader to think of speech as a rational, corrective tool. Echo's curious association with reason will be considered in the next chapter in the setting of Provençal poetry and the *Roman de la Rose*.

Ovide Moralisé

The popularity of the anonymous *Ovide moralisé* is evidence of the pedagogical success of the earlier commentaries in the thirteenth-century schools.[63] This success is evident in borrowings but is even more manifest in the undertaking itself.[64] The earlier works taught later generations how the study of the *Metamorphoses* could be defended. Objections such as those made by

Conrad of Hirsau that Ovid's work contained heretical matter because it described radical alterations in the human form made in God's image could be countered by insisting that internal, not external change was signified by Ovid's work.[65] This psychological argument made it possible not only to defend Ovid's major work, but to draw it closer to the Bible itself and put it in a form that would permit its use in the preparation of sermons. Instead of providing abstractions to investigate the material world and the aberrations of human psychology, fables in the moral commentaries become examples of lessons already found in scripture. Theology, not philosophy, comes to frame the application of fable. The Bible, not the *Timaeus*, becomes the authority that guides the interpretation of Ovid.

It is quite common among scholars to view the change from philosophy to theology as a sign of rigidity. In contrast to the subtle use of fable as an instrument that permitted access to the world, the *Ovide moralisé* with its 36,092 lines has appeared as a tedious, pedagogical machine. The work as a whole, however, deserves to be studied carefully, as Paule Demats has shown. While the earlier commentaries search the *Metamorphoses* for a code that will make creation more accessible to rational investigation, the moralizations make another contribution. They rediscover the narrative integrity of Ovid's text and the relation between fable and history. This happens in several ways. By being drawn closer to the Bible, Ovid's work becomes an expression of biblical history, and the fables come to signify the degeneration as well as restoration of mankind. The narrative itself also takes on an importance not emphasized in commentaries since the *Narrationes*. This is most obvious in the careful attention given to the fables. Almost half of the *Ovide moralisé* is devoted to retelling the Latin story in French. Expansion rather than abbreviation is encouraged. Such expansion involves more than the amplification of narrative. It also becomes a means of approaching biblical history through story.

The rhetorical proem to the *Ovide moralisé* (I.1–70) makes it immediately apparent that theology, not philosophy, provides the setting for the author's work. Unlike the earlier commentaries there is no formal discussion of transformation. Since scripture shows that everything is for man's edification, study of the *Metamorphoses* may be undertaken without fear. The proverb which begins the work makes this evident.

> Se l'escripture ne me ment,
> Tout est pour nostre enseignement
> Quanqu'il a es livres escript,
> Soient bon ou mal li escript. (I.1–4)

[If that which is written does not lie
Everything written in books can edify
Be it either good or bad.]

The very ability to undertake the project is ascribed to God; "En Dieu me fi de cest afaire" (26). With humility the author will uncover the meaning Ovid has hidden in his overtly false fables. For the sake of brevity he will choose only those stories which are "bone et profitables" (54). Above all the author declares his desire to be corrected if his remarks do not accord with the teachings of the church.

An example of the author's reluctance to use Ovid's text for philosophical discussion appears in his comment on the first lines of the *Metamorphoses*, "in nova fert animus mutastas dicere formas/corpora" (1–2). Rather than make logical distinctions as Arnulf did, the author simply places a warning before his reader.

'Les cors qui en formes noveles
Furent meuz,' mes teulz faveles
Ne doivent audience avoir:
Homs raisonables puet savoir
Que bien dist, ce croi, li autours,
Quar, ançois que li Creatours
Creast le monde, il n'iert encors
Ne ne pooit estre nul cors
Qui nove forme receüst.
Quel cors iert il dont Dieus deüst
Forme traire au comencement?
Il n'iert riens fors lui seulement,
Qui en sa devine pensee
Avoit toute forme pensee
Tele come il la donneroit
Au cors, que de noient feroit,
Sans aïde de nulle rien,
Sans point de present mairien. (1.79–96)

['Bodies changed into new forms'—such sayings deserve no attention. A reasonable man is able to recognize, I believe, that the author speaks correctly for, before the creator created the world, there was not yet, nor could there be, any body which could receive a new form. What body was there from which God was supposed to produce form in the beginning? There was nothing except him alone who, in his divine thought, had conceived all form just as he would give it to the body, which he would make from nothing, with no help, without any matter present.]

The passage serves as a reminder of how attitudes toward the *Metamorphoses* had changed during the previous century. Two centuries before such an objection was enough to question whether Ovid's work should be studied at all. For this author it is a warning not to become entangled in Ovid without the guidance of scripture.

Although it is necessary for the sake of discussion to distinguish between the French version of Echo and Narcissus and its commentary, it must be made with knowledge that both provide interpretations of the fable. The narrative interpretation is apparent in the relocation of the Latin fable into a contemporary setting. One by one the author shifts the fable's main figures from a Greek pastoral setting to French society where they come close to being romance characters. This is important because it shows the author thinks of Ovid's figures as more than vehicles for abstraction. Rather than a water nymph ravished by the river Cephisus, Liriope appears as "une dame de grant parage" (3.1301). Her identity as a mother concerned about the future of her beautiful son is stressed more than in Ovid. Instead of a sixteen year old Theban boy, Narcissus is a handsome twenty-one year old gentleman, a "vallet de bele faiture" (3.1382). Echo, in turn, is identified as a reasonable young girl; "Echo, pucele raisonnable" (3.1343). Pagan references are filtered out. For example, the comparison of Narcissus to Bacchus and Apollo is not found in the French work. While a spurned young man prays to Nemesis for justice in Ovid's text, the sex of the young person is not identified by our author and God, not Nemesis, receives the prayer (3.1533–34).

But while certain details are removed from Ovid's story, other elements are made more specific or given special amplification. Echo's identification as a reasonable young girl was mentioned above. The author emphasizes this by giving specific description of her ability to manipulate language. The description of her as a "pucele raisonnable" (3.1343) is drawn from Ovid's notation of her as *resonabilis Echo* (3.358). Here Ovid's resounding Echo seems translated as reasonable Echo. Three times Echo's ability to speak is described by the word "araisonner" (3.1395, 1396, 1403) which usually means 'to speak or address.' The French word, however, taken from the medieval Latin word *adrationare*, reveals how closely related speech is to reason.[66] Of course the importance given to Echo recalls her special role in Arnulf and John. In fact her association with reasonable speech here may help explain why she was attributed such importance previously. In the next chapter we will see even further evidence of her rational identity. The important thing to notice here is that the convergence of reason and Echo is not unusual.

Echo's reasonable ability contrasts sharply with the depiction of Narcissus' lack of reason. Falling in love with his own image, Narcissus is overwhelmed by "estrange rage" (3.1585). Throughout the rest of the story the author emphasizes the folly or absence of reason that accompanies Narcissus' condition. He has been deceived by a foolish love, "fole amours deceu" (3.1590); his hope is foolish and vain, "esperance fole et vaine" (3.1595). The point in the story where Ovid dramatically portrays Narcissus' insanity is even more intensified. The author depicts the demented Narcissus turning away from the pool now described as a "faulz mirooir" (3.1761). When his tears cause the image to fade he does not simply cry for the return of the familiar face but becomes enraged like a beast; "si cria com beste enragie" (3.1768). Appropriately Ovid's reference to Narcissus in Hades is translated into a place befitting Christians who have fallen into bestial behavior.

> En enfer voit, et la remire
> En l'eaue noire et tenebreuse
> Sa samblance laide et hideuse. (3.1830–32)
>
> [He sees even in hell and there views his foul and contorted image in the black and shadow-filled water.]

The flower which remains after Narcissus vanishes gives the author a chance to conclude the translation by stressing the irrationality that has led to Narcissus' destruction.

> De teulz flours est toute porprise
> La fontaine ou cil, par folie,
> En soi mirant perdi la vie. (3.1844–46)
>
> [The fountain where, like a fool, he lost his life while looking at himself is entirely surrounded by such flowers.]

The moral is indicative of what we have found throughout the fable. The desire to apply the fable to a contemporary setting, the removal of pagan figures, the depiction of Echo's capacity for reason which in turn stresses the irrationality of Narcissus—all emphasize the author's moral attitude. This is amplified even more in the glosses.

Arnulf's identification of Echo and *bona fama* provides the foundation for the commentary. But here Echo's identity as "bone renomee" (3.1465) is applied more directly to society and what people will do for good reputation. Many people will do anything for reputation and praise.[67] Some appear simple and pious but are filled with guile and hypocrisy.[68] Though they deceive the world by the shadow of their false fame they are found out.[69]

Interestingly the amplified consideration of "bone renomee" resolves any ambiguity concerning fame noted in Arnulf's commentary. While the desire for fame may lead to evil, fame itself is not bad. For our author the fact that Echo will not speak to anyone until she is addressed, indicates that true fame only comes to those whose reason is demonstrated by good works.

> Echo n'araisone nullui
> Qui premerain n'aregne lui,
> Quar nulle bone renomee
> Ne puet estre a home alevee,
> S'ains n'a quelque bone oeuvre faite. (3.1497–1501)
>
> [Echo answers no one who does not address her first, for man never receives good reputation without having done some good work.]

Further on we learn that it is appropriate that Echo have no body because it is impossible to see fame. Fame is nothing more than speech (*parole*, 1518) generated by people. Like an echo it seems to produce sounds without lying.[70] Within this setting Narcissus becomes an exemplum of wasted fame.[71] Because of his presumption and pride he failed to fulfill his reputation and came to nothing.

The identification of Narcissus with destructive pride, already evident in the translation and the commentary on Echo, permits the author to draw correspondences between the fable and biblical history.

> Orgeulz desconfit home et fame.
> Par orgueil cheïrent jadis
> Li fol angle de Paradis. (3.1874–76)
>
> [Pride destroys man and woman; long ago through pride the foolish angels fell from heaven.]

But to stress only Narcissus' association with pride would substantially misrepresent the gloss. The fable exemplifies not only pride but supplies a framework for understanding this sin as well. This is done by repeatedly associating pride with the fountain.

Actually the fountain is more important than Narcissus. Narcissus after all is already dead while the fountain remains to entrap and destroy the living. The most extended evidence of this is found in the miniature history invented to link Narcissus to the present.

> Dou non Narcisus est nomee
> La fontaine et bien renomee,
> S'a non 'fontaine Narcisi.'
> La flours, et la vile autresi,

Apele on Narci, qui ore est
La ou fu jadis la forest
Ou la fontaine estoit assise. (3.1847–53)

[The fountain is called Narcissus and is well-known as 'The Fountain of Narcissus.' The flower is called 'Narci' as is the town which stands where the forest used to stand that surrounded the fountain.]

The lines show the author extending the fable beyond Ovid's etiological account of the narcissus flower. Not only has Narcissus given his name to a flower but to a specific fountain and finally even to a town in which the fountain stands as a monument. By linking the fountain with a town the author shows where earthly delights, once associated with the fountain, most threaten his contemporary audience. The town has become the place most filled with deceit likely to lead man away from God. The author is obviously not referring to a single town but is rather addressing criticism and warning to all towns about their pride. While the description points toward an idea about change in time it ultimately would stress the timeless danger present in pride. What was forest has become town and what was threatening in the forest remains threatening in an urban setting. This urbanization of the fable—which also involves a movement away from the original pastoral setting—is a good example of how fable could be expanded into a larger narrative. Here the fable is on the way to becoming a narrative more like a romance.

Mirrors are also an expression of the worldly delights represented by the fountain. They appear four times in the commentary: "faulz mireoirs de cest monde" (3.1909); "il mireoirs perillous" (3.1925); "li mireoirs de la fontaine" (3.1883); and "ce falible mireoir" (3.1938). The reference to mirrors indicates another attempt on the part of the author to apply the fable to a contemporary setting. The deceptive qualities of reflection were surely known more through experience with mirrors than with fountains. It is possible that the reference to mirrors is even an indication of the increased production and distribution of mirrors in the thirteenth century.[72]

More than any of the commentaries already considered, the French work amplifies description of the deception related by the fable. The commentary, like the translation, is also filled with references to folly. Here, however, the author is even more able to stress how the world's deceptive shadows debilitate and make one susceptible to ever increasing folly. This is not to say we find more sophisticated psychological description. What we find instead is dramatic exaggeration. Ovid describes Narcissus plunging his arms into the pool. Our author suggests that being enamoured of the false mirrors of the world leads one not only to break the surface of the water but actually to plunge into the depths only to discover madness.[73]

The conclusion of the commentary makes it obvious that the location of such suffering is not only this world. For attraction to a transitory shadow one can lose eternal glory and be sent to hell and eternal damnation.

> Pour fol tieng et pour esperdu
> Qui pert la pardurable gloire
> Pour tel faulse ombre transitoire,
> Ou n'a que fainte vanité
> Et faulse falibilité
> Qui les cuers art et les cors paine
> Et les ames a dolour maine,
> A pardurable dampnement
> Ou puis d'enfer parfondement. (3.1956–64)

> [He should consider crazed anyone who loses eternal glory for such a false, transitory illusion where there is only feeble vanity and false error which burns the heart, causes pain to the body, and causes the soul to suffer eternal damnation in the profound pit of hell.]

Once again we must not overemphasize or isolate the moral conclusion. The *Ovide moralisé* cannot be opened as an enormous filing system of strictly arranged moralizations that may be read as detached from the text. The moral conclusion is part of an ongoing narrative and evolves from an ambitious recasting of Ovid's entire text. The author has turned a work which he regarded as an encyclopedia into poetry. He, not Ovid, is the poet of these fables. It is quite appropriate to think of the work as a nursery for poetic invention.

The dissolution of sharp demarcation between story and commentary also has importance for the generation of new narrative. As we have seen, the French work makes the moral glosses an actual part of the text. This affects the status of both the text and the commentary. By placing interpretation on the same level as the text, the privileged status of Ovid's text is devalued. Rather than appearing as an *auctor* surrounded by glosses, Ovid's own identity comes to be less important than the meaning he comes to generate. This levelling gives new importance to the commentary for, raised to the level of the poetic text, the commentary itself becomes part of the story. Although the importance of this levelling must not be exaggerated the assimilation of translation and commentary shows an important way vernacular poetry could evolve from the study and commentary of Latin texts. The very assimilation of the Latin text through translation and commentary alters substantially perception of the Latin story. This comes not only from the new meaning that adheres to the original text but from the new setting and plots which help reformulate moral meaning. The Latin text invites interpretation only to be replaced by what it has engendered. The *Ovide moralisé* ultimately points towards a growing interest not only in moralization but in the imaginative expansion of Ovid's own text.

Ovidius Moralizatus

In contrast to the French *Moralisé*, Pierre Bersuire's commentary provided an abbreviated collection of moralizations in a form easy to consult.[74] Instead of amplified narration fused with commentary we find short Latin prose summaries of the fables followed by lists of moralizations. The lists are in such a form that they could easily be added onto and the complicated history of the work's transmission shows that this was often the case.[75] In general Bersuire's text represents an attempt to reorganize mythographic material in a form even more suitable for consultation.

Bersuire's traditional approach to fable is evident in the encyclopedic structure of the larger work of which the *Moralizatus* is part. Though rarely consulted as part of the larger work today, the *Moralizatus* was originally conceived and published as part of a much larger encyclopedic work which examined how the physical world supplied moral lessons corresponding to the teachings of the Bible. The *Reductorium morale* functions quite literally as a universal guide. Bersuire's reference to Rabanus Maurus in the Proemium identifies the very encyclopedic tradition he is working in.[76] We must be careful to distinguish such encyclopedic texts from the mythographic traditions referred to earlier. The comprehensive nature of Bersuire's *Reductorium* places it in a category that includes expansive Christian compilations such as Isidore of Seville's *Etymologiae*. In an important way the work exemplifies a renewed interest not simply in detail, but in its systematic classification. Bersuire's work is part of a renewed interest in encyclopedias that intensifies right into the Renaissance.

Bersuire's *Moralizatus* was probably not prepared for use in the classroom but for occasional consultation by the educated clergy. Seen from the vantage point of Bersuire's project the *Metamorphoses* once again stands out not as a poetic work but as an encyclopedia of fables. A reference to Ovid in the Proemium shows that Ovid is only considered an appropriate source for fable because his work is so complete.

> hinc est quod in presenti opusculo non intendo nisi rarissime literalem sensum fabularum tangere, sed solum circa moralem expositionem et allegoricam laborare sequendo librum Ovidii qui Metamorfoseos dicitur ubi recte videntur quasi per modum tabule universe fabule congregari (88).
>
> [In the work before the reader I do not touch upon the literal significance of fables except in rare cases. Instead, I will concern myself with moral explication and allegory following Ovid's books called the *Metamorphoses* where fables seem rightly assembled as in an encyclopedia.]

Ovid's collection gives Bersuire orientation and provides him with a path he can follow.

Bersuire's desire to include all that has relevance for his consideration of fable accounts for his addition of a chapter describing the physical appearance of the major gods and goddesses in the pagan pantheon. The chapter, known today as *De formis figurisque deorum*, has received much attention from art historians who have used it to show how indebted artists of the period were to literary rather than pictorial representations of the gods.[77] It is also of interest because Petrarch probably encouraged the project. Unfortunately the rather specialized attention given to *De formis* has kept scholars from asking what its addition to the *Moralizatus* may imply about mythographic traditions. Organized according to the major gods, *De formis* represents a pattern of mythographic organization that goes back at least to Fulgentius. Albericus' commentary (also known as the Third Vatican Commentary) and Boccaccio's *Genealogie deorum* are contemporary examples. The placement of this chapter next to fifteen chapters that follow the structure of Ovid's work suggests that Bersuire is actually bringing two different mythographic traditions into his encyclopedia. Bersuire's attempt to bring all this material into a single work must be regarded as an influence of the older Christian encyclopedic tradition. The juxtaposition of the pantheon and the tradition following Ovid's own schema continues into the Renaissance. The relation of *De formis* to descriptions of the gods found in renaissance handbooks such as Cartari, Ripa, and Conti, is a good indication of Bersuire's influence.

By seeking correspondences between Ovid and Biblical passages, Bersuire shapes a reference work that may be consulted with greater facility than the *Ovide moralisé*. As Bersuire suggests in the Proemium, the work provides a means of confirming the mysteries of faith: "ad moralizandum fabulas poetrarum manum ponere ut sic per ipsas hominum fictiones possim morum et fidei misteria confirmare" (88). The comment shows that fables are to be employed not only as rhetorical exempla to attract the attention of a restless congregation but as a kind of figurative shorthand to aid in the demonstration of scriptural truths. Bersuire's running assignment of scriptural passages to Ovid's text graphically illustrates how the Bible functioned as a privileged, ordering text that governed interpretation.

The commentary on Echo and Narcissus provides a table of meaning.[78]

> Revera talis sententia Tiresie cothidie verificatur in multis quia s. multi sunt qui spiritualiter viguerunt s. se vel suam pulchritudinem summam vigent, ita quod pulchritudinem suam quantum ad formam pulchritudinem animi, quantum ad scienciam. (. . .) Quod etiam de multis in ecclesia et religione potest dici. Qui tamen pulchritudinem mortalem et virtutem quam habent considerant, in vanagloriam elati alios contempnunt et vituperant, et se immoderate reputant, et sic per inanem gloriam et superbiam pereunt et in florem vane ypocrisis transeunt et anime eorum finaliter ad inferos descendunt. (. . .) Vel dic quod ista umbra temporalia mundi bona disignat. Que revera in fonte mundane prosperitatis homini solent arridere, et quasi osculum et amplexum spondere et vix per votum possunt acquirere vel habere, ita quod pre disiderio et ambitione et avaricia terrenorum quandoque solent perire, et sic in florem mutari dicuntur, et solent cito deficere et eorum gloria evanescere et dormire. Ecc. 30: qui apprehendit umbram (. . .) Echo fuit quedam nimpha loquacissima. (. . .) Ista possunt historialiter allegari contra lenones et lenas et vetulas rufianas que adulteriis favent, et dum sua opera lubrica faciunt, Iunonem i. zelotipes et parentes iuvencularum in verbis tenent. (. . .) Vel dic aliter quod Echo signat adulatores (113–15).
>
> [The truth of Tiresias' words is demonstrated daily in many things. For example, there are many who flourish spiritually. They watch out for their own lofty beauty—that is they care for their own physical beauty as much as they care for the condition of their souls or their learning. (. . .) This may be said about many in the church and in holy orders. Even so, whoever has the same beauty and virtue as they do, they find guilty of vanity. These people they condemn and despise. These they consider immoderate but for their own empty glory and pride they perish as vain hypocrites and become as flowers which pass away and their souls fall with certainty into hell. (. . .) You may also think that such material shadows signify the world's delights. Indeed, whoever is accustomed to laugh at men in the worldly fountain of prosperity and whoever offers kisses and embraces and is scarcely able to gain any in return, this person for his desires and ambitions and earthly avarice will certainly perish and, as it is said, be transformed into a flower. Indeed, this person will be carried away and his renown will disappear and even go to sleep. Ecclesiasticus 30: Whoever sees his shadow (. . .). Echo was a certain talkative nymph (. . .). Historically this is a charge against whores and pimps and lusty old

> women who encourage adultery. While they do their filthy work they capture with their words Juno—that is those who are jealous and the parents of young people. (. . .) Or, you may even say that Echo signifies those who flatter.]

In contrast to the other commentaries, Bersuire's examination of the fable urges specific application. Tiresias' warning *si se non noverit* is especially directed at those in the church. The observation that pride may actually be most obstinate in those who criticize vanity in others shows Bersuire applying the story with added sophistication.

With Echo in particular there is a specification of meaning not present in earlier works. Rather than being associated with *Fama*, Echo is identified as a figure applicable to prostitutes, or others involved in illicit sexual practice. The shift shows that Bersuire pays special attention to Ovid's description of Echo as one with knowledge of Jove's sexual play with mountain nymphs rather than Echo's association with sound. Regarding Echo as a person rather than a personification, Bersuire shows that his application of fable involves concerns which are far more practical.

As we read the gloss we sense how the audience to which the commentary is directed has changed since the time of the earliest commentary. While the *Narrationes* seem directed at guiding the study of fable, Bersuire's commentary is directed at its application beyond the classroom. The *Moralizatus* shows little interest in Ovid as a poet but instead transforms his work into a sermon handbook with implicit directions for further amplification. Narcissus might be used to warn against the danger of spiritual pride in a sermon delivered before the clergy. Echo might be appropriate for a sermon to the clergy or laity warning against the deception inherent in concupiscence.

The way the text lends itself to amplification is seen if we compare it with the earlier version published by Badius Ascensius in 1509. The later text makes criticism of certain vices more explicit. The earlier version criticizes women who talk back to their husbands.[79]

> Vel dic quod tales echo sunt quaedam litigiose et brigose mulieres vel quidam servitores queruli quae ultimum verbum semper volunt habere: et ad omnia quae dicuntur a maritis atque dominis respondere. Et si ab eis reprehenduntur semper murmurant.

> [You may also say that an echo is like certain stubborn women and quarrelsome servants who always want to have the last word. To everything which is said by their husbands or servants they have something to say. If they are reproached by anyone they always grumble.]

The Paris manuscript makes more explicit criticism of pride and vainglory in the church: "Quod etiam de multis in ecclesia et religione potest dici." This statement, not found in the early text, may even be related to Bersuire's own experience. From 1351 to 1355 he was imprisoned by the Bishop of Paris for heresy.[80]

The French *Ovide moralisé* and the Latin *Ovidius moralizatus* tell us little about Ovid's own narrative. Instead they take us farther away from Ovid and transform his text into a diagnostic manual. Each segment becomes a window through which the student may learn to identify and treat human frailty. Yet we must not think of the commentaries as a wall with many windows that look out upon vastly different views. We should rather think of them as opening onto a common landscape. Here the landscape of Boeotia, still accessible to the educated Roman who had studied Greek, either through trips or through guidebooks such as Strabo's *Geography*, is replaced by a very different terrain. What is an ingenious display of skill in combining Theban stories in Ovid becomes in the *Ovide moralisé* a collection of settings that evolve into a sequence of moral conclusions and in Bersuire's text a list of lessons that may quickly be accommodated to scripture. With his multiple readings of each fable, Bersuire represents the commentary tradition at its farthest reach from Ovid.

The single most important accomplishment of early Ovidian commentary is the way it shows how Ovid's transformations could be interpreted by abstraction. Such a position made it possible to defend the study of Ovid's work and use individual fables as abstractions that could explain both the material and spiritual world. Ovid, who was much honored as a poet of love psychology, here becomes respected as a mythographer or scholar of fable. The double identification of Ovid as poet and Ovid as mythographer continues through the Renaissance and even into modern times.

Echo and Narcissus receive only limited treatment in the commentaries. Even though the story was used to depict the process of falling in love, as we shall see next, we find little about love psychology in the commentaries. The reason for this is quite simple. In the classrooms where moral truths were to be revealed, there would have been little room for comments on the psychology of human passions. Yet even though the fable is not given the detailed attention we are familiar with from modern discussion, we must not think its treatment superficial. To view Narcissus only as a warning against self-love and pride is to ignore the way commentaries reach such meaning. In the *Narrationes* simplification of plot and vocabulary suggests Christian order is being imposed on the fable. In Arnulf and John of Garland, Echo, not Narcissus, provides the abstraction that leads to the interpretation of the fable.

Identified as *fama*, or *gloria*, because of her association with speech and ultimately with the element air, Echo provides a framework in which Narcissus is judged. In later moralizations the fable has multiple applications to a contemporary setting. When we look at the evolution of the commentaries we see that they more and more become glosses on glosses and engender a proliferation of meaning. As we will see in our next chapter, even more extended commentary on Narcissus is found when the fable is incorporated into another text. In an important way poetic texts too are glosses which simply continue methods found in commentaries.

While the commentaries created a system of access to Ovid's text, they did not pronounce the final word on its meaning. By providing a ready body of exempla that could be drawn on, they created ground fertile for further meaning. The study of Ovid for Latin grammar and rhetoric or for sermon exempla stressed how fables could be used for further invention or moral instruction. For this reason the study of Ovid was not static but continually engendered new meaning and new poetry. Once incorporated into another text the meaning attached to the fables by commentaries could be expanded or even abandoned. It is to the expanded meaning of Narcissus in the *Roman de la Rose* that we turn next.

CHAPTER THREE

The Invention of Personal History

The schools that showed students how to read Latin fables and control their meaning in abbreviated form also provided training in the application and amplification of the truth they discovered in classical texts.[1] Vestiges of the pedagogical methods used to teach Ovid are evident in both parts of the thirteenth-century *Roman de la Rose*. In the early section completed by Guillaume de Lorris in the first half of the thirteenth century, the moralization following the inset story of Narcissus is an example of a method taught in the schools. The manipulation and eventual displacement of the fable in Jean de Meun's conclusion of the poem, completed in the last quarter of the century, also show how the use of a fable was guided by teachers who taught students the use of commentaries. Yet the poem is hardly fashioned as mechanically as these remarks might suggest. While the commentaries provide insight into the way Ovid was taught and convey the authority which Guillaume and Jean would have acknowledged in Ovid's texts, they tell little about how a fable like Narcissus encouraged narrative invention in the *Roman de la Rose*.

This chapter shows how the Narcissus fable came to engender narrative in the *Roman* and even more explores the ways the fable supplied matter for the representation of evolving psychological awareness. An important assumption underlies this discussion. The fable's capacity to represent mental life and psychological crisis within other narratives cannot be assumed and is hardly manifest within the fable itself. Such universal application of the fable must be discovered within other narrative. It is the capacity of the fable to elaborate psychological crisis and invite its resolution that stands behind the title of this chapter. By formulating a new mode of portraying psychological crisis and its resolution, the *Roman* represents the invention of a new means of depicting personal history. In contrast to the more limited use of the fable as a negative exemplum signifying the death and isolation that comes from self-love, the *Roman* encompasses a new strategy for using the fable. In addition to using the fable to describe the Lover's experience and longing, the *Roman* defines the experience represented by Narcissus as a psychological configuration that must be overcome if the Lover is to discover his sexuality, not through introspection, but through engagement in the world.

While the poem is often introduced as an allegory that tells much about conventions of courtly love, these terms have tended to become critical concepts that deflect attention from the Ovidian components that make up the work. It is better to approach the *Roman* first as an educational poem based on Ovidian pedagogy, not as an allegory of love or a poem encoded with conventions of courtly love. While Guillaume is certainly not the first vernacular poet to use Narcissus for the representation of love psychology, he is the first to address in detail the resolution of the problems the fable raises. He does this by applying the educational strategy suggested by Ovid's *carmina amatoria* to the fable derived from the *Metamorphoses*.[2] By bringing Ovid's *ars* to the Lover through a series of personifications, Guillaume confronts tension inherent in the ideal of courtly love and points toward its resolution through education and self-knowledge.[3]

Another distinction must be made as well. While the Lover is shaped with matter from the fable, Guillaume's intention is not to make him suffer Narcissus' fate. The Lover is not Narcissus and it is a serious error to restrict study of the story by assuming a simple correspondence between the moral affixed to Narcissus and the Lover. The history of Narcissus invokes a continuum of events by which the Lover's actions may be scrutinized but not irrevocably condemned. To regard the significance of the moral terminus found in commentaries is to simplify the use of the fable. Guillaume urges comparison of the Lover and Narcissus in order to transfer psychological detail from the fable to the Lover and to delineate his psychological progress. The use of Ovid's fable would intensify examination of the Lover's actions, not condemn them.

An important indication that Guillaume uses Narcissus to portray the education of the Lover—not his moral condemnation—is found in his demonstration that the Fountain of Narcissus is a particular manifestation of the Fountain of Love. Within the poem sensual phenomena previously associated with the destruction of Narcissus become incorporated into a new *historia* that both affirms love and assimilates the sensual confusion present in the fable. Through Guillaume's story, the fable comes to represent not an aberration of human psychology but a common psychological experience. This is supported by the scientific matter that informs the fountain allegory. Influenced by medical ideas that diagnosed love as a disease and by ophthalmology that described the eye's anatomical structure, the fountain allegory functions as a central component in the universal application of the fable. Ovid's scientific role in *both* parts of the poem has not been sufficiently recognized.

Jean's continuation of Guillaume's work should also be thought of in reference to Ovid. Jean inherited the Lover's unresolved attraction for the Rose fashioned from Ovid's fable as well as the dialectical *remedia* explored through personification allegory. The problem posed by Guillaume involved not simply describing the consummation of the Lover's desire—in itself this was easy, as the anonymous conclusion to the poem shows. A far more important problem concerned developing a redefinition of love that would justify such consummation. Criticism of Ovid's fable is central to Jean's redefinition of love. While Guillaume's discussion shows how well the fable could be used in poetry of love psychology, Jean's reaction shows that it obstructs the representation of love's consummation. For Jean, the Lover had to be divorced from Narcissus if the Lover's desire was ever to be fulfilled. Seen within the Ovidian structure of both parts of the poem, Narcissus becomes a narrative with ideological significance, for it marks an experience in the progression from an ideal conception of love to its material redefinition. Within the *Roman* the fable helps trace a shift from an isolated courtly ideal to a problematic engagement in self-awareness and the world.

Troubadour Poetry

For orientation to the *Roman de la Rose*, it is helpful to consider the presence of Narcissus in several twelfth-century works. My intention is not to account exhaustively for the use of the fable before the *Roman*. This has already been done by Frederick Goldin.[4] I would simply observe several ways the fable was applied to love psychology before Guillaume's poem, and stress how it came to portray a process of maturation and education.

Narcissus is referred to directly in at least three troubadour lyrics.[5] In a poem by Bertran of Paris the fable is mentioned among a repertoire of classical stories that a poet could be expected to tell.[6] More developed use of the fable is found in two other poems. In Peirol d'Auvergne's poem "Mout m'Entremis de Chantar Voluntiers," the poet compares himself to Narcissus to explain the foolishness of desire that has little hope of being fulfilled.[7] Reference to Narcissus' beauty, folly, and the reminder that he was one who loved his own shadow, shows Peirol using the kind of formalized account of the fable found in commentaries.[8] The other stanzas of the poem show that

Peirol constructs his lyric on more than an amplification of Narcissus. In stanza IV the poet shifts his attention to Echo. Abandoned and with little hope for private conversation ("privat parlamen," 26), the Lover decides to become silent: "my tongue will I hold in check. That at least will speak no more to her on this matter." [Mas la boca tenrai ades e fre./Aquilh sivals non l'en dira mais re! 34–35.] In the final lines the voice of the poet ironically contradicts the isolation required by the foregoing argument.

Lo vers tramet midons per tal coven
qu'a tot lo menhs, s'autre pro no m'en ve,
quan l'auzira, li membrara de me. (43–45)

[The *vers* do I send my lady on such terms that if no other benefit accrues to me therefrom, when she hears it she will at least remember me.]

The lines recall Echo's final remembrance of Narcissus. Even though the poet is removed from his lady, his voice may return materialized in verse. Echo, not Narcissus, becomes the poet's strategic persona.

The best known application of Narcissus in Provençal poetry is found in Bernart de Ventador's poem, "Can vei la lauzeta mover."[9] Since it compares the mirror of Narcissus with the eyes of the Lady it has become the *locus classicus* for many discussions of love engendered by the eye.

Anc non agui de me poder
ni no fui meus de l'or'en sai
que.m laisset en sos olhs vezer
en un miralh que mout me plai.
Miralhs, pus me mirei en te,
m'an mort li sospir de preön,
c'aissi.m perdei com perdet se
lo bels Narcisus en la fon. (17–24)

[I have never had the power of myself.
I have not been my own man since that moment
when she let me look into her eyes
into a mirror that gives great pleasure, even now.

Mirror, since I beheld myself in you,
the sighs from my depths have slain me,
and I have lost myself as fair Narcissus
lost himself in the fountain.]

The lyric depends on a selective manipulation of the fable, for it screens out all detail except the mirror-like fountain. By animating the death-giving mirror of Narcissus, Bernart transfers the psychological confusion which accompanies self-love to love for another. Like Narcissus the Lover has lost power over himself, but unlike Narcissus the impotence he experiences comes not from himself or an inanimate mirror but from the eyes of a lady, which have the power to give life. Like Narcissus, the Lover desires and suffers, but unlike Narcissus, the Lover's torment is not permanent. For Bernart, Ovid's fable is not a source for an exemplum but a story which helps him formulate an argument for compassion.

As in Peirol's lyric, the poet's own identity does not remain fixed with Narcissus but is transferred to Echo. This marks an important shift because it shows the Lady, not the Lover, is the real victim of pride.

> De las domnas me dezesper;
> ja mais en lor no.m fiarai;
> c'aissi com las solh chaptener,
> enaissi las deschaptenrai.
> Pois vei c'una pro no m'en te
> vas leis que.m destrui e.m cofon,
> totas las dopt' e las mescre,
> car be sai c'atretals se son. (25–32)
>
> [I give up all hope in women.
> I shall not put my faith in them again;
> as much as I used to hold them up,
> now I shall let them fall,
> because I do not see one who is of any use to me
> with her, who destroys me and brings me down.
> I shall fear and distrust them all,
> because they are all alike, I know it well.]

In part the Lover's response imitates the prayer of the spurned lover who prays for justice in Ovid's text. The declared intention to withdraw, however, shows the Lover's reaction also parallels Echo's proclaimed renunciation of Narcissus.

The special significance given to Echo in these poems complements the interpretive function Echo receives in the commentaries by Arnulf and John of Garland. At the same time that the fable is applied to a contemporary relationship, it too gives strategic force to Echo as one who holds the potential to break isolation. Narcissus does not represent the Lover, but, as in the commentaries, defines phenomena that must be overcome.

The poems are important because they represent the first developed use of Ovid's fable in a setting of love psychology. The application of the fable to relationships between men and women carries an important assumption as well. Use of the fable requires that detail that we would consider unusual or abnormal be approached as if it were normal. The allegorical, or more precisely euhemeristic habits given to students when they learned Latin and studied fables, made it natural that the unusual detail or event was read as if it were a moment in a normal sequence of events. In an age that is urged to seek out the unusual or abnormal as a mark of hidden or unconscious contradiction, we are not used to thinking of a hermeneutic that could turn abnormality and distance into what was common and close.

The Norman *Lai de Narcisus*

The best example of an extended application of Ovid's fable to courtly love before the *Roman de la Rose* is found in the late twelfth-century Norman *Lai de Narcisus*,[10] which reformulates the fable into a miniature romance.[11]

The Norman poem changes the Latin fable into a story of education and growth by inventing a figure to take Echo's place, and transforming Nemesis into Amors. By replacing Echo with Dané, the poet avoids the abstraction inherent in Ovid's etiological subplot about the origin of reflected sound. Instead of directly confronting details such as Echo's strange speech and petrification, the poet shapes a figure more like the medieval Thisbe.[12] Dané's intense suffering when alone, nocturnal planning to meet Narcissus in a wood outside the city wall, and ultimate death with Narcissus show that in this Norman story Echo and Narcissus are at least partly modeled after Pyramus and Thisbe. Here we also find the desire, already seen in Peirol and Bernart, to regard Ovid's fable as a story about love between a couple. In general the removal of specific references to Echo allows the poet to amplify the woman's experience far more than was the case in the fable or in the lyrics.[13] This has considerable importance in the poem, for Dané's suffering becomes both the justification and prefiguration of Narcissus' experience. What Dané learns, Narcissus too must learn.

While retribution remains an abstract personification in Ovid's fable and is appealed to only after Narcissus has rejected all those who love him, retribution emerges from Dané's own experience in the Norman poem. This is possible because the Norman poet transforms Ovid's distant source of retribution into private experience. Amors, however, does not function simply as a personification. Instead Dané's attraction to Narcissus and the agitation it causes lead to introspection and self-examination. Painful internal experience is intended to take the place of counsel that she might otherwise receive from her father or nurse. Love first becomes conceptualized and then personified so that it is possible for her to seek aid. Amors becomes her teacher as well as her source of revenge.

The revenge sought by Dané does not inflict purposeless suffering on Narcissus, as was the case in the fable. Here punishment is made to coincide with education. The stages of Narcissus' education are carefully marked. When he first meets Dané, he declares their mutual ignorance of love. His own childlike attitude becomes evident when he asks if the image he seeks in the fountain is a fairy, nymph, or goddess. The fact that he also regards Dané as a goddess or fairy when he first sees her, shows that the image in the pool already may be associated with his eventual reunion with her. Once more he declares his ignorance before love (739) but this time his confession is only preparation for his recognition that Dané's tutor has become his as well.

> Amors est mastre qui me duist,
> Qui dedens le cors m'art et cuist.
> Il m'aprent tote sa nature
> Et si m'angousce sans mesure. (775–78)
>
> [Amors is the teacher who instructs me, who burns and scorches me within my body: he teaches me all his nature and causes me suffering without measure.]

Through suffering he recognizes not only the reflected image but the suffering he can bring to another. This is entirely different from the fable where retribution remains an abstraction. Ovid's Narcissus never knows why he suffers or that he is being punished. He knows nothing of Tiresias and the prophecy which governs his life. Where Ovid followed the moment of self-recognition with intensified suffering and death, the Norman poet used self-recognition as a departure for confession of one's dependence on others.

The placement of Tiresias' prophecy in the poem demonstrates the author's pedagogical intent. In the fable it appears only at the beginning. At the end of the poem the poet has Narcissus himself recall Tiresias' words and declare that he now understands their meaning (849–50). Rather than remaining forever senseless before his image, the Norman Narcissus learns that self-knowledge comes from love that must ultimately lead beyond one's self. The education Amors has given to Narcissus leads not to insanity but reason.

The motif of education we find here becomes even more important in the *Roman de la Rose*. While the *Lai* retains the structure of Ovid's fable, the *Roman* uses the fable for the creation of an entirely new narrative.

Guillaume de Lorris

We come to the Fountain of Narcissus after moving through a formalized pastoral terrain filled with much detail. Yet, this detail does not impede our progress or the sensation that we reach the fountain quickly and that its appearance, rather than being surprising, is quite expected. In careful succession we rise with the young man, leave the town, follow the bank of a great river and pass into the garden. Only when we come upon the fountain does our focal point become more specific as the narration halts for recollection of the Narcissus fable and closer inspection of the fountain.

Before considering the significance of this attentive examination, however, we need to examine the composition of the initial pastoral setting with the Latin text of Ovid's fable.[14] When we do this we see that Guillaume has used *loci* from Ovid's text for the invention of his own description. In addition to having provided Guillaume with a story or plot that could be evoked by specific reference to Narcissus, the fable offered a thesaurus of grammatical and rhetorical detail which could be used independently of the plot. We remarked above that the fountain and its story seem curiously expected when they appear in the garden. Such a sensation is appropriate when the pastoral setting is already infused with Ovidian matter.

Upon leaving the town, the Lover comes to a familiar and beautiful river which quickly occupies his attention. So clear and fresh are the waters that he compares them to water from a fountain or well (103–13).[15] It is not the fountain or well that Guillaume drew from the Latin text but the Lover's attraction to the beautiful location and his physical contact with the water. In the Latin text it is literally the "face" or appearance of the place that attracts Narcissus and anticipates the face he soon meets in the secluded setting: "faciemque loci fontemque secutus" (414). In Guillaume's poem too it is the beauty of the place that attracts the Lover: "si m'abelissoit et seoit/a regarder le leu pleisant" (117). ["I was pleased and happy to look upon that charming place," p. 32.]

The appearance of the river signals the initiation of a special experience.

> De l'eve clere reluisant
> mon vis refreschi et lavé
> si vi tot covert et pavé
> le fonz de l'eve de graveile. (118–21)

[As I washed my face and refreshed myself with the clear, shining water, I saw the bottom of the stream was all covered and paved with gravel. p. 32]

Face-washing does not become part of the description fortuitously, but is an invention based on Ovid's account of the exhausted Narcissus seeking to refresh himself by drinking (413–17). By emphasizing face-washing rather than drinking—an action that poisons Narcissus in the fable—Guillaume stressed the refreshing quality of water and even its ability to awaken. Significantly, at the same time that Guillaume drew upon the fable he distinguished the Lover from Narcissus. The distinction between the water's reflective and transparent qualities already suggested by Ovid's *inlimis* and *argenteus* (407) is broadened. In contrast to Ovid's text, it is not the reflective nature of water which is most important but its translucence. As the Lover refreshes and washes his face (and thus his eyes) his vision is heightened and he catches sight of the gravel on the river bottom. By providing the Lover with a focal point beneath the water, Guillaume again distinguished the Lover's experience from Narcissus'. Even more, the sight of gravel through the water conveys the presence of a secret which remains to be revealed. The use of *covert*—a word used elsewhere to indicate concealment[16]—even suggests that the Lover's eyes which now see only gravel may in time discern more. Actually the perception of gravel through water signals the initiation of a psychological process conveyed through visual imagery.

The form of this process and the special meaning of the river become more evident when we realize that the meadow which appears after the reference to gravel (120–23) creates a movement similar to the shift we later find at the fountain from the crystals to the Rose. Here, the field of vision remains larger; later it becomes more specific, narrowing finally to a particular Rose. The reason for this movement may be found in the fable. Even though the Lover is distinguished from Narcissus, the intense desire which grows in Narcissus as he drinks also applies to the Lover.

> dumque sitim sedare cupit, sitis altera crevit,
> dumque bibit, visae conreptus imagine formae
> spem sine corpore amat, corpus putat esse, quod unda est. (415–17)
>
> [While he tries to quench his thirst another thirst rises within him, and while he drinks he is overwhelmed by the form he sees. He loves an unsubstantial hope and believes that a body which is only water.]

As the Lover refreshes himself he too comes to experience desire, but a desire which is more abstract. Ovid's *spem sine corpore amat* also applies to the Lover and provides psychological detail that accounts not only for an invention but an innovation. In contrast to Ovid, Guillaume delayed the Lover's discovery of an object of love. This delay is an innovation. The celebration of love in poetry invariably occurs after love has already been experienced. The courtly love lyric often meditates on absence but an absence which follows at least some visual contact with the loved one. Here, it is not the effects of love which are described but the longing for the experience itself. While Narcissus finds the object of his love immediately before him, the Lover must begin a quest for experience that will fulfill his desire. Like Narcissus the Lover "loves a hope" but his hope remains detached from any particular object. Hope draws the Lover into the pastoral setting. As he looks into the water, and then rises to follow the riverbank, he is drawn by desire for some still undiscovered object. We must think of the Lover's movement along the riverbank and the vision directed beneath the water's surface as intimately related, for Guillaume used the river not only as a geographical guide but as a representation of introspection. Washing his face and looking into the stream are actions which alert us to a psychological experience. As we follow him along the riverbank and into his *aventure* we enter his fantasy.

Guillaume did not draw specific matter from the fable again until the Lover has made his way deep into the secluded part of the garden. The pastoral setting of the fable accounts for this. Almost immediately upon leaving the river, the Lover confronts the personifications on the garden wall and then the groups of figures in the garden. These are moments of fellowship and make specific use of the pastoral fable inappropriate. Elements from the fable appear again only when the Lover leaves the dance and enters the forest.[17]

Guillaume also made use of a motif often overlooked in discussion of the fable. Hunting, which provides the social setting for Ovid's story, is also carried over into the portrayal of the Lover and actually gave Guillaume a means of formulating the Lover's desire. As the Lover penetrates the wood he appears as a hunter of sensual and eventually sexual experience. At first he desires to do no more than wander outside the city ("talant d'aler," 94); when he comes to the river it provides him with direction, and by the time he reaches the garden wall he is prepared to use any art or device to gain entry ("par quel art ne par quel engin/je porroie entrer el jardin," 497–98). Once in the garden his desires are ordered by the dance executed by people who are well-educated ("bien enseignies," 1280). Finally, it is the dance and the appearance of its leaders (1283–84) which urge him to inspect the garden by himself (1285–87). When we learn of his actions we see that he has been engaged in a methodical hunt.

> Mes j'alai tant destre et senestre
> que j'oi tot l'afere et tot l'estre
> dou vergier cherchié et veü. (1415–17)

[However, I went so far, to the left and to right, that I searched out and saw the entire condition and nature of the garden. pp. 49–50]

The movement both right and left accords with the symmetrically planted trees in the garden (1360–66). The sensual order of the dance continues in the orderly plantation of fruit and nut trees. The order points to more than ornamentation. It reveals a grove arranged to facilitate the sight of a hunter not unlike the poplar stands one finds in Touraine today. This is, of course, precisely the case, for the garden is not only the place where the Lover hunts but where he is hunted.

The entire time the Lover moves among the geometrically arranged trees, Amors stalks him as a hunter follows his prey. The arrangement of trees permits the Lover to search out and inspect each detail and also permits Amors to keep the Lover easily in sight.

Et li dex d'Amors m'a seü
endementieres aguetant
con li vanieres qui atant
que la beste en bon leu se meite
por lessier aler la saeste. (1418–22)

[And the God of Love followed me, watching me all the time, as does the hunter who waits until the animal is in a good position before he lets fly his arrow. p. 50]

These lines give the most complete expression to the hunt and appropriately come just before the Lover sees the Fountain of Narcissus.

En un trop biau leu arivé,
en un destor, ou je trové
une fontaine soz un pin. (1423–25)

[At last I arrived at a very good spot, where I found a fountain under a pine. p. 50]

In the fable it is Nemesis who transforms the adolescent hunter, who laid nets for deer (356), into one who is entrapped. Here, as in the *Lai de Narcisus*, Amors takes the place of Nemesis and affirms that the Lover is both hunter and hunted. Arriving at the fountain under the eyes of Amors, the Lover has come to a place where his identities as hunter and hunted will intersect.

Guillaume also prepares us for his retelling of the fable by including moral abstractions and iconographic detail related to the fable. Interestingly, the fable is evoked in such a manner when the Lover is in a social setting. Papelardie (405–38) warns against "gloire vaine" (437); Oiseuse carries "un miroër" (555); Amors knows how to punish "l'orgueil de gent" (867). These details are part of Guillaume's portrayal of an adolescent learning to control his senses.

The consistent reference to face, images, and appearances found in the garden creates a profusion of sensual phenomena analogous to what we find in the fable. In the shimmering water of the river, the Lover refreshes his face ("mon vis," 119). When he comes to the garden wall images and appearances abound. "Ymage" and "semblance" occur in remarkable succession.[18] In the garden the faces ("semblances," 1283) of the dancers correspond to the "semblances" on the walls of the garden. It is these images which draw the Lover deeper into the trees. In the wood, as we have seen, he becomes even more a hunter of images. Considered together, these details intensify an atmosphere already shaped with matter from the fable.

We have seen in our earlier chapters how Narcissus became an exemplum for sensual confusion related to vision. As we follow the Lover we see that he does not completely comprehend what he sees. When he comes to the painted sculptures on the garden wall he pays careful attention to their physical detail and craftsmanship. His empirical interest in these "ymages" is much the same as his interest in the "graveile." Nowhere, however, is there anything to suggest he understands their significance. We must not think of these personifications as abstractions removed from the Lover. They are rather part of a moral universe that he cannot yet apply to himself.

The personified figures within the garden complement the personifications on the garden wall. Together they exemplify an entire system of values which the Lover can move within without fully understanding. Guillaume's poem does not lend itself to strict moral interpretation as Robertsonian critics would have it, but neither is its courtly setting empty of value. The poem creates a setting in which moral values are present but suspended until they become acknowledged through the Lover's education.[19]

The garden is not a classroom but a kind of nursery for the senses which directs the lover to the fountain and the real inception of knowledge. For this reason it is entirely appropriate that when Oiseuse opens the gate, the Lover is unaware of the threat posed by a guide who is a personification of leisure in the *Remedia amoris* (139–40) and an ancestor of the False Duessa, Falerina, and Armida.[20] His acceptance of such a figure for a guide neither condemns him, as Fleming suggests, nor justifies interpretation that would see Oiseuse as a figure for the *otium* required by philosophy.[21] Oiseuse represents the suspension of time necessary for the very existence of the garden itself and gives formal expression to the suspension experienced by Narcissus in Ovid's fable. The mirror she carries does not immediately signal vanity but represents the introspective state of the Lover and anticipates her role as guide and representative of conditions necessary for his discovery of the fountain. Outside the garden the river has the role of guide; within the garden Oiseuse becomes *directrice*.

The Lover's reaction to the songbirds provides a particularly revealing example of his incomplete understanding. From the beginning of the poem, the song of birds marks the progress of the Lover's desire and represents the sensual experience he hunts for. He desires to leave the town to listen to the birds (95); the sound of birds intensifies his desire to enter the garden (495–98); and when he is inside the garden wall the birds sound angelic (662). The last image complements his general experience of the garden as a "paradis terrestre" (634).

Yet incongruity also appears. As the Lover moves through the garden, the birds are compared not only to angels but to sirens.

> Tant estoit cil chanz doz et biaus
> qu'il ne sembloit pas chant d'oisiaus,
> ainz le peüst l'en aesmer
> au chanz des seraines de mer,
> qui par lor voiz qu'eles ont saines
> et series ont non seraines. (667–72)
>
> [It was so sweet and beautiful that it did not seem the song of a bird; one could compare it rather with the song of the sirens of the sea; who have the name siren on account of their clear, pure voices. p. 39]

The etymological definition which relates siren to *sain* (sane, healthy) and *seri* (serene, calm, harmonious) gives special significance to their positive meaning and at first suggests that the poet has drawn upon Macrobius' discussion of sirens as figures related to cosmic harmony.[22] Such an interpretation would justify their earlier comparison with angels. Yet, while tempting, such an interpretation is subverted by the text which places the sirens in the sea. While these sirens may sound angelic, they also evoke a warning which appears in the mythographers.[23] The etymology we find in the French text may even function as an ironic commentary on the Lover's misconception when we realize that contemporary commentaries trace the root of sirens to the Greek word σειρω and the Latin word *trahere*, literally meaning to draw or pull as with a rope.[24] Significantly the comparison is also at odds with the effect the birds have on the Lover. Even though he claims they bring sanity, they actually induce irrationality when he listens to their song from outside the garden.

> Quant j'oï les oisiaus chanter,
> forment me pris a dementer

par quel art ne par quel engin
je porroie entrer el jardin. (495–98)

[When I heard the birds singing, I began to go out of my mind wondering by what art or what device I could enter the garden. p. 37]

Here the word *dementer* shows that the song of the yet unseen birds causes the Lover great distress and almost makes him lose his senses.

While the Lover is familiar with sirens and angels, he cannot distinguish between them or apply their meaning to himself. The detail is important because it shows that while the Lover is formally educated, he does not know how to use his knowledge. The detail is part of a larger configuration as well. Even though he knows how to dress according to his rank and age, he still must learn to act within a courtly setting. The insufficient understanding or misapplication of a moral figure associated with sound also anticipates his incomplete understanding of visual phenomena at the fountain. When associated with the sirens, the birds represent the deceptive phenomenon linked to Echo.

To this point the *materia*, not the *historia*, of Ovid's text has been most important. This changes, however, when the fountain appears, for it immediately becomes a formal expression that gives focus to details from the fable already in the poem.

The shift to the history of Narcissus is made carefully. Coming to "un trop biau leu" the Lover sees the fountain with the words "estoit morz li biau Narcisus" (1436). The history emerges quite literally from the letters carved into the stone and the *translatio* that immediately follows becomes a textual version of the story. Together, the fountain and its evocation of Narcissus become the center of a configuration of *materia* that reaches backward and forward into the text.

Translatio

The story told by Guillaume (1437–1504) is not a translation of Ovid's fable but a carefully abbreviated version which offers interpretation through translation. Like the *Lai de Narcisus*, it is told as an account of recent events. The mythographic or marvelous details are left out. Juno, Jove, Liriope, Tiresias, Nemesis, Echo's strange speech and petrification, the transformation of Narcissus into a flower—none of this is present. Instead, Echo and Narcissus are given identities which accord with the aristocratic and courtly setting of the poem. Narcissus is a "demoisiaus" (1437) and Echo "une haute dame" (1442).

As in Provençal poetry and the Norman *Lai* the story concerns the potential love of a couple rather than the relation between Narcissus and his image. Even though Echo loved Narcissus more than anyone alive (1443), she did not gain his favor. She is a "loial amant" (1463) whose own beauty, careful entreaties and prayers (1450) were villainously denied ("si vilmant," 1464) because Narcissus was occupied with his own beauty.

Guillaume sketches their unsuccessful relation by distinguishing between the animalistic behavior of Narcissus and the reasonable behavior of Echo. Where Ovid stresses Narcissus' lack of feeling by comparing him to marble (419), Guillaume attributes animal qualities to him. He is filled with savagery or fury ("fierté," 1448) and has a heart which is bestial ("farasche," 1457). The description fits with Ovid's identification of Narcissus as a hunter and the description of his eventual loss of sense (474). In the French text his insanity is more diagnostically attributed to his *ire*. His wild behavior also shows him to need education in the ways of love. The absence of knowledge implicit in Ovid's Narcissus is expressed directly by Guillaume. Echo's prayer is not simply that he be punished—the request of the anonymous follower in the fable—but that he learn the pain of a loyal lover: "si poroit savoir et aprendre/quel duel ont li loial amant,/qui les refuse si vilmant" (1462–64); ["that he might know and understand the grief of those loyal lovers who are so basely denied," p. 50].

Untamed and without sense Narcissus is the opposite of Echo. As "une haute dame" (1442) she expects her love to be returned. This accounts for her distress when ignored and explains why her prayer for Narcissus' education ("savoir et aprendre," 1462) is reasonable: "Ceste priere fu resnable,/ et por ce la fist Dex estable;" (1465–66); ["since the prayer was reasonable, god confirmed it," p. 50]. The reasonable quality given to her prayer is not a translation of Ovid's *precibus iustis* (406) but comes from perceiving Echo's response to Narcissus' behavior as logical.

The inset story has a function that goes beyond its own self-contained narrative. It recalls and orders details already present in the poem. Like the river (110–11) and the fountains confronted by the Lover in the garden (1390), the fountain Narcissus comes to is "clere" (1468). The "grant orguil" (1488) for which Narcissus is punished by Amors recalls his already acknowledged power to punish arrogance (866–70). The description of Narcissus approaching the fountain is a miniature portrayal of movements already undertaken by the Lover.

> que Narcisus par aventure
> a la fontaine clere et pure

se vint soz le pin ombroier
un jor qu'il venoit de chacier,
qu'il avoit soffert grant traval
de corre et amont et aval,
tant qu'il ot soif por l'aspreté
dou chaut et por la lasseté
qui li ot tolue l'alaine.
Et quant il vint a la fontaine
que li pins de ses rains covroit,
ilec pensa que il bevroit. (1467–78)

[One day when Narcissus was returning from hunting he came by chance to rest at the clear, pure fountain under the pine. He had endured such labor in pursuing the hunt by hill and valley that he was very thirsty, what with the fierce heat and the fatigue that had left him out of breath, and when he saw the fountain, covered by the branches of the pine, he thought that there he would drink. p.50]

The setting causes the fable and the narrative to converge. The clear fountain shaded by trees and the eye-catching pine remind us that the fountain discovered by the Lover is the same one that once destroyed Narcissus. Here too the hunting imagery and the physical thirst that draws Narcissus to the fountain remind us of similar details used in the description of the Lover.

The intersection of the two stories does not, however, identify the Lover as Narcissus. It is rather an invitation to evaluate the Lover's actions in comparison with Narcissus should he approach the fountain. Only in the future could the Lover become more like Narcissus. For this reason the fable conveys not simply moral warning but holds the possibility that it may be prophetic, marking not only the intersection but integration of the stories.

The evaluative function of the fable in Guillaume's poem is not only found in the parallel between the Lover and Narcissus. It is also evident in the form of the story. This is obvious when we compare Guillaume's version of the fable with the *Lai de Narcisus*. While the *Lai* is an amplified narrative, Guillaume's *translatio* is arranged as an abbreviated moralization. It begins just as commentary on the fable might commence. Narcissus, the subject of the fable, is identified first and then in the course of several lines the plot is sketched and the end revealed.

Narcisus fu uns demoisiaus
qui Amors tint en ses raisiaus;
et tant le sot Amors destraindre
et tant le fist plorer et plaindre
qu'il li covint a rendre l'ame,

car Equo, une haute dame,
l'avoit amé plus que rien nee,
et fu por lui si mal menee
qu'ele dit que il li donroit
d'amor ou ele se mouroit. (1437–46)

[Narcissus was a young man whom love caught in his snares, love knew so well how to torment him, to make him weep and complain, that he had to give up his soul. For Echo, a great lady, had loved him more than anything born, and was so ill-used on his account that she told him that she would die if he did not give her his love. p.50]

It is appropriate to think of this abbreviated version as formally related to the compressed version of the fable we found in the *Narrationes*, and in the commentary of Arnulf of Orleans. The exemplum drawn at the end of the story makes the moral function of the story even more obvious.

Dames, cest essample aprenez,
qui vers vos amis mesprenez;
car se vos les lessiez morir,
Dex le vos savra bien merir. (1505–8)

[You ladies who neglect your duties toward your sweethearts, be instructed by this exemplum, for if you let them die, God will know how to repay you well for your fault. p. 51]

The attached moral suggests the systematic arrangement one would expect to find in a school exercise. But there is more to the moralization than this, and it would be wrong to regard it as an appeal with no bearing on the progress of the Lover. By abruptly breaking the continuity of the narration, the gloss calls attention to itself.[25] Although the narrative has established a parallel between Narcissus and the male Lover, the exemplum unexpectedly shifts the significance of the fable to women.[26] The very moment we expect the moral to be applied to the Lover, such application is deflected. This is important, for it momentarily suspends our comparison of the Lover and Narcissus, thereby raising a question about the applicability of the fable. A precedent for such a shift certainly comes from the rhetorical use of Narcissus in Provençal lyric. But here something else is at work as well. By directing the example away from the Lover, Guillaume prepares for the Lover's own decision that Narcissus can teach him nothing that he does not already know.

While Guillaume's rhetorical strategy parallels the Lady's association with Narcissus in early poetry, it is even more related to Ovid's text. In the fable too (432–36) the narrator interrupts to warn Narcissus of his error, dramatically heightening our awareness of Narcissus' misperception in the process.

Similar to the narrator's appeal in the fable, the voice of the narrator in the French poem gives a warning strategically removed from the Lover. Like the warning in Ovid's fable, this voice too prepares for the possibility of eventual entrapment.

The story evoked by the words carved in the marble fountain represents what has passed through the Lover's mind. It is a good example of the way fables could portray mental processes. At first the memory of Narcissus' fate causes the Lover to question whether he should look into the fountain.

> Quant li escrit m'ot fet savoir
> que ce estoit trestot por voir
> la fontaine au bel Narcisus,
> je me suis trez un poi ensus,
> que dedenz n'ousai esgarder,
> ainz comançai a coarder,
> que de Narcisus me sovint
> cui malement en mesavint. (1509–16)

> [When the inscription had made clear to me that this was indeed the true fountain of the fair Narcissus, I drew back a little since I dared not look within. When I remembered Narcissus and his evil misfortune I began to be afraid. p. 51]

Then in several remarkable lines, the Lover concludes that his reaction is foolish.

> Mes me pensai que a seür
> sanz peor de mauvés eür,
> a la fontaine aler pooie;
> por folie m'en esloignoie (1517–20)

> [But then I thought that I might be able to venture safely to the fountain, without fear of misfortune, and that I was foolish to be frightened of it. p. 51]

We are not told precisely why he was afraid to look into the fountain, or what removes his fear. Nonetheless, it is obvious that his initial reluctance comes from fear that he could be captured by his reflection like Narcissus. The fear disappears when subjected to rational examination. He is not so foolish as Narcissus and knows—through the example of Narcissus—about the insubstantial nature of reflections. The use of *folie* (1520) stands out because it is the same word often used to describe Narcissus. A reversal has taken place as well. Just as Narcissus was foolish to be deceived by his reflection, the Lover would be foolish to stay away from the fountain. In contrast to Narcissus, the Lover believes he approaches the fountain through reason.

At the same time that the Lover's response is reasoned, it is limited. Yet he too will undergo a profound change at the fountain. Even though the Lover's knowledge of Narcissus' fate will protect him from being deceived by reflections on the water's surface, he has no awareness that the fable may be applicable to him in ways he cannot yet conceive. For this reason there is a paradox in the Lover's decision. While his actions are governed by reason, his use of reason remains restricted. He would use his knowlege for guidance but, as we found in his application of *seraines*, he can use his knowledge only with limited effect. Narcissus not only warns about reflections but about reliance on the faculties in general. The error he commits involves his incapacity to understand the ways the fable *could* be applicable to him. We think of the moral force of Narcissus wrongly if we regard it as a fable that only conveys an abstract warning about vanity, pride, or self-love. The fable conveys these meanings *not* through abstraction but through psychological detail. It is precisely the reliance on the senses without comprehension of their propensity for error that gives Narcissus moral significance. Ironically, the Lover's error lies in the incomplete perception of the very fable that warns against trust in one's own perception.

The Lover's response to the fable belongs with other cases of errors in judgment that involve the misapplication of *historia*. It is especially instructive to compare the manner in which the Lover responds to the fable with the use of Narcissus in Dante's *Paradiso* (III.1–33).[27] When translucent, shimmering faces appear before the pilgrim, he vigilantly turns away from them to seek their true faces. His action would demonstrate the knowledge of optics he has drawn from Ovid's fable. But as he learns from Beatrice, he has made an error. The shadowy faces he turns away from are real heavenly phenomena. Rather than excessive trust in vision, his fault now becomes excessive trust in his earthly senses and in the fables related to them. The comparison we would make between the Lover and the pilgrim comes not only from the incomplete or insufficient knowledge they gain from the fable but from the way response to the fable is linked to epistemological problems. In each case the fable becomes a vehicle that permits the representation and comprehension of new vision. The fable is so important because it can be used to mark shifts in perception. For the pilgrim such vision involves the new spiritual optics of the heavenly spheres. For the Lover it involves comprehension of the new vision afforded by love at the fountain.

The Fountain

As the Lover approaches the fountain, the text resonates with matter from the Latin fable.

De la fontaine m'apressai;
quant je i fui, si m'abessai
por voair l'eve qui couroit
et la graveile qui bouloit
au fonz, plus clere qu'argenz fins.
De la fontaine c'est la fins,
en tot le monde n'a si bele.
L'eve est tot jorz fresche et novele,
qui nuit et jor sort a grant ondes
par .II. doiz cleres et parfondes.
Tot entor croist l'erbe menue,
qui vient por l'eve espesse et drue
ne en yver ne puet mourir,
ne l'eve sechier ne tarir.
El fonz de la fontaine aval
avoit .II. pierres de cristal
qu'a grant entente remirai.
Mes une chose vos dirai
qu'a merveille, ce cuit, tendroiz
maintenant que vos l'entendroiz. (1521–40)

[I approached the fountain, and when I was near I lowered myself to the ground to see the running water and the gravel at the bottom, clearer than fine silver. It is the fountain of fountains; there is none so beautiful in all the world. The water is always fresh and new; night and day it issues in great waves from two deep, cavernous conduits. All around, the short grass springs up thick and close because of the water. In winter it cannot die, nor can the water stop flowing. At the bottom of the fountain were two crystal stones upon which I gazed with great attention. There is one thing I want to tell you which, I think, you will consider a marvel when you hear it: p. 51]

The passage recalls events already described in the poem. The "graveile" (1524) he sees recalls the "graveile" (121) seen at the bottom of the river. Here, however, the description of the gravel, "plus clere qu'argenz fins" (1525), imitates Ovid's description of the water: "fons erat inlimis, nitides argenteus undis" (407). Now the reflective nature of the water in Guillaume's earlier description of the river ("l'eve clere reluisant," 118) is transferred to the bottom of the fountain. Ovid's description of the grass surrounding the fountain ("gramen erat circa, quod proximus umor alebat," 411) becomes part of the setting as well, and is amplified to convey the timeless, suspended nature of the fountain. Even the stress on reflection evident in the Latin text through repetition ("dumque," 415, 416) and syntax (425–26) is brought into the French text through the repetition of end rhymes, at first in lines 1525 and 1526 and later in lines 1573, 1574, 1575, 1576.

The description of the fountain directs our eyes into the water two times. The first time we see the "graveile" as we did in the river and learn that the fountain is an artesian well with two sources (1521–30). Then after shifting our attention to the grass surrounding the fountain (1531–34), Guillaume once again directs our attention to the bottom of the fountain where two crystals now appear as well. The intensified perspicacity we find here is also present in the Latin text.

> dumque bibit, visae conreptus imagine formae
> spem sine corpore amat, corpus putat esse, quod unda est.
> adstupet ipse sibi vultuque inmotus eodem
> haeret, ut e Pario formatum marmore signum. (416–19)

> [While he drinks he is overwhelmed by the form he sees. He loves an unsubstantial hope and believes that a body which is only water. In speechless wonder he hangs there motionless in the same expression like a statue carved from Parian marble.]

In the Latin text the combination of three words related to vision (*visa*, *imago*, *forma*) creates an abstract, technical idea of the process involved in sight. The first time Narcissus looks into the water he sees the image of a form; "visae conreptus imagine formae" (416). Next, he sees a face, "vultus" (418), which signifies that the abstract form has become more specific. Then the face too is further specified as his attention focuses on eyes which appear like twin stars: "spectat humi positus geminum, sua lumina, sidus" (420). The reference to twin stars is important, for it is the descriptive detail behind the twin crystals in the French text.

The segmented description of the images in each text suggests a process by which the field of vision is narrowed and carefully focused. Just as Ovid's description shifts from the image of a perceived form (416) to *lumina* (420), Guillaume shifts from *graveile* to *cristal*. The detail stresses the care with which Guillaume has studied the Latin text and points to the intricacy with which he has related the events at the river and the fountain.

At times critics have assumed that the crystals are the eyes of the woman because love generated by the pupillary mirror in the eyes of a woman occurs in Provençal poetry.[28] The identification of a textual source for the crystals has special importance for this discussion. By observing that the crystals are drawn from the star-like eyes of Narcissus, we are given reason to think that the crystals are related to the Lover's eyes. The later description of Narcissus as one who saw both his face *and* eyes ("mira sa face et ses ieuz vers," 1571) shows that Guillaume had Ovid's text in mind in his representation of the Lover at the fountain.

The description of the Rose as a rose with its own physical qualities further suggests the incongruity of regarding the crystals as an allegorical expression of a woman's eyes. The Rose never becomes a personification but remains a symbol throughout Guillaume's poem. This does not mean, however, that we are driven to a harsher, censorial position either, for the crystals are *not* a reflection of the Lover's eyes. To see the events at the fountain as pointing to self-love is too restrictive an accommodation of the text to the moral sense of the fable. Instead, the appearance of the crystals within the fountain signals the beginning of a more precise allegory of the Lover's vision. This allegory further marks the Lover's separation from Narcissus. At the very moment that we might expect Guillaume's use of Narcissus to lead to moral censure, it leads to further psychological investigation.

When the Lover looks into the fountain, there is a shift in the narrative. For hundreds of lines we have been taken by a steady progression of visual detail across the garden landscape. When we look into the fountain and see its minute internal structure our focal point becomes specific and even microscopic. The description of detail beneath the water draws close attention to the sequence of events and creates an intimacy suggesting access to a mystery. Indeed, we learn that Guillaume himself thinks of the events as a "mistere" (1600). Guillaume's allegory, however, does not simply create a mystery; it works above all to provide rational explanation. What is sought is "la verité de la matere" (1599). The additional description which follows the mention of the "cristal" (1536) is a technical commentary identifying these crystals and creating an allegory of vision itself.

Quant li solaus, qui tot aguiete,
ses rais en la fontaine giete
et la clarté aval descent,
lors perent colors plus de cent
ou cristal, qui par le soleil
devient inde, jaune et vermeil.
Si est cil cristaus merveilleus,
une tel force a que li leus,
arbres et flors, et quan qu'aorne
le vergier, i pert tot a orne.
Et por la chose feire entendre,
un essample vos voil aprendre:
ausi con li mireors montre
les choses qui sont a l'encontre

et i voit l'en sanz coverture
et lor color et lor figure,
tot autresi vos di por voir
que li cristaus sanz decevoir
tot l'estre dou vergier encuse
a celui qui en l'eve muse;
car torjors, quel que part qu'il soit,
l'une moitié dou vergier voit;
et c'il se torne, maintenant
porra veoir le remenant;
si n'i a si petite chose,
tant soit reposte ne enclouse,
dont demontrance ne soit feite
con s'ele ert ou cristal portrete. (1541–68)

[When the sun, that sees all, throws its rays into the fountain and when its light descends to the bottom, then more than a hundred colors appear in the crystals which, on account of the sun, become yellow, blue, and red. The crystals are so wonderful and have such power that the entire garden appears there all in order. To help you understand, I will give you an example. Just as the mirror shows things that are in front of it, without cover, in their true colors and shapes, just so, I tell you truly, do the crystals reveal the whole condition of the garden, without deception, to those who gaze into the water, for always, wherever they are, they see one half of the garden, and if they turn, then they may see the rest. There is nothing so small, however, hidden or shut up, that is not shown there in the crystal as if it were painted in detail. p. 51]

When the rays of the sun penetrate the clear water and touch the crystals, colors appear (1541–46). Then, as if related to the presence of the colors the crystals have the power to order all that is in the garden ("pert tot a orne," 1550). To further instruct his audience, Guillaume uses an exemplum. The crystals are like mirrors which reflect the color and form of any object placed before them. But while the crystals are free from deception and can reveal the entire garden, they can only reflect half of the garden at a time (1561–64). If one looks at the crystals from the opposite side of the fountain another side of the garden comes into view. Their ability to reflect half of the garden at a time does not imply weakness, for they are capable, through movement, of showing the entire garden. The commentary stresses the physical power of the crystals. They are able to transform the sunlight into color, order the garden, and when directed at different portions of the garden bring forth its smallest detail. The truth of the image seen in the crystals and the explanatory form of the commentary itself is present in the use of *demontrance* (1567), a word of argument and proof.

This allegory of vision invites us to ask what significance crystalline stones have in twelfth-century lapidaries.[29] The most important lapidary in the twelfth and thirteenth centuries was *De lapidibus* by Marbode of Rennes (1035–1123).[30] This encyclopedic work, written at the beginning of the twelfth century, exists in many French versions.[31] Two stones, *crystallo* and *beryllus*, attract special attention.

The stone commonly identified as *crystallo* in Marbode's work (*De lapidibus*, 41) is known today as transparent quartz. Its name comes from the Greek word *krystallos*, which means rock crystal or ice. Its resemblance to ice was attributed to its supposed formation in ancient glacial ice. Although associated with ice, one of its primary virtues is that it creates heat and fire when used as a burning glass.

> Sed certum cunctis, nec stat dubitabile cuiquam
> Quod lapis hic soli subjectus concipit ignem
> Admotosque sibi solet hunc accendere fungos. (556–58)
>
> [But true it is that held against the rays/ of Phoebus it conceives the sudden blaze,/And kindles tinder, which, from fungus dry/Beneath its beam, your skilful hands apply.]

While it is tempting to wonder if crystal's ability to conceive fire from sunlight could also be understood as a figurative representation of the conception of amatory flames, nothing in the account points in this direction.

Beryl (*De lapidibus*, 12), on the other hand, another crystalline stone confused with rock crystal in the Middle Ages, was said to have the virtue of generating love: "Hic est conjugis gestare refertur amorem" ["With mutual love the wedded couple binds"]. Its association with light rays under water and eyesight, together with its amatory power, suggests a configuration that takes us closer to the mysterious virtues of Guillaume's fountain crystals. The amatory function of beryl, related specifically to conjugal love in Marbode's text, is made more general in the French translations. The first version from the twelfth century declares that beryl "ome e feme fait entramer."[32] Although the entries show that certain stones were thought to generate love and reminds us that the attention Guillaume gave stones is not unusual, it does not account for the crystals' function in the more detailed visual process described in the text. To more fully understand the operation of the crystals in Guillaume's allegory of vision we must consider accounts of the visual origin of love in more detail.

Accounts of the visual origin of love were common and appear at least as early as Plato's *Phaedrus*.[33] They are found in the church fathers,[34] in treatises devoted to love,[35] and in Ovid and other Roman poetry.[36] Even more detailed attention is found in medical or optical handbooks. Due perhaps to the modern propensity to think of vision phenomenologically rather than physiologically, this medical material continues to receive little attention. In the twelfth century the situation was quite different. Because of growing commerce with the Middle East and Spain, medical handbooks became available and circulated widely. For this reason the anatomical study of the eye's structure came to be an important component in the psychological discussions of vision. The significance medicine has for *De amore* by Andreas Capellanus is a good example.[37] Detailed accounts of vision based on knowledge of optics and physiology hardly remain foreign to twelfth-century poetry. A remarkable passage in Chrétien de Troyes' *Cligés* provides an instructive survey of such discussion and helps us rethink our understanding of Guillaume's fountain and its relation to optics.[38]

Soon after Alexander arrives at King Arthur's court, he falls in love with Sordemours. In a long speech (618–864) he describes his ailment and seeks to understand how love can have such a powerful effect. As his discourse proceeds it becomes more and more analytical until it concludes with an account of how the image of the loved one enters the eyes and affects the heart.[39]

> If the dart entered through the eye, why does the heart in the breast complain, when the eye, which received the first effect makes no complaint of it at all? I can readily account for that: the eye is not concerned with the understanding, nor has it any part in it; but it is the mirror of the heart, and through this mirror passes, without doing harm or injury, the flame which sets the heart on fire. For is not the heart placed in the breast just like a lighted candle which is set in a lantern? If you take the candle away no light will shine from the lantern; but so long as the candle lasts the lantern is not dark at all, and the flame which shines within does it no harm or injury. Likewise with a pane of glass, which might be very strong and solid, and yet a ray of the sun could pass through it without cracking it at all; yet a piece of glass will never be so bright as to enable one to see, unless a stronger light strikes its surface. Know that the same thing is true of the eyes as of the glass and the heart is accustomed to see itself reflected, and lo! it sees some light outside, and many other things, some green, some purple, others red or blue; and some it dislikes and some it likes, scorning some and prizing others. But many an object seems fair to it when it looks at it in the glass, which will deceive if it is not on its guard. My mirror has greatly deceived me. (697–741)

The passage sets forth in a simple manner ideas central to the twelfth-century understanding of vision. To explain why the heart, not the eye, complains when the dart enters, Chrétien appealed to faculty psychology. The eye does not suffer because it is only the receptor of the visual images, not the rational faculty whose function it is to interpret the visual stimuli. By itself the eye has no sensation.

With the example of the candle and lantern, Chrétien set forth the two conditions regarded as essential for sight: a source of light and a means of directing it. The example probably comes from Empedocles through Aristotle.[40] The candle is a representation of the animal or visual spirit which flows from the heart to the brain and radiates from the eyes. Although the example points to an extramission theory of vision, such theories were not based wholly on a conception of an internal light source but required a theory of external illumination as well.[41] Chrétien followed accounts in which external light is a precondition for the efficacy of the visual ray.

Another precondition for vision appears in the necessary relation between light and color. Only through color do we know of light's existence.[42] The eye is like a lantern in the way it holds and directs the visual spirit and also like a glass. If light comes only from an inner source, the heart sees a reflection of itself in the glass. If there is a strong external light, the glass becomes transparent and the heart is flooded with colored images that it either likes or dislikes. The judgment of objects points again to an underlying notion of faculty psychology in which visual stimuli are analyzed by the rational faculty. What is of greatest importance, however, is that even though the rational faculty is engaged, it may be deceived by an unexpected visual ray which affects the heart directly.

I have already suggested that it is important to think of Guillaume's description of the crystals as a technical commentary. The process he describes becomes more apparent when placed alongside Chrétien's text. For Chrétien the visual process takes the following form: external light strikes the surface of the eyes and, as color, permits the perception of many objects. Some Alexander likes, some he dislikes. As the objects are perceived, another light penetrates the eyes, deceives the judgment, and enflames the heart. Although Guillaume did not portray the process in the same analytic manner, his allegory depicts a similar process. Sunlight strikes the crystals beneath the water and produces color. The mirror-like surface of the crystals shows forth the garden and its detail. Suddenly among the many things observed in the crystals, an object appears which deceives the Lover and occupies his entire attention. As we study Guillaume's text in regard to psychological accounts of vision, details which first apppear to have no defined relationship become integrated in a configuration that accounts for vision allegorically.

Here the fountain is not simply a monument that commemorates Narcissus as it is in the *Ovide moralisé*. Its allegorical meaning is intimately related to the Lover's own faculty of perception, for as a receptacle of images the fountain is a representation of the human eye.

That Guillaume should have used the fountain as a figure for the allegorical representation of vision is not as unusual as it might at first appear. Marbode's lapidary has already shown how stones were given visual and amatory significance. Early discussion of vision made the relation of the eye to water specific. In *De sensu* Aristotle observed that "the visual organ is composed of water." He went on to notice, however, that by itself water is insufficient for vision. Vision involves reflection. In contrast to Plato and Democritus in particular, Aristotle analyzed not only the phenomena of reflection in regard to vision but its location. The distinction drawn by Aristotle is important for our consideration of Guillaume.

> Democritus . . . is right in his opinion that the eye is of water; not, however, when he goes on to explain seeing as mere mirroring. The mirroring that takes place in an eye is due to the fact that the eye is smooth, and it really has its seat not in the eye which *is seen*, but in that which *sees*. For the case is merely one of reflection. But it would seem that even in his time there was no scientific knowledge of the general subject of the formation of images and the phenomena of reflection. It is strange too, that it never occurred to him to ask why, if his theory be true, the eye alone sees, while none of the other things in which images are reflected do so. *De sensu* (438a)

Vision is possible *not* because the eye reflects external objects on its surface that may be seen by an external observer, but because objects are reflected *within* the perceiving eye. Guillaume's description of the reflective ability of the crystals must be seen in regard to this distinction. The image reflected by the crystals should be understood *not* as the images which rebound off the smooth surface of the eye, but as images which are reflected within the eye.

According to Aristotle, the reflective agent of vision is located deeper within the eye.

> The soul or its perceptive part is not situated at the external surface of the eye, but obviously somewhere within: whence the necessity of the interior of the eye being translucent, i.e. capable of admitting light. *De sensu* (438b)

To understand with exactitude how Guillaume's description of crystals beneath the water can be a representation of a reflective agent essential for sight we must turn to medical accounts of the eye.

Beginning in the eleventh century, accounts of the eye became available in the Latin West that explained the parts of the eye and their function in detail unknown since the end of the classical period. In these discussions one could learn of the existence of a glass-like lens suspended in the eye's fluid. Since the time of Galen, the lens was referred to as the crystalline humor. It was Hunain ibn Ishaq (d. 877), also known to the West as Johannitius, who first taught the Latin Middle Ages about the crystalline humor in a work known today as *The Ten Treatises on the Eye*.[43] In the Middle Ages the work was known as the *Liber de oculis* in a translation attributed to Constantinus Africanus at the end of the eleventh century.[44]

When we look at the *Liber de oculis* we are immediately struck by the primary importance given to the crystalline humor in the process of vision.

> Sunt enim de diversis multisque partibus compositi: visus enim non fit nisi una suarum partium, id est humore qui crystalloidos dicitur. Ceteri vero humores et panniculi non sunt nisi propter juvamentum crystalloides. p. 167
>
> [The eye is composed of many different parts. Vision, however, arises from only one of these parts which is called the crystalline humor. The rest of the humors and small tissues exist only to aid the crystalline humor. p. 3]

Hunain then proceeds to discuss the characteristics of the eye's dominant humor.

> Est autem crystalloidos humor albus et lucidus, non omnino rotundus quia aliquantulum planus: qui locatur in medio oculorum. Est albus et splendidus ut cito varios suscipiat colores. Album enim et splendidum corpus coloribus velociter opponitur, sicut videmus fieri in claro vitro. p. 168
>
> [The crystalline humor is white and luminous. It is not completely round, however, because it is somewhat flat. It is situated in the middle of the eye. It is white and shiny so that it may quietly receive a variety of colors. With its white and shiny quality, it rapidly reflects colors just as we find in clear glass. p. 3]

Following this the precise location of the crystalline humor is described. It is sustained by the clear vitreous humor which resembles glass. In front of it is an aqueous humor which separates the structure from the cornea. Beneath the crystalline and vitreous humors is the optic nerve which leads to the brain. The crystalline humor is crucial to the process of vision because it is the receptacle for color and form and the means by which they are conveyed to the optical nerve and the brain.

Hunain's description of the eye's structure provides important detail for our understanding of Guillaume's fountain, for it indicates that the crystals beneath the water, with their ability to receive color from the sun's rays, are most likely a physical allegory of the crystalline humor situated within the watery substance of the eye. The crystals' receptivity to color, their ability to order the visual imagery of the garden, and their inability to reflect the entire garden at once, point to the process of vision as understood at the beginning of the thirteenth century.

Details in Guillaume's text suggest that it may even be possible to extend the physical allegory of the fountain beyond the crystals. We saw above that the eye consists of three humors—the crystalline, vitreous, and aqueous humors. The presence of a bubbling source (1528–30) which passes through a shiny, silvery bottom that in turn supports the crystals, may point toward an allegorical representation of the eye's major structures. The bubbling source passing through the silvery gravel (1525) may be a representation of the visual spirit issuing from the optic nerve and passing through the vitreous and crystalline humors. Guillaume describes the source in the following manner:

> L'eve est tot jorz fresche et novele,
> que nuit et jor sor a grant ondes
> par .II. doiz cleres et parfondes. (1528–30)
>
> [The water is always fresh and new; night and day it issues in great waves from two deep, cavernous conduits. p. 51]

The two *doiz* (1530) or channels correspond to the two crystals and seem to be a representation of the optic nerves leading into the eyes. These nerves were considered remarkable in the twelfth and thirteenth centuries because they were thought to be hollow. Hunain says this about the optic nerve:

> Quia ipse solus est concavus cuius concavitas sensui ostenditur. Que concavitas tendit se celare, quod facile sensui patet, si anathomia cernatur. p. 173
>
> [(It differs from the other nerves in that . . .) it alone is hollow and may be seen. This hollowness, which tends to conceal itself, may be seen easily if it is studied anatomically. p. 21]

The fact that Jean de Meun later described the source at the bottom of Guillaume's fountain as two hollow conduits ("deus doiz creuses," 20439), further suggests that they may represent a contemporary idea of the hollow optic nerves.

We hardly need to make Guillaume into an early thirteenth-century ophthalmologist to account for the incorporation of such technical matter into his poem. Ovid not only supplied the *geminum sidus* which led to the crystals; he also provided justification for the physical allegory we have just examined. Following the description of Narcissus' futile efforts to grasp his reflection, Ovid adds what was regarded in the twelfth and thirteenth centuries as a technical commentary on his own text.

> quid videat, nescit, sed quod videt uritur illo,
> atque oculos idem; qui decipit, incitat error.
> credule, quod frustra simulacra fugacia captas?
> quod petis, est nusquam, quod amas, avertere, perdes!
> ista repercussae, quam cernis, imaginis umbra est. (430–34)
>
> [What he sees, he does not recognize; but what he sees he burns for, and the same delusion at once mocks and entices his eyes. Oh foolish boy, why vainly try to hold a fleeting image? What you seek is nowhere; turn away and you will lose what you desire. What you see is the shadow of a reflected image;]

It is passages like this that permitted Ovid to be regarded as a philosopher. For a modern reader, analytical and diagnostic passages like this stand out because they interrupt the narration and shift the rhetorical tone. Often they are cited as examples of Ovid's humor. But such a view obstructs the scientific impression they conveyed to early readers. Simone Viarre has shown how passages like these were incorporated into scientific literature of the period.[45] William of Conches, for example, refers to Echo and Narcissus in a discussion about sound in *De substantiis*[46] and in *De naturis rerum* Alexander Neckam uses a discourse on mirrors for a digression on Narcissus.[47] In both cases the reference to the fable occurs in the context of the traditionally linked discussions of vision and hearing. What we find in Guillaume's text is an example of the way Ovid could provide descriptive detail as well as the larger scientific, or more precisely, psychological framework with which to comprehend this detail. While the crystals are drawn from *geminum sidus*, their allegorical representation is justified by Ovid's own technical commentary.

Understanding how Guillaume's fountain works as a physical allegory does more than account for details that have often been regarded as incongruous. It also helps explain the progression of events from the moment the

Lover sees the crystals in the water to the moment he is struck by Amors' first arrow. These events mark a process of psychological change that prepares for the precise moment Amors strikes the Lover. Shifts in the narrative indicate the decisive moments in the psychological process and may be abbreviated in the following way.

I. Recollection of Narcissus and decision that the fable is not applicable to the Lover (1509–20)
II. Approach to the fountain and the description of physical qualities of the crystals (1521–68)
III. Condemnation of the perilous crystal-mirror and declaration of their universal applicability (1569–1600)
IV. Reflection of the Lover in the crystals and admission of deception (1601–12)
V. Appearance of the rose bed in the crystals (1613–52)
VI. Attraction to a single rose (1653–78)
VII. Attack of Amors begins (1679)

The progression we find here reminds us that the moment of love comes only after careful attention is given to the crystals. The sequence also reminds us that it is too simplistic to think of the Lover falling in love at an actual fountain. The fountain, as we have seen, is an allegory of the Lover's sight in conjunction with his internal senses. The discovery of the crystals (section II above) represents the Lover's discovery of his own eyes. The abrupt shift from the affirmation of the crystals in section II to their condemnation in section III represents the Lover's recognition that vision is the primary agent of love. One's eyes are perilous because they initiate a process that may be irrevocable. Section IV portrays the continuation of the process already underway. The confession that he has seen his reflection in the crystals ("Mes de fort eure m'i miré," 1605) shows that the Lover has fulfilled the requirements for love mentioned previously (1573) and indicates that he is on the road to love.

> Qui en ce miroër se mire
> ne puet avoir garant ne mire
> que il tel chose as ieuz ne voie
> qui d'amors l'a mis tost en voie. (1573–76)

> [Whoever admires himself in this mirror can have no protection, no physician, since anything that he sees with his eyes puts him on the road to love. p. 52]

While sections I-IV portray an internal process in which vision is identified as an instrument of "volenté pure" (1584), section V marks the beginning of an outward process in which vision selects a single desired object. The appearance of the rose bed in the crystals in section V shows the audience what the Lover sees and prepares for his selection of a particular rose.

The movement from the general to the specific in sections V and VI continues a pattern already seen in the Lover's movement from the expansive river to the secluded garden, from the innumerable details of the garden to a single fountain, and from the silvery gravel in the fountain to the crystal-like stones. The progression from rose bed to particular rose, as well as the entire progression from universal to specific in the garden is a representation not only of the eye's ability to shift from the general to a specific meaningful detail, but of the direction of desire through the agency of vision. Only at the moment the Lover's eye focuses on a particular rose does Amors release the first dart. Up to this moment Guillaume defines the physical apparatus and psychological process necessary for love's conception.

To account fully for the use of optical imagery in the psychological process discussed above, we must return to two passages which appear incongruous if we stress the relation between the crystals and the Lover's own eyes. In the lines cited above, and later in the poem, the Lover sees himself reflected in the crystal-like mirrors.

> Adés me plot a demorer
> a la fontaine remirer
> et as cristaus, qui me mostroient
> mil choses qui entor estoient.
> Mes de fort eure m'i miré. (1601–5)

> [I wanted to remain there forever, gazing at the fountain and the crystals, which showed me the hundred thousand things that appeared there; but it was a painful hour when I admired myself there. p. 52]

How is it possible for the Lover to see his reflection in his own eyes? To account for this we must remind ourselves that the crystalline humor was thought to make sight possible through *internal* reflection within the eye. All sight, in essence, must be conceived of as involving internal reflection of an external object. From such a physical understanding of the eye, it follows that the only time a person could see himself reflected in the internal mirror of his eye would be when his reflection appeared on a smooth, external surface. Such a surface could be either an inanimate one such as water or the animate surface of another eye.

The passages cited above also indicate that the physical conception of love takes place in two steps. First, one needs to see one's reflection on another reflective surface. Then one must see "tel chose" (1575) that actually incites love. Although it is not directly stated, the "tel chose" is the visual ray that comes from the eye of another. The importance of an external visual ray for the inception of love is not made apparent in the discussion of the crystals but is implicit in the darts Amors shoots into the Lover's eyes. Such an idea is also found in the description of the Fountain of Love which is portrayed *not* as the eye which is the source of love's seed but rather as the eye in which the seeds are sown. This is made explicit in the text. "Sema d'Amors ici la graine/qui toute acuevre la fontaine" (1587–88). The past tense of the following passage makes this even more emphatic.

> Por la graine qui fu semee
> fu ceste fontaine apelee
> la Fontaine d'Amors par droit. (1593–95)
>
> [Because of the seed that was sown this fountain has been rightly called the Fountain of Love. p. 52]

It is of utmost significance that Guillaume referred here to the external visual ray obliquely, carefully excluding any reference to the eyes of a woman. Even when the Lover's eyes are struck by the darts of Amors, the eyes of a woman are not mentioned.

There are good reasons for the absence of any reference to the Lady's eyes. We mentioned earlier that specific reference to the physical body of the woman would clash with her symbolic presence in the poem as the Rose. But there is another reason as well. By not identifying the external source of the reflected image, Guillaume kept open to question the precise origin of love. Because we are never shown the eyes of the woman, we must imagine their presence. We create the idea of an actual beloved to take the place of the empty image before Narcissus and by so doing are drawn closer to the text. Yet paradoxically, Narcissus remains present. The absence of any reference to the Lady's eyes emphasizes the abstract nature of the Lover's devotion and makes it inevitable that we compare the intensity of his desire for a removed object to Narcissus' desire for his image. Once again the experience of the Lover and Narcissus are entwined.

The physical allegory present in Guillaume's account of the Fountain of Love also shows that a general notion of faculty psychology underlies the progression of events in the poem. Medical accounts of the eye were not limited to the physical structures alone but described in relation to the internal senses. Such physical examination of the eye had led to physical study of the brain and the cellular model of faculty psychology.[48] Philosophical discussion in the twelfth century also shows considerable interest in faculty psychology.[49] Within such a framework Guillaume's poem is not only an allegory of love but an allegory about the rational assimilation of emotion related to love. In the vocabulary of faculty psychology, the poem portrays the integration of the *virtus cognitiva*, *virtus imaginativa*, and the *virtus memorativa*.

These functions may be found in the poem, but they are not present in any systematic way. The poem actually goes beyond faculty psychology in its portrayal of the development of knowledge. Because of its formulation of the internal senses as fully developed functions, faculty psychology proposes what is essentially a static ideal, rather than a process accounting for the development of reason. Only through experience permitted by vision or the *virtus imaginativa* is the *virtus cognitiva* called upon to account for deception. Error finally rests not with the imagination or in the eyes, but with the faculty of reason. Guillaume's poem presents an allegorical account of change and development which cannot be accounted for by faculty psychology alone. It expands the fixed nature of medieval psychology and anticipates developmental psychology. Within the poem the account of love's inception becomes a means for describing the acquisition of identity and the evolution of personal history.

The psychological process portrayed by Guillaume is not restricted to the young adolescent Lover, but is applicable to all of aristocratic society.

> Maint vaillant home a mis a glaive
> cil miroërs, car li plus saive,
> li plus preu li mieuz afetié
> i sont tost pris et agaitié.
> Ci sort as genz noveile rage,
> ici se changent li corage,
> ci n'a mestier sens ne mesure,
> ci est d'amer volenté pure,
> ci ne se set conseiller nus. (1577–85)

> [This mirror has put many a valiant man to death, for the wisest, most intelligent and carefully instructed are all surprised and captured here. Out of this mirror a new madness comes upon men: Here hearts are changed; intelligence and moderation have no business here, where there is only the simple will to love, where no one can be counseled. p. 52]

The universal disruption caused by the crystals is not associated with the Fountain of Narcissus but to the more universal Fountain of Love. Guillaume does not transform one into the other as Köhler suggests but shows that the

Fountain of Narcissus is actually another designation of the Fountain of Love. Narcissus is representative of one disastrous experience at the Fountain of Love. The experience of love brought about through the eyes overwhelms reason. Love disrupts intelligence, moderation, the ability to receive counsel. These were the values of an entire class, the attributes disrupted by love in a tradition that continued into the renaissance epic. It is hardly a coincidence that several lines later (1596–97) Guillaume referred to the literary works which were an ideological expression of this level of society.

Guillaume's strategy for resolving the crisis of love follows the rational spirit of Ovid's work as well as its *materia*. The declaration we find at the beginning of the *Remedia amoris* that Ovid's science of love has turned *impetus* to *ratio* ("Et quod nunc ratio est, impetus ante fuit," 10) also describes Guillaume's *Roman de la Rose*. Use of Ovid's fable allowed discussion of love psychology and established the need for education in love. When the Lover is stunned by the darts of Amors, he is truly ready to begin his education. This is also signaled by the shift from description to dialogue that takes place at this point in the narrative. The Lover's conversation with Amors and the cast of figures he meets exemplify the rational inquiry that continues to underlie the poem. The guidance the Lover is given marks a shift not only from description to dialogue but from one Ovidian model to another. While the first part of the poem is constructed through the amplification of a fable from the *Metamorphoses*, later it is modeled after Ovid's *carmina amatoria*. Having shaped the Lover's dilemma with Narcissus, Guillaume sought to resolve it with strategy drawn from the *Ars amatoria* and the *Remedia amoris*.

We cannot judge the success of Guillaume's strategy because he left his poem unfinished. We know that the unfinished poem attracted the attention first of an anonymous poet, and then of Jean de Meun. Writing a conclusion was partly a rhetorical problem that involved working out an appropriate curriculum for the Lover to follow. An even greater problem concerned inventing a redefinition of love that would permit love's consummation.

Jean de Meun

Where Guillaume focused on the *mistere* of Narcissus, Jean de Meun used the fable in a more restricted way. Rather than amplifying detail from Ovid's text, he elaborated matter from Guillaume's poem. For this reason it is appropriate to think of the second part of the poem as a commentary on the first. While our study of Guillaume's text showed how the Latin fable was scanned for narrative and rhetorical detail and consulted for scientific insight, in Jean's section the fable was used as a component in an ideological discussion. Though less concerned with the imitation of Ovid, Jean's use of fable is hardly superficial. His sophisticated manipulation of fable actually undermines the dominance given to Narcissus in Guillaume's poem. In Nature's discussion of deception and finally in Genius's gloss of Guillaume's garden, we find an ordered critique of Narcissus and the use of the fable in love psychology. This criticism prepares for the eventual replacement of the fable altogether with Pygmalion.

Reason and Echo

While Jean's use of fable is close to commentaries such as John of Garland's *Integumenta Ovidii* or Alberic of London's mythographic compendium, his knowledge of mythography led him not to the static implementation of fable but to its inventive expansion.[50] It is as if the mythographic tradition we have studied in Chapter II taught Jean a new alphabet whose letters could be ever combined in ways that would give new meaning. The use of Narcissus in Reason's speech provides a good example of such invention. In the middle of her appeal to the Lover, Reason offers herself to the Lover as a companion.

> Si avras en cest avantage
> amie de si haut lignage
> qu'il n'est nule qui s'i conpere,
> fille Dieu, le soverain pere,
> qui tele me fist et forma.
> Regarde ci quele forme a
> et te mire en mon cler visage.
> N'onques pucele de parage
> n'ot d'amer tel bandon con gié,
> car j'ai de mon pere congié
> de fere ami et d'estre amee,
> ja n'en seré, ce dit, blamee;
> ne de blame n'avras tu garde,
> ainz t'avra mes peres en garde
> et norrira nos .II. ensemble.
> Di je bien? Respon, que t'en senble?
> Li diex qui te fet foloier,
> set il ses genz si bien poier?
> Leur apparaille il si bons gages
> aus fols dom il prent les homages?
> Por Dieu, gar que ne me refuses.
> Trop sunt dolentes et confuses

puceles qui sunt refusees,
quant de prier ne sunt usees,
si con tu meïmes le prueves
par Equo, sanz querre autres prueves. (5783–5808)

[Furthermore, you will have a lover of such noble family that there is none to compare with her; I am the daughter of God, the sovereign father who made and shaped me so. Look at my form and at yourself in my clear face. No girl of such descent ever had such power of loving as I, for I have leave of my father to take a friend and be loved. I shall never be blamed for it; nor need you worry about sin, since you will be in my father's keeping, and he will feed us both together. Do I say well? Answer me: how does it seem to you? Does the god who has made you mad know how to pay his followers well? Does he dress them at such cost, these fools whose homage he demands? Before God, take care lest you refuse me. Maidens unaccustomed to begging are thrown into great sorrow and turmoil when they are refused. You can prove this fact yourself by the case of Echo, without seeking other proofs. p. 117]

The passage reaffirms the association between the Lover and Narcissus established by Guillaume. It once more places Echo within the reasonable context we have already found her in Provençal poetry, the *Lai de Narcisus*, and in Guillaume's poem.

When Jean depicted Reason asking the Lover to look into her eyes, he turned a motif of courtly love upside down. Here an act that previously engendered an irrational response would signify the restoration of reason. The passage is more than a humorous aside, for it demonstrates that the exchange between Reason and Lover is actually a redefined version of the Lover's experience at the Fountain of Love. By asking the Lover to look at her beautiful form and into her clear face so he may see his reflection, she actually identifies herself as his mirror, or more precisely, as a manifestation of the Lover's own reason. Reason has the power to restore the Lover's senses. The warning that concludes Reason's speech is serious, for it shows us that, if the Lover ignores Reason's appeal, he will suffer as Narcissus suffered through the continued alienation of reason.

Jean's association of Reason and Echo also points toward a relation between vision and speech that is not made in Guillaume's allegory of the fountain. As Reason asks the Lover to see his image in her face, we discover a quite conscious relation drawn between the self-recognition of one's visual image and the ability to seize such self-recognition in language. While Guillaume's allegory is constructed from visual imagery and becomes reasonable when the visual details are fit into a physical process, Jean's description of

Reason as Echo indicates that the rational process he would portray is far more dependent on the use of language.

Nature

Nature's discourse on mirrors and dreams pushes the examination of reason and fable further and should be approached as a commentary on the problem of sensual deception raised by love and illustrated by Narcissus in Guillaume's poem. Nature's scientific discussion is a scholarly amplification of matters raised by the allegory. In particular Nature seeks to account for the phenomenon that Guillaume does *not* treat in detail. While Guillaume's allegory provides a representation of the eye's function, it does not include a discussion of the conditions under which visual deception occurs. We jump abruptly from praise of the crystals as true mirrors to their condemnation as instruments of deceit. In Nature's discourse on deception, Jean sought to account for this shift. Guillaume raised the problem of deception; Jean explained how it is possible.

In her lecture Nature provides example after example to illustrate the subjective nature of the senses. The purpose of these examples is to emphasize the importance of deception as a means of exercising, and thereby developing reason. A number of scholarly discussions have shown that these examples are drawn from thirteenth-century discussions of faculty psychology.[51] We must stress, however, that it is not the examples themselves that are most significant but the reason for their inclusion, which may be found in the visual phenomena discussed by Albertus Magnus and Alhazen, the optical authorities cited by Nature.

Albertus Magnus' commentary on Aristotle's *De anima*, or his presentation of vision in the *Summae de creaturis*, shows that his interest in physical phenomena was determined by efforts to understand the operation of the mind.[52] The fact that a stick appears bent when one part of it is under water, demands rational explanation.[53] Particularly interesting is the examination of internal senses to which the study of external phenomena leads.[54] The imagination is of special interest in Albert's discussion because he found it to be a faculty which, when used with care, can strengthen reason.[55] The deceptive optical phenomena which abound in these discussions and even the representation of deceptive phenomena through imagination become a means for affirming rational inquiry. Simply stated, error engenders reason.

In contrast to earlier optical discussion such as Hunain's *Liber de oculis*, Alhazen's *Perspectiva* contained not only more sophisticated integration of geometry and physiological investigation of the eye, but more detailed interest in the process by which visual images were assimilated by the internal senses.[56] This is given less attention in modern discussions, which are primarily concerned in analyzing Alhazen's proof of the intromission theory of vision and his application of geometry to light rays.[57] Alhazen sought to explain not only why images reflected by mirrors are reversed but included in his examination phenomena which represent the relation of the external and internal senses. He desired, for example, to comprehend how the eye recognizes letters, forms words, and makes these marks intelligible to the rational faculty.[58] By calling attention to Alhazen and his newer analytical optics, Jean criticized Guillaume's less sophisticated account of vision.

Both Alhazen and Albert used common physical phenomena to demonstrate the efficacy of reason. This interest in physical phenomena as a means of demonstrating and even testing the rational faculty stands behind Nature's discourse on mirrors and dreams. Perhaps the best example of Nature's use of physical phenomena is the remarkable intersection of reason and imagination we find in her combination of a magnifying glass and the fable of Mars and Venus.

Immediately after referring to Alhazen's book on optics (18004–13), Nature proceeds to describe the special power of the magnifying glass (18014–30). Then, as if to further demonstrate the great power of such an optical glass, Nature asks her audience to imagine what would have happened if Mars and Venus had taken such a glass to bed with them. Would they not have uncovered the trap set for them by Vulcan? The incongruity and hyperbole of the comparison strikes one as both amazing and amusing. But once again our smiles must not impede us from seeing the test of reason which stands behind the comparison.[59] The addition of a scientific instrument to Ovid's fable requires the imaginative refabrication of plot and encourages the rational investigation of the invention. Nature's example becomes analogous in function to the example of natural phenomena found in Albertus or Alhazen. Ultimately the question concerning Mars and Venus's use of such a glass is irrelevant. Jean makes it apparent that they would have found a way to make love without the glass. Certainly this inability to obstruct the sexual union of Mars and Venus points toward the union that lies at the end of the Lover's quest. Nevertheless, the glass brings nuance to one's comprehension of the fable, even though its presence does not affect its outcome. In part the addition of the magnifying glass represents the assimilation and even testing of a new scientific instrument within a traditional moral narrative. Above all it urges the audience to examine Vulcan's net and learn what is revealed by its magnified links.

The subtle net forged by Vulcan does not stop adultery, but rather publicizes it by allowing Mars and Venus to be displayed before the gods. The publicity brought about by the net, as well as its ability to entrap, suggest that the net has qualities very much like fabulous narrative itself.[60] Previously Nature recommended a glass for reading small letters; here she places the glass in the fable to urge the careful examination of fabulous narrative. Inherent in the juxtaposition of optical instrument and fable is the capability of each to cause error or induce correction. Like a magnifying glass, a fable can reveal meaning which is otherwise difficult to discern. Yet, like optical phenomena, fables too can mislead if they are not properly understood. The association of the glass and the fable urges us to find in Nature's demonstration a lesson about how reason might be used to reveal fabulous traps. What the Lover should learn from Nature's instruction is that a fable—like an eye or optical instrument—may be used to discover deception or bring deceit. Ultimately Nature's example must be construed as part of a censorial lecture against the Fountain of Love which captures Narcissus and threatens to do the same to the Lover.

While Nature is capable of explaining deceit that may originate in vision, she is not herself able to formulate the imaginative vision that finally is used to replace Narcissus. Such an imaginative task is left to Genius.

Genius

In his long sermon before the final assault on the Castle of Venus, Genius provides the Barons with arguments inciting their sensual combat. The detailed critical gloss he makes on Guillaume's fountain and his efforts to ridicule its deficiencies through comparison with the "biau parc" are part of an ongoing strategy to criticize and finally replace Narcissus as the central fable in the *Roman*. The criticism directed at the fountain is exact and shows that Jean examined Guillaume's text carefully. The commentary proceeds by questioning how anyone could be attracted by a fountain that has so many negative qualities. The fountain is bitter, venomous, and cruel. The Lover himself refers to it as "la fontaine perilleuse" (20379). This is the fountain where Narcissus perished.

> c'est la fonteine perilleuse,
> tant amere et tant venimeuse
> qu'el tua le biau Narcisus
> quant il se miroit iqui sus. (20379–82)

> [It is the perilous fountain, so bitter and poisonous that it killed the fair Narcissus when he looked at himself in it. p. 334]

The double source should especially raise questions, Genius argues, for it fails to acknowledge the spiritual source of all things.

> El sort, ce dit il, a granz ondes
> par deus doiz creuses et parfondes;
> mes el n'a mie, bien le sai,
> ses doiz ne ses eves de sai;
> n'est nule chose qu'ele tiegne
> qui tretout d'ailleurs ne li viegne. (20395–400)

> [He says that the fountain comes in great waves from two deep springs. But I know well that its springs and waters do not come of itself. There is nothing about it that does not come to it from elsewhere. p. 334–35]

The invocation of a universal which extends beyond the implicit limits of the original setting leads to the ridicule of the physical allegory. The irony of the sanctimonious criticism stands out when we recall that Genius is actually in the process of masterminding a sexual union. Criticism of the fountain depends on the omission of positive qualities included by Guillaume. The crystals' ability to order, show form and color, reflect the garden without deception and make one see even the smallest detail—all this is left out. In contrast to the wondrous spiritual source of the carbuncles in the fountain of the *biau parc*, Guillaume's crystals are made to seem utterly mundane. Besides showing only half of the garden at the same time, they depend on the sun. Even the accuracy of the earlier description is challenged, for how could one expect to see a reflection in a fountain where the water flows ceaselessly? Such detail shows that Jean subverted the physical allegory by approaching it as if it were a simple literal description. Rather than an eye, Jean had his audience think of the fountain as a cloudy well.

The calculated reinterpretation of the fountain also permits Jean to playfully twist the meaning of the original visual allegory. His repeated used of *trouble* (20404, 20410, 20418, 20424) not only portrays the cloudy and opaque nature of the water but describes eyes which cannot see well (18093, 18209). Thus, at the same time that the commentary would lead us to think of the fountain in literal terms, it makes a joke about the weakness of Guillaume's invention—or about the frailty of his vision.

The evocation of a universal that would logically subsume Guillaume's garden was also part of Jean's plan. Such strategy was, of course, a continuation of a tactic important for Guillaume as well. Just as Guillaume showed that the Fountain of Narcissus was logically included in his conception of the Fountain of Love, Jean demonstrated that Guillaume's entire garden may be subsumed under an even larger abstraction in the "biau parc." What is at play here is a sequence of ever larger abstractions. Viewed as a movement toward ever larger categories, the poem moves further and further from Ovid's Narcissus.

Genius's gloss of the fountain hardly represents Jean's entire attitude toward fable. Genius himself has a great arsenal of fable which he uses in his rhetorical bombardment of the Barons. Jean's inclusion of Cadmus and the founding of Thebes is of special interest because it shows that his criticism of Narcissus also fits within the structure of Theban history recounted in Book III of the *Metamorphoses*.

> Cadmus, au dit dame Pallas,
> de terre ara plus d'un arpent
> et sema les denz d'un sarpent,
> don chevalier armé saillirent
> qui tant antr'eus se combatirent
> que tuit en la place moururent
> for .V., qui si compaignon furent
> et li voldrent secours doner
> quant il dut les murs maçoner
> de Thebes, don il fu fondierres.
> Cist assistrent o lui les pierres
> et li peuplerent sa cité,
> qui est de grant antiquité.
> Mout fist Cadmus bone semance
> qui som peuple ainsic li avance. (19706–30)

> [Cadmus at a word from lady Pallas, plowed more than an arpent of ground and sowed the teeth of a serpent. From these, armed knights sprang up and fought one another until they all died on the spot except five who were his companions and wanted to give him help when he had to build the walls of Thebes, the city that he founded. With him they laid the stones and populated his city, he thus advanced his good people. If you also begin well, you will advance your lines a great deal. p. 325]

Cadmus, who sowed seeds as an act of Reason—stressed through his association with Pallas—and founded a great city, provides a model suitable for imitation, not the foolish Narcissus who lost his reason and contributed nothing to Thebes.

The critique of Guillaume's Narcissus finally leads to the replacement of the entire fable. To a Lover preoccupied with visual imagery like Narcissus, Reason offers rational argument in speech and thus for a moment can pose as Echo. Addressing the physics and psychology of deception, Nature can evaluate phenomena not treated in Guillaume's physical allegory. With his greater imaginative powers, Genius is able to offer a vision of another pastoral landscape which can take the place of Guillaume's garden. Within the dialectical examination that revealed the fabulous impediment to the Lover's progress, Jean replaced the fable which served as an expression of the Lover's impotence.

The introduction of Pygmalion comes as a further sign of the careful symmetry that Jean sought to develop in shaping his poem. A garden provides a conceptual orientation at the beginning of Guillaume's poem; at the end another garden appears to provide focal point for action. Now further symmetry appears. Just as Guillaume interrupted the Lover's approach to the fountain by retelling the story of Narcissus, Jean interrupts the assault on the Castle of Venus with Pygmalion.

By placing Pygmalion into the narrative, Jean also continued the process by which even greater abstractions were evoked to reveal the limitations of those already operative in the poem. Yet to speak of the poem's course as a logical process in which one invention is made to envelop another does not fully convey the dialectical progression from one abstraction to another. The poem does not jump from idea to idea but unfolds from earlier configurations. New fountains, gardens, and fables unfold from old ones. At the end of the poem Pygmalion unfolds from Narcissus, portraying the psychological growth of the Lover.

Finding that he is in love with a statue that he has carved, Pygmalion decries his inability to possess the object. Yet, even in his misery he announces that at least he is not like Narcissus who never could possess the image before him.

> Si n'ain je pas trop folement,
> car, se l'escriture ne ment,
> maint ont plus folement amé.
> N'ama jadis au bois ramé
> a la fonteine clere et pure,
> Narcisus sa propre figure,
> quant cuida sa saif estanchier?
> N'onques ne s'an pot revanchier,
> puis an fu morz, selonc l'estoire,
> qui oncor est de grant memoire.
> Don sui je mains fos toutevois,
> car, quant je veil, a ceste vois
> et la praign et l'acole et bese,

s'an puis mieuz souffrir ma mesese;
mes cil ne poait avoir cele
qu'il veait en la fontenele. (20843–58)

[But I do not love too foolishly, for, if writing does not lie, many have loved more dementedly. Didn't Narcissus, long ago in the branched forest, when he thought to quench his thirst, fall in love with his own face in the clear, pure fountain? He was quite unable to defend himself and, according to the story, which is still well-remembered, he afterward died of his love. Thus I am in any case less of a fool, for, when I wish, I go to this image and take it, embrace it, and kiss it; I can thus better endure my torment. But Narcissus could not possess what he saw in the fountain. p. 341]

The devotion Pygmalion shows the statue becomes a parody of the Lover's actions before the Rose and an ironic commentary on the conventions of courtly love. Immediately after Pygmalion distinguishes himself from Narcissus, he also compares his own hopeless state with that of lovers who follow courtly convention.

D'autre part, en maintes contrees,
ont maint maintes dames amees
et les servirent quan qu'il porent,
n'onques un seul besier n'en orent,
si s'an sunt il forment pené. (20859–63)

[Besides, many lovers in many countries have loved many ladies and served them as much as they could without a single kiss from them, although they exerted themselves strenuously. p. 341]

Pygmalion's allusion to this tradition and his reaction to the statue show that his actions still have much in common with Narcissus. This is also evident in Jean's continuing satiric allusion to Narcissus. Having complained of the cold kisses he receives from the statue, Pygmalion suddenly worries that he has offended the figure before him. The passage mimics Narcissus' fear that the image before him has left him, when his tears drop into the water and blur his reflection. Even Pygmalion's lament over his strange love may be related to Narcissus' complaint to the woods about his strange fate. Only when the statue miraculously begins to breathe and offers herself to Pygmalion does allusion to Narcissus cease.

In contrast to Narcissus who sees only dead images of himself, Pygmalion generates living images. But while Pygmalion's success frees him from sterility, his new experience also leads to new suffering. Pygmalion's family history becomes an exhibition of sexual aberration. Paphos, Pygmalion's daughter, gives birth to Cinyras who later commits incest with his daughter

Myrrah. Adonis, the issue of their union, displays even more dramatically the erratic nature of sexuality and the uncertainty that accompanies human sexuality.

Such problems show that Pygmalion not only replaces Narcissus but supplies commentary on Jean's conclusion. The sexual play with the statue, its animation, and Pygmalion's eventual union with the new creature, prepare for the sexual act that culminates the poem. Even more, the problematic sexuality of Pygmalion's offspring hints that pain as well as pleasure will follow the assault on the Castle of Shame.

Even though pain dominates the lives of Pygmalion's children, we must also see the outcome of the story as a celebration of life's continuation. With Pygmalion Jean evoked an idea of love that had procreation as its very goal. Love involving devoted suspension before an idealized object has given way to action and fruition. To the visual seeds of Guillaume's fountain, Jean added physical seeds. Even at the very end of the poem as the Lover scatters his seeds on the bud and desires to "tout cerchier/jusques au fonz du boutonet" (21694–5) ["examine everything right down to the bottom," p.353], Jean intended us to compare the Lover's physical action with his earlier inspection of the Fountain of Love and the seeds planted there. The shift from visual to physical experience describes not a renunciation of early experience but affirms psychological growth and a process of evolving maturity.

Our study of the *Roman de la Rose* has sought to do more than catalog the appearances of Narcissus in this expansive French poem. It has examined the use of Ovid's fable in the psychological investigation of love. We have seen the fable used in different ways in each part of the poem. In Guillaume's poem Narcissus is used for description, rhetorical strategy, and scientific commentary. In regard to the last category the fable is used as a departure point for a physical allegory of the fountain. By applying the fable to normal love psychology, Guillaume extended the relation between Narcissus and psychology and dramatized the suspension of the senses inherent in the experience of love. At the same time as Guillaume's poem may be regarded as the most complete expression of courtly love conventions, it may also be considered to contain implicit criticism of these conventions, particularly through the efforts made to resolve the Lover's crisis.

Jean's portion of the poem adopts and amplifies the educational form of Guillaume's poem. The comments made by Reason, Nature, and Genius attack the limitation of Guillaume's Lover and prepare for the eventual replacement of Narcissus by Pygmalion, a fable suggesting that even though he may remain ignorant, the Lover will enter history through sexual union.

It is not strange that we should think of history at the end of the poem.

History has been present throughout as a force balancing the Lover's isolation. It is history that is kept outside the garden, and it is to history the Lover must finally return. The garden in which Oiseuse personified the suspension of time must be dissolved. At the beginning of his dream the Lover leaves a wide river for introspection at the fountain. At the end his forceful actions mark his return to time. Macrobius' *Somnium Scipionis* not only reminds us that the entire poem suspends time as a dream but that the suspension takes place against the vast panorama of universal history. With the *Roman de la Rose* it is particularly Reason who uses history to appeal to the Lover. This of course is appropriate, for it is Reason with her superior vantage point who is able to comprehend the relation of events. Because the Lover remains without experience, Reason's historical arguments can have no effect on him. They do affect Jean's audience, however, by emphasizing the expanse of time from which the Lover remains isolated. Only through sexual experience at the end of the poem will the Lover be able to enter history. Our study of Ovid's Narcissus in the *Roman* has shown that the very fable which represents the suspension of time actually becomes the vehicle which leads back to history.

By using Narcissus for the portrayal of normal love psychology, the *Roman* also established justification for the continued use of the fable. Narcissus is not simply a negative exemplum warning against pride and self-love but a narrative inviting the resolution of deception through new vision. By depicting Narcissus forever looking into the fountain, Ovid created a fable that forever invites new visions that may entice Narcissus away. The great interest in Ovid's fable after the *Roman* shows that the French work taught many subsequent poets how to answer Ovid's invitation.

Conclusion

Ovid's fable posed an invitation for medieval and renaissance poets to invent new visions and narrative strategies that would resolve the confusion portrayed in Narcissus' experience at the fountain. In my concluding remarks I want to identify aspects of the fable which are instrumental in provoking response. Three closely related features deserve special attention—the fable's marvelous quality, its phenomenological detail, and its capacity as a short narrative to represent moments of psychological change and thereby individual growth. By looking at each of these features, I will be able to review parts of my previous discussion and also suggest why the fable continues to engender interest even today.

The marvelous qualities of Ovid's fable provoked a desire in pagan and Christian culture alike to ask what lay beyond the story's literal untruth. Within Christian schools a marvelous narrative like Narcissus engendered even greater faith that such fictions held valuable meaning. Macrobius' definition of *fabulosa narratio* provided early theoretical justification for such faith when it was needed. By using different modes of allegory as well as reformulating the plot of Ovid's narrative, commentaries located meaning within larger philosophical and religious preoccupations. Since I have discussed allegory above, I want to draw attention to the interpretive function of plot here. An abbreviated plot accompanies each of the commentaries we have looked at. These simple narratives articulate the sense of the fable and may become an aid either in construing the more complicated Ovidian text or in replacing it altogether. In both cases they work to redefine and even censor the original plot by establishing a rudimentary frame in which to think about the fable. Here plot is not a structure for entertainment but for signification. Such simplification of plot is an important means of remaking a narrative without including fabulous details and may be compared to rhetorical strategy that restates arguments in a form that makes them easier to refute.

The radically condensed plot in John of Garland's *Integumenta* as well as the broadly embellished plot in the *Ovide moralisé* screen Ovid's text by either transforming it into a form that is closer and more accessible or by ignoring parts of it altogether. Both also pose an invitation for imaginative elaboration as well, John's through a formulaic terseness that urges amplification and the French poem by demonstrating the license that may be taken in applying the fable.

Another aspect of the abbreviated plots found in commentaries and handbooks concerns narrative invention and can only be mentioned. As the reconfiguration of plot translates supernatural into natural events, it also shapes new narratives. This may be illustrated by pagan and Christian examples. Unable to accept the mythological account of Narcissus' death, Pausanius seeks to understand the boy's end as an accidental drowning caused when he fell into water while seeking the image of his twin sister. This euhemeristic translation of the fable not only rationalizes the story but invents another narrative. Such rationalization of Narcissus probably stands behind Boiardo's placement of female faces in fountains in *Orlando inamorato* (see appendix). In the *Ovide moralisé* the translation of the fable into a contemporary setting anticipates the allegorical invention of the Town of Narci and the extension of the fable to society as a whole. While allegory certainly contributes to the invention of narrative, efforts to rationalize the marvelous also work to formulate new narratives.

The phenomenological matters of vision and sound which dramatically contribute to the supernatural qualities of the story also counter the marvelous detail and make the story accessible. At one extreme the phenomena and experience included in the fable are common and a necessary precondition to human knowledge. The narrator's instructive warning to Narcissus conveys knowledge dependent on a shared experience of reflection and signals the moment at which the story makes its most universal appeal. At the other extreme Ovid's description of Narcissus' insane reaction to his reflection appears unnatural and teases one into a reexamination of phenomena, the senses that regulate them, and the nature of knowledge itself. The reactions caused by the fable—one urging identification with Narcissus and the other separation—explain why the fable seems paradoxically true and false. As we have seen, the association of reflected light and sound deserves comparison with the relation of these phenomena in Greek and Roman philosophy. Roman debates on skepticism also affect Ovid's portrayal of sensual disorientation and deserve further attention.[1] A precondition for such investigation is the simple but crucial recognition that Ovid's fable transforms mythological material related to Ceres, Bacchus, and Juno into an epistemological narrative.

Whether or not the fable was affected by Augustan philosophy, the skepticism suggested by the fable becomes acknowledged in a Christian setting. Plotinus' philosophical use of Narcissus to warn against the senses foreshadows the Neoplatonism that accompanies the fable within Christian culture. At the same time that it challenges the reliability of the senses, it admonishes faith in a metaphysical system that offers greater security than eyes or ears. Milton's silent use of the fable in his portrayal of Eve's early moments in Eden (*Paradise Lost*, IV:449–491) makes this point at the end of the Renaissance (see appendix). The phenomenological problems presented by the story make it into a privileged narrative both for the investigation of light and sound and for meditations on the limits of human knowledge. Its capacity to make ephemeral phenomena accessible stands behind its protoscientific application in the Middle Ages and explains why the *Metamorphoses* came to be used as an encyclopedia of natural phenomena.

The ease with which mirrors or other reflective surfaces replace Narcissus explains still other responses to the story. In the medieval texts we have studied, the place of Narcissus is secondary. Rather than being drawn to a figure before a fountain, commentators and poets are attracted to the visual and aural phenomena which are universally shared. It is not Narcissus which the Lover finds in the *Roman de la Rose* but his fountain. What we witness in the evolving Christian response to the fable is the displacement of the Ovidian plot by mirror metaphors. This is a crucial aspect in the reception of the fable, for it works to replace Ovid's text with imagined versions that give special attention to visual phenomena at the expense of sound and speech. Such a visually oriented model continues to be employed in the application of the fable in psychoanalytic theory. The fable's reception testifies to the privileged position of visual metaphor within Graeco-Latin tradition.

Condensation of the fabulous narrative into mirror metaphors affects our perception of the fable in an even more direct manner. By locating the primary agent of meaning in mirrors or reflecting surfaces, medieval tradition transformed everyone into a potential Narcissus. This universalization of the fable becomes even more fixed as the fable comes to depict love psychology. An important distinction follows from this. While the association of Narcissus and love psychology is certainly not invented by the Middle Ages, the application of the fable to *normal* love psychology may be justifiably thought of as a medieval invention. The extension of the fable to heterosexual relationships comes partly from approaching Echo and Narcissus as actual figures. Even more it takes place when the eye replaces the fountain as the agent of disorientation. At first the fable is limited to the initiation of love and the depiction of amorous longing for the absent loved-one. But even within this setting, the apparent isolation caused by love is complemented by asserting

Echo's active role. In simple terms hearing rectifies visual deception. While a Provençal poet like Bertran de Born uses Narcissus as a persona to represent love's visual origin, he also uses Echo as a persona to draw the Narcissus-like lady from isolation. The rhetorical use of Echo to develop strategies that transcend amorous isolation is expanded in the *Roman de la Rose*. For Guillaume de Lorris and Jean de Meun the fable not only diagnoses the amorous disease that afflicts the lovers, but prescribes the remedy through the rational qualities associated with Echo. These remedies are manifest in the allegorical dialogues which follow the Lover's experience at the fountain. In effect a critique of love's idealization and the divorce from society it portends makes up the greater part of the French poem. While the fable depicts suspension and isolation, it also argues for resolution that takes place in history.

The fable's capacity to portray psychological crisis and to invite resolution explains the popularity of Ovid's invention beyond the setting of love psychology. Dante's use of the fable in the *Divina commedia* provides an example of this. In Inferno XXX:124–29, the fable helps portray Master Adam, the Florentine counterfeiter, and Sinon the Greek, who tricked the Trojans into accepting the wooden horse. Even more it signals the danger of the pilgrim's own attraction to the spectacle before him and the stories he hears. Virgil's warning and the response it provokes show that the epistemological problem described in the fable becomes a means to give the pilgrim a mental life. This is also the case in Paradiso III:17–18. Thinking the angelic figures he sees are only shadowy reflections, the pilgrim prepares to protect himself from deception by recalling the lesson of Narcissus. Told that the images he sees are not illusory but spiritual figures, the pilgrim learns that he can no longer trust his earthly senses or the morals that have guided them. In both cases Narcissus signals a moment of psychological and spiritual growth.

Throughout this study attention has been given to the fable's evolving capacity to represent change and maturation. The *Roman* shows the fable to be appropriate for depicting adolescent change within amorous settings. Britomart's painful identification with Narcissus in Spenser's *Faerie Queene* (III.2.44) is a particularly developed later example of this (see appendix). However, as the above example from Dante shows, the fable surely need not be restricted to youth. One cannot help but notice how psychoanalytic theory has rediscovered in the fable a developmental model. Use of Narcissus by psychiatrists from Freud to Kohut attests not only to the predominantly visual orientation to the fable, but shows that the story continues to function as a quasi-scientific device.[2] Obviously interpretations of the fable by Freud or Kohut differ from John of Garland's. Nonetheless modern psychoanalytic use of the fable still tacitly assigns the plot an analytical function comparable to those given *integumenta*. The fable is not given an explicit moral meaning by Kohut; it signifies a neurotic or negative disturbance that requires rectification. It is used more as a narrative vehicle for psychological inquiry.

These responses, found in commentaries and poetry, seek to give answers to the puzzling fable by invariably placing it in another narrative setting. Pausanius and the *Ovide moralisé* are examples of this. The general response to Echo and Narcissus is not unlike the reaction to other fables. As a short form the single, isolated fable exists in potentiality and only receives meaning by becoming part of some other discourse. Not until it is given a context either through attribution of meaning in commentary, application in another larger narrative form, or elaboration of another narrative, is the fable's significance realized. The meaning of Echo and Narcissus is always manifest in larger settings. In the *Metamorphoses* the fable is not isolated but works both as a testimony to Tiresias' prophetic skill and as an example of the fragile nature of human communication. When the fable becomes detached from the historical setting of ancient Thebes in the Christian era, it comes even more to challenge the medieval audience to give it meaning. The negative meaning it receives as a story depicting the isolation and death that comes from self-love, urges the invention of strategies that would save one from Narcissus-like isolation and be drawn into history. Narcissus becomes not only a means for depicting sterile introspection but a way for directing one toward society.

Interest in Echo and Narcissus does not come from efforts to control the marvelous or from fascination with epistemological phenomena alone but also emerges from the fable's narrative qualities. In contrast to Virgil's episode of Dido and Aeneas, for example, Ovid's fable offers special advantages for further invention. Dido's tragic end and Aeneas' ordained mission are part of a story whose end is known. This is not the case with Narcissus, for even at the end of the story he is portrayed as perpetually transfixed before his image. Narcissus is without a history because there is no end to his entrapment. For this reason Narcissus asks to be given an end and placed in narratives where his experience becomes descriptive of psychological change and a component in the representation of individual history.

This book has examined an important Ovidian contribution to the romance epic tradition. Considered within the *Metamorphoses*, Echo and Narcissus fit among a sequence of stories about language and difficulties in communication. Within medieval commentaries, we studied the abbreviated versions of the fable suitable for Latin education. Within the *Roman de la Rose* and other poems we examined the way the fable was used for rhetorical argument, psychological detail, and amplification. We have done more than observe the appearance of a particular fable in the Middle Ages. We have considered the transformations of the fable from its Ovidian setting to those created when it was rewritten in other texts. Above all we have seen that the fable of Echo and Narcissus generates narratives, and that these narratives seek to resolve the suspension portrayed in the fable through strategies that surmount the isolated vision of Narcissus in a more expanded vision provided by history.

Appendix

This appendix includes three brief discussions of the narrative function given to Ovid's Narcissus fable in renaissance epics by Boiardo, Spenser, and Milton. These remarks show that, as in the *Roman de la Rose*, Ovid's fable is not affixed to these poems as a moral exemplum alone but that it is a narrative component for the representation of transition from personal isolation to the affirmation of historical mission.

Boiardo

While wandering in India, Orlando and his friend Brandimarte come upon a fountain identified as the Fountain of Narcissus (II.17.49).[1] The discovery of the physical fountain permits Boiardo not only to remind the reader of the fable but also to invent its history and warn of the continuing danger it poses. After Narcissus' death so much beauty remained in his body that another nymph, Silvanella, fell in love with the dead form (II.17.56). Unhappy because she could never possess Narcissus, Silvanella enchanted the fountain and made its water reflect the face of a young girl whose beauty was so great that any man who saw it could not leave the fountain. When a young knight in the company of a beautiful woman comes upon the fountain, he sees the beautiful image and is so bewitched that he abandons the real woman he is with for the image in the water. Saddened by the loss of her knight, Calidora devotes herself to protecting others from the fate of Larbin. It is she who tells Orlando the story of the fountain.

The history Boiardo invented is a commentary on the fable and the danger of the idealized image of woman. His extension of the fable shows that the self-deception associated with Narcissus does not involve simply seeing images of oneself in mirrors but concerns the fantasies one carries within oneself.

The importance the episode has for the poem is indicated by the care Boiardo took to frame it. Before Orlando reaches the fountain, Boiardo declares that what follows will permit him to gather together his diverse stories in "one substance" ("una sustanza" [II.17.38]). Immediately after the fountain's history is related he makes his most detailed statement on his joining into a single narrative the martial stories of Charlemagne and the love stories of Arthur's court (II.18.1–3). Ovid's fable is at the very center of Boiardo's poem.

The significance given to the history of Narcissus is not difficult to understand, for it reveals the major psychological structure operative in the narrative. At the very beginning of the poem the sight of Angelica disrupts the attention of all the major knights in Christendom. Like Larbin, the knight who leaves Calidora for the idealized image in the fountain, Orlando's attention shifts from his wife to the marvelous presence of Angelica. Before Orlando learns the story of Narcissus, he survives the garden kingdoms of Dragontina, Falerina, and Morgana, each of which manifests elements of his fantasy and faults in his perception of Angelica. The deceptive fountains and lakes which provide access to these realms of fantasy are all manifestations of the false image which appears in the Fountain of Narcissus.

The warning Orlando receives from Calidora not only clarifies what has happened; it also explains what happens to him later in the Forest of Arden. Looking into a stream, he wonders to see that it is filled with singing and dancing women. Intent on learning more about the figures before him he enters the water. Here, enchanted by love, he sees himself mirrored in the crystal clear water and loses his sense (III.6.9). The description of his own reflection among the smiling faces beneath the water gives even more formal expression to his Narcissus-like act. The profound danger present in Orlando's actions becomes even more obvious when we realize that at this very moment the Saracens are beseiging Paris. Just as he did at the fountain itself, Boiardo emphasizes the thematic significance of this event by placing it in a special narrative frame. The presence of a sheet of parchment with writing on both sides momentarily turns the scene we have imagined into the page of a book. Suddenly we find before us motifs known to us through commentary on Narcissus. On one side we read:[2]

> Desio de chiara fama, isdegno e amore
> Trovano aperta a sua voglia la via.
>
> ["Aloofness, lust for fame, and love
> Find a way open to their will."]

When the parchment is turned over we read:

Amore, isdegno e il desiare onore
Quando hanno preso l'animo in balia,
Lo sospingon avanti a tal fraccasso,
Che poi non trova a ritornare il passo. (III.7.13)

["Disdain, the search for honor, love
When they control a person's soul,
Propel it forth with so much force
It cannot trace a backwards course."]

For a moment the lines signal the moral significance of the events described in the text and function like a proverb in an emblem book. The desire for love, pride, and fame, and the confusion they bring once more show that Orlando's error, like that of Narcissus, threatens to drive him mad.

Spenser

After seeing the image of Artegall in Merlin's magic crystal, Britomart incorrectly compares herself to Narcissus (III.2.44).[3] Even though the fable is wrongly applied, its use demonstrates Britomart's adolescent experience and creates an interpretive problem that Glauce seeks unsuccessfully to resolve (III.2.45–46). Britomart's prolonged anguish shows that only a more elaborate argument can draw her from the isolated fate she assigns to herself. Spenser shapes this argument in Merlin's prophetic account of Britomart's future experience (III.3.19f). In contrast to the sterile fate Britomart assumes is left for her, Merlin reveals that the image she has seen in the glass is one that she must seek in the world. Incorrectly understood, the image in the mirror designates Britomart's fantasy alone; correctly understood the image directs her into the world.

The two interpretations given to the image create a polarity that gives orientation to Britomart's quest. She is unable to discover the meaning of the knight's image immediately but must learn its significance. Experience with the magic crystal marks the beginning of her education. As she looks for Artegall the misjudgment first exhibited in her response to the mirror returns to temporarily suspend her progress. Her misunderstanding of Malecasta's sensual intentions (III.1.50), her encounter with the Red-Cross Knight (III.2.5), and her Petrarchan complaint at the seashore emphasize that her education is not complete.

Finally Britomart's worldly education permits her to comprehend the threat posed by isolation. Overwhelming the Narcissus-like Marinell who lives in isolation and who is "love's enemie" (III.4.26), Britomart shows that she has conquered her own isolation (III.4.16). Her progress is even more apparent when we reach Malbecco's Castle where she is able to identify her own Trojan ancestry and establish its relation to British history (III.9.44f).

Spenser's use of the fable is also remarkably pedagogical—his story of Britomart is really an account of a progression through a renaissance curriculum which begins with fable and ends with history. Spenser follows the sequence of genres thought appropriate for strengthening personal virtue and civic responsibility. By moving from easier to more complicated forms, Spenser is able to mark Britomart's advance. Her cautious attitude toward Ovidian fables in the Castle of Busirane reveals her progress. Once ready to apply Narcissus to herself, she now is able to regard Ovidian love stories without harm.

Milton

Milton's imitation of Ovid's fable in Eve's account of her first moments in Paradise (*Paradise Lost* IV.449–81) marks a shift away from the overt use of the story found in the other texts we have looked at.[4] Here, as in other texts, we find the fable used for the representation of disorientation and correction but now within Milton's account of the faculties responsible for mankind's turn away from God.

Initially Milton's use of the fable stresses the affinity between the disruptive consequence of self-love witnessed to in scripture and the fate of Narcissus. Understandably, the vanity commentators found in Narcissus complements the vanity Biblical commentators attributed to Eve. But the stories entwine in subtler ways as well. God's commandment that Adam and Eve not eat of the Tree of Knowledge is complemented by Tiresias' prophecy about Narcissus. On a broader level it is Ovid's dramatization of the place of language in the growth of knowledge that facilitates Milton's incorporation of Ovid's story.

The importance given to Echo in other texts is also found in Milton's poem. Here the corrective function of speech in Ovid's text corresponds to the corrective force of God's Word. Milton's use of the corrective function of speech is a manifestation of the corrective mirror of scripture referred to in 1 Corinthians 13:12. The material mirror that destroys Narcissus is balanced by the corrective mirror of God's Word. For Eve such a choice is present when she must choose between the pleasing visual image before her and the corrective words offered by God's voice.

Although Eve's creation account contains the most extended allusion to Ovid's story, it is misleading to limit discussion of Narcissus to the pool scene. The configuration we find in the pool scene is a more explicit expression of others encountered by Satan and Adam. Satan is attracted to his own reflection allegorically portrayed by Sin. Adam is drawn to his reflection in Eve. The pool scene gives orientation to Milton's ideas of human psychology much as Boiardo's fountain scene becomes central to the analysis of Orlando's error, or much as Merlin's magical crystal reveals the beginning of Britomart's education.

Notes

Chapter One

1. All references are to the Teubner edition of Ovid's *Metamorphoses*, ed. William S. Anderson (Leipzig: B. G. Teubner Verlagsgesellschaft, 1982), which differs slightly from the Loeb edition. Translations are my own but owe much to those by Frank J. Miller included in the Loeb edition, Ovid, *The Metamorphoses*, 2 vols., 3rd ed. (Cambridge: Loeb Classical Library-Harvard Univ. Press, 1977).

2. A useful survey of Ovidian scholarship and some of its problems is found in Simone Viarre, *Ovide: Essai de Lecture Poétique*, Collection d'Etudes Latines, fasc. 33 (Paris: Société d'Edition les Belles Lettres, 1976); also useful but not as comprehensive is the English survey provided by John Barsby, *Ovid* (Oxford: Clarendon Press, 1978); Edgar Martini, *Einleitung zu Ovid* (Darmstadt: Wissenschaftliche Buchgesellschaft, 1970) provided impetus for the other surveys.

3. The best studies of the Narcissus episode are Heinrich Dörrie, "Echo und Narzissus (Ovid, Met. III. 341–510) Psychologische Fiktion in Spiel und Ernst," *Der Altsprachliche Unterricht*, 10 (1967), 54–75; and Joachim Schickel, "Narziss: Zu Versen von Ovid," *Antaios*, 3 (1962), 486–96. Brooks Otis, *Ovid as an Epic Poet*, (Cambridge: Cambridge Univ. Press, 2nd rev. ed, 1970) provides the best orientation to the thematic structure of the *Metamorphoses*. Walter Ludwig, *Struktur und Einheit der Metamorphosen Ovids* (Berlin: W. de Gruyter, 1965) is also important and will be referred to in the final section of this chapter.

4. Evidence of this may be found in the bibliography that accompanies Franz Bömer's useful textual commentary, *Metamorphosen: Ein Kommentar* [*Buch I-III*] (Heidelberg: Carl Winter, 1969); Simone Viarre, *Ovide: Essai de Lecture Poétique*, emphasizes the need for narrative study of Ovid's poem; 90–91.

5. This is partly due to the influence of iconographic studies on medieval and renaissance texts. Three generations of literary scholars have been influenced by the Warburg Institute and scholars such as Irwin Panofsky and Edgar Wind. Their studies admonish the cultivation of possible sources for painting and the use of Ovid and his

commentators as potential handbooks. While they encourage the use of Ovid as a painting manual, they rarely draw attention to the *Metamorphoses* as a poetic text.

6. See John Brenkman, "Narcissus in the Text," *Georgia Review*, 30 (1976), 293–327.

7. See the bibliographies on narcissism in Shirley Sugerman, *Sin and Madness: Studies in Narcissism* (Philadelphia: Westminster Press, 1976) and in Peter Homans, *Jung in Context* (Chicago: Univ. of Chicago Press, 1979).

8. A concise survey of the genre debate surrounding the *Metamorphoses* may be found in E. J. Kenney, "The Style of the *Metamorphoses*," in *Ovid*, ed. J. W. Binns (London: Routledge & Kegan Paul, 1973), 116–53.

9. The *Metamorphoses* was first referred to as *La Bible des Poètes* in Antoine Verard's 1493 edition of Pierre Bersuire's fourteenth-century moralization. See D. C. Allen, *Mysteriously Meant* (Baltimore: Johns Hopkins Press, 1970), 169.

10. Louise Vinge, *The Narcissus Theme in Western European Literature up to the Early Nineteenth Century* (Lund: Gleerups, 1967).

11. See for example Heinz Kohut, *The Analysis of the Self: A Systematic Approach to the Psychoanalytic Treatment of Narcissistic Personality Disorders* (New York: International Universities Press [The Psychoanalytic Study of the Child, 4], 1971.

12. By emphasizing examination of a single story at a time, source study led to the assumption that the *Metamorphoses* was a large gallery in which figures could be rearranged at will. An example may be found in Antonio Menzione, *Ovidio: Le Metamorfosi* (Turin: Biblioteca della rivesta di studi classici, 1964) where stories are broken from their context and displayed as examples of a variety of topics.

13. Brooks Otis, *Ovid as an Epic Poet.*

14. Walter Ludwig's *Struktur und Einheit* presents such a view.

15. In this section I am indebted to the orientation provided by Vinge and to the major study of the mythological ground of the Narcissus story by Friedrich Wieseler, *Narkissos: Eine Kunstmythologische Abhandlung nebst einem Anhang über den Narcissen und ihre Bezeihung im Leben, Mythos und Cultus der Griechen* (Göttingen: Dietrich'schen Buchhandlung, 1856).

16. After recounting two versions of the fable, Pausanias observes that the flower called narcissus preceded the fable. "The flower narcissus grew, in my opinion before this, if we are to judge by the verses of Pamphos. The poet was born many years before Narcissus the Thespian, and he says that the Maid, the daughter of Demeter, was carried off when she was playing and gathering flowers, and that the flowers by which she was deceived into being carried off were not violets but the narcissus." Pausanias, *Description of Greece*, 6 vols., trans. W. H. S. Jones (Cambridge: Loeb Classical Library-Harvard Univ. Press, 1961), 10.31.8–9; (IV,311).

17. "And also the narcissus whom the Earth, in accordance with the plans of Zeus, guilefully let grow for the child who was as fresh as a corolla, in order to please Him who receives many guests. The flower glowed with a marvellous lustre and astonished all who lived at that time, immortal Gods and mortal men alike. A stalk with a hundred heads had grown forth from the roots and all the heaven on high, the whole of the earth and the pungent swell of the ocean wave smiled at the

perfume from this cluster of flowers. With surprise the child stretched out both her arms at the same time to catch hold of the lovely plaything: but in the Nycaean plain the earth with its vast ways opened up and there emerged with his immortal steeds, the Lord of so many guests." (Cited in Vinge, 34)

18. See Wieseler, *Narkissos*, for use of the narcissus flower in funeral wreaths, 126–35; for use of the Narcissus story on sarcophagi see Wieseler, *Narkissos*, 18.

19. See Hyman Spotnitz and Phillip Resnikoff, "The Myths of Narcissus," *Psychoanalytic Review*, 41 (1954), 178.

20. "Dieser Name hängt ohne Zweifel mit νάρκη, ναρκᾶν zusammen, Wörtern die in der Griechischen Sprache hauptsächlich von den Wirkungen des Frostes, des Schreckens, der Ohnmacht, des Todes gebraucht werden." Wieseler, *Narkissos*, 79.

21. "It is bad for the sinew and causes a dull headache, its name being derived from the word narce, torpor, and not from the youth in the myth." ["nervis inimicum, caput gravantem et a narce narcissum dictum, non a fabuloso puero"] Pliny, *Natural History*, 10 vols. (Cambridge: Loeb Classical Library-Harvard Univ. Press, 1951), 21.128 (VI, 254–55).

22. Strabo makes the following observation: "Near Oropus is a place called Graea, and also the temple of Amphiaraüs, and the momument of Narcissus the Eretrian, which is called 'Sigelus's' (Σιγηλόν) because people pass it in silence." *The Geography of Strabo*, 8 vols., trans. Horace Leonard Jones (New York: Loeb Classical Library-G. P. Putnam's Sons, 1927), 9.2.10 (IV, 293).

23. Sophocles, *Oedipus at Colonus* (ll. 673–93), trans. Robert Fitzgerald in *Greek Tragedies*, 3 vols., ed. David Grene and Richard Lattimore (Chicago: Univ. of Chicago Press, 1960), III, 107–87.

24. The flower is used in conjunction with a pool that Dionysus uses to entrap the nymph Aura (48:582); the narcissus flower is mentioned several other times as well: 10:215; 11:323; 15:353. Nonnos' work, which recounts the birth and life of Dionysus, also includes a detailed account of Cadmus and his children. When looking at this genealogy one is struck by Nonnos' arrangement of stories. Nonnos, like Ovid, places the story of Actaeon before Semele. In the place we find the Narcissus narrative in Ovid, Nonnos tells the story of Persephone in a depiction reminiscent of Narcissus. "Once she was amusing herself with a resplendent bronze plate, which reflected her face like a judge of beauty; and she confirmed the image of her shape by this free voiceless herald, testing the unreal form in the shadow of the mirror and smiling at the mimic likeness. Thus Persephone gazed in the selfgraved portrait of her face, and beheld the self impressed aspect of a false Persephoneia (5:587–600). Since it is unlikely that Nonnos knew Ovid's work, there is reason to consider whether Nonnos' work makes use of source also known to Ovid. Nonnos, *Dionysiaca*, 3 vols., trans. W. H. D. Rouse (Cambridge: Loeb Classical Library-Harvard Univ. Press, 1940), I, 211.

25. Cited in Vinge, 20.

26. "In the territory of the Thespians is a place called Donacon (Reedbed). Here is the spring of Narcissus. They say that Narcissus looked into this water, and now understanding that he saw his own reflection, unconsciously fell in love with himself, and died of love at the spring. But it is utter stupidity to imagine that a man old

enough to fall in love was incapable of distinguishing a man from a man's reflection. There is another story about Narcissus, less popular indeed than the other, but not without some support. It is said that Narcissus had a twin sister; they wore similar clothes, and went hunting together. The story goes on that Narcissus fell in love with his sister, and when the girl died, would go to the spring, knowing that it was his reflection that he saw, but in spite of this knowledge finding some relief for his love in imagining that he saw, not his own reflection, but the likeness of his sister." Pausanias, 311.

27. See G. S. Kirk, *The Nature of Greek Myths* (Harmondsworth: Penguin Books, 1974) especially ch. 2, "The Relation of Myths to Folktales," 30–37. Although Kirk agrees with Franz Boas (*Tsimashian Mythology*, 1916, 880) that there is a "continual flow of material from mythology to folktale and vice versa and that neither group can claim priority" (31), he still makes an informal distinction between myth and folktale on the basis of sophistication (33–34).

28. See Georges Lafaye, *Les Métamorphoses d'Ovide et leur modèles grecs* (Paris, 1904; rpt. Hildesheim: Georg Olms, 1971).

29. See *Plato's Cosmology*, trans. F. M. Cornford (London, 1937; rpt. Indianapolis: Bobbs-Merrill Co., 1975), 45b–46d, 152–59; Aristotle, *De anima*, 2.7–8 (419b–21a) vol. 3 of *The Works of Aristotle*, trans. J. A. Smith (Oxford: Clarendon Press, 1931); Lucretius, *De rerum natura*, ed. Cyril Bailey, 2nd ed. (Oxford: Oxford Classical Texts-Clarendon Press, 1922), 4.215–819.

30. References are to Apollodorus, *The Library*, 2 vols., trans. James. G. Frazer, (Cambridge: Harvard Univ. Press—Loeb Edition, 1921); see esp. the genealogy of Cadmus, Vol. 1: 3.4–3.5; 312–335.

31. L. P. Wilkinson emphasizes the puzzle-like quality of Ovid's work in "The World of the *Metamorphoses* in *Ovidiana: Recherches sur Ovide*, ed. N. I. Herescu (Paris: Société d'Edition les Belles Lettres, 1958), 231–44.

32. Bömer, 540; See also Wieseler, 99–123.

33. The suggestion for such structural simplification comes both from imitations of this exchange in Renaissance poetry and Heinrich Dörrie, 62.

34. Hugh Parry, "Ovid's Metamorphoses: Violence in a Pastoral Landscape," *Transactions and Proceedings of the American Philological Society*, 95 (1964), 268–82; esp. 276. The major study on Ovid's use of natural setting is Charles Segal, *Landscape in Ovid's Metamorphoses: A Study in the Transformation of a Literary Symbol*, *Hermes Zeitschrift für klassische Philologie*, 23 (1969).

35. This has been suggested by Schickel, 486.

36. For comparison of *umbra* and death see Lucretius, *De rerum natura*, 4:26–45.

37. See n. 17 above.

38. See n. 23 and 24 above.

39. Although several theories of vision were known to the Romans, Ovid seems closest to an extramission theory which explained sight as the projection of a visual ray that excited the object in the field of vision and stimulated the return of the object's image to the eye. For an excellent survey of ancient ideas about vision see

David C. Lindberg, *Theories of Vision from Al-Kindi to Kepler* (Chicago: Univ. of Chicago Press, 1976).

40. Plato, *The Phaedrus* trans. R. Hackforth, in *The Collected Dialogues*, ed. Edith Hamilton and Huntington Cairns (New York: Pantheon Books, 1961), 475–525; see esp. 252a–257b.

41. John Brenkman has argued that writing is actually denoted by Ovid's depiction of speech acts. Writing, though suppressed in the text, manifests itself through the graphic portrayal of speech. It is possible to reach a similar conclusion without recourse to the deconstructionist theory behind Brenkman's argument. The care Ovid takes with syntax and line arrangement, his manipulation of written words that give Echo a voice, the narrator's intervention—each of these points to a similar conclusion.

42. Herman Fränkel takes such a position in his *Ovid: A Poet between Two Worlds* (Berkeley: Univ. of California Press, 1945), a book instrumental in beginning reassessment of the *Metamorphoses*; 75.

43. Otis divides the *Metamorphoses* into four sections: I) The Divine Comedy, 1–2; II) The Avenging Gods, 3:1–6:400; III) The Pathos of Love, 6:401–11:795; and IV) Troy and Rome, 12–15. These divisions actually represent the rigorous application of divisions already suggested by other Ovidian scholars such as L. P. Wilkinson, *Ovid Recalled* (Cambridge: Cambridge Univ. Press, 1955). Wilkinson suggested four sections: I) Prologue and Cosmogony, 1:1–1:451; II) The Gods, 1:452–6:420; III) Heroes and Heroines, 6:421–11–193; and IV) Historical Personages, 11:194–15; 148. Wilkinson's divisions are adopted by Karl G. Galinsky, *Ovid's Metamorphoses: An Introduction to the Basic Aspects* (Berkeley: Univ. of California Press, 1975), 85.

44. See Robert Coleman, "Structure and Intention in the Metamorphoses," *Classical Quarterly*, N.S. 21 (1971), 461–77, and Galinsky, *Ovid's Metamorphoses*.

45. The importance of Ludwig's approach has been pointed out by Otto Due Steen: "From our point of view Ludwig's results are important because they are not only based upon analysis of the poem itself but also take into account a literary tradition which would have made it natural for Ovid's readers to recognize a universal history as a working principle in the *Metamorphoses*." Otto Due Steen, *Changing Forms: Studies in the Metamorphoses of Ovid* (Copenhagen: Gyldendal, 1974), 135–36.

46. Division of time into cosmological, mythical, and historical periods is found in Varro. Ludwig notes the following: "Varro unterschied drei Epochen der Menschheitsgeschichte: die erste reichte *ab hominum principio ad cataclysmum priorem* und wurde *propter ignorantiam* als ἄδηλον *intervallum temporis* bezeichnet; die zweite, von der Flut des Ogygus, bis zur ersten Olympiade sich erstreckend, heiß, *quia in eo multa fabulosa referuntur*, μυθικόν *intervallum temporis*, die dritte war das anschließende ἱστορικόν *intervallum temporis, quia res in eo gestae veris historiis continentur*" (79). See also Francesco della Corte, "L'idea della preistoria Varrone," *Atti del Congresso Internazionale di studi Varroniani* (Rieti: Centro di Studi Varroniani, 1976), 111–36.

47. Ludwig surveys the problems the *spatium mythicum* posed for ancient histo-

rians. Some, like Herodotus, Thucydides, and Ephorus, regarded the historical interpretation of mythical material with reserve. Others like Hellanicos, Soilus of Amphipolis, and Anaximenes of Lampsakes, did compose universal histories that traced the evolution of the world from its creation. According to Ludwig, interest in encyclopedic histories intensified in the first century B.C. The histories of Castor of Rhodes and Diodorus are indications of this interest. See Ludwig, 78.

48. According to Arnaldo Momigliano synchronisms permitted ancient historians and chronographers to coordinate the *spatium mythicum* and the *spatium historicum*. See Arnaldo Momigliano, "Time in Ancient Historiography," in *Essays in Ancient and Modern Historiography* (Middletown: Wesleyan Univ. Press, 1977), 179–204; 192.

49. Ovid suggests that the rise and fall of cities may lie behind his conception (15:420–35). Configurations of cities appear elsewhere in the *Metamorphoses* as well, for example, 6:412–21. Thebes, Colchis, Athens, Cnossus, Troy, and Rome are especially prominent.

50. See *De inventione* (I.1–3) where Cicero discusses both the constructive and destructive functions of speech in history. Cicero, *De inventione; De optimo genere oratorum; & Topica*, trans. by H. M. Hubbell (Cambridge: Loeb Classical Library-Harvard Univ. Press, 1949).

51. See Hyginus, *Fabulae*, ed. H. I. Rose (Leyden: A. W. Sythoff, 1933), 170–71.

Chapter Two

1. Many works on Ovid in the Middle Ages and Renaissance have helped in the preparation of this chapter. For a comprehensive bibliography of Ovidiana see Simone Viarre's monograph *La Survie d'Ovide dans la littérature scientifique des XIIe et XIIIe siècles*, Publications du centre d'études supérieures de civilisation médiévale, IV (Poitiers: Université de Poitiers, 1966), 161–71; for additions to this bibliography see Viarre's more recent *Ovide*, 123–34. The best bibliographic survey of the Ovidian commentary tradition in particular is found in D. C. Allen's *Mysteriously Meant*, 163–99. Fausto Ghisalberti's editions and studies of Ovidian commentary (cited in the notes below) have been of utmost importance. The single best study of medieval Ovidian commentary, apart from individual editions is Paule Demats', *Fabula: Trois études de mythographie antique et médiévale* (Geneva: Droz, 1973). See also Judson B. Allen, *The Friar as Critique: Literary Attitudes in the Later Middle Ages* (Nashville: Vanderbilt Univ. Press, 1971) and his more recent *The Ethical Poetic of the Latin Middle Ages* (Toronto: Univ. of Toronto Press, 1982).

2. The first important outline of Ovidian commentary is found in Rudolph Schevill, *Ovid and the Renaissance in Spain* (Univ. of California Publications in Modern Philology, 4, 1913; rpt. New York: Georg Olms, 1971). The first major study of Ovidian commentary, Lester Kruger Born's "Ovid and Allegory," *Speculum*, 9 (1934), 362–79, is still useful. Jean Seznec's *The Survival of the Pagan Gods*, trans. Barbara Sessions (Princeton: Princeton Univ. Press, 1953), still provides useful orientation to topics such as euhemerism. Seznec's work is a testament to the icono-

graphic approach to source study and is probably the Warburg document that has most influenced literary studies.

3. E. K. Rand determined that Ovid had several different identities in the Middle Ages which included roles as *Ovidius ethicus* and *Ovidius theologus*. He concluded that the later evolved from the former without recognizing the importance of yet another Ovid, *Ovidius philosophus*. E. K. Rand, *Ovid and His Influence* (Boston: Longmans, Green and Co., 1928).

4. Demats' book is cited above; Viarre has traced in detail Ovid's acceptance as a philosopher in the twelfth and thirteenth century in *La Survie d'Ovide* cited above. American scholars such as Winthrop Wetherbee have also studied Ovidian commentary but have approached it through medieval philosophy and psychology rather than through the study of the *Metamorphoses*. See Winthrop Wetherbee, *Platonism and Poetry in the Twelfth Century: The Literary Influence of the School of Chartes* (Princeton: Princeton Univ. Press, 1972).

5. Philostratus, *Imagines and Callistratus Descriptions*, trans. Arthur Fairbanks (New York: Loeb Classical Library—G. P. Putnam, 1931, 89–93; (I.23) 391–95. Karl G. Galinsky suggests that pantomime took the place of tragedy, which was falling out of favor during Ovid's lifetime. See *Ovid's Metamorphoses*, 68.

6. Plotinus says, "Let him who can follow and come within, and leave outside the sight of his eyes and not turn back to the bodily splendours which he saw before. When he sees the beauty in bodies he must not run after them; we must know that they are images, traces, shadows, and hurry away to that which they image. For if a man runs to the image and wants to seize it as if it was reality (like a beautiful reflection playing on the water, which some story somewhere, I think, said riddlingly a man wanted to catch and sank down into a stream and disappeared) then this man who clings to beautiful bodies and will not let them go, will like the man in the story, but in soul, not in body, sink down into the dark depths where *Nous* has no delight, and stay blind in Hades, consorting with shadows there and here. This would be truer advice, 'Let us fly to our dear country.'" (*Iliad* 2.140). Quoted in A. H. Armstrong, *Plotinus* (London: George Allen & Unwin, 1953), 136–37.

7. Clement of Alexandria writes about women who pay great attention to their physical beauty, "If any one were to call these courtesans, he would make no mistake, for they turn their faces into masks. But us the Word enjoins 'to look not on things that are seen, but the things that are not seen; for the things that are seen are temporal, but the things that are not seen are eternal' (2 Cor. 4:18). But what passes beyond the bounds of absurdity, is that they have invented mirrors for this artificial shape of theirs, as if it were some excellent work or masterpiece. The deception rather requires a veil thrown over it. For as the Greek fable has it, it was not a fortunate thing for the beautiful Narcissus to have been the beholder of his own image." *The Instructor*, III.2 in Vol. 4 of *The Ante-Nicene Christian Library*, ed. Alexander Roberts and James Donaldson (Edinburgh: T. and T. Clark, 1871), 111–342; 280–81.

8. Narcissus appears in the index to the *Fabulae* as fable 214 but is missing because of a lacuna in the text between fables 207–218. The editor of the *Fabulae*, H. I. Rose, has suggested that the Narcissus text appears in Lanctantius Placius' com-

mentary on Statius' *Thebaid*, VII.341. The passage in the commentary reads as follows: "Narcissus venandi studisosus fuit. quo labore fatigatus venit ad fontem, ut restingueret sitim. qui in fontis speculo imaginem suam vidit et amavit, cum putaret alienam. et cum coepisset eius disiderio cotidie intabescere, in florem sui nominis est mutatus." Quoted in H. I. Rose, *Hygini Fabulae*, 143n. See also the helpful notes by Mary Grant, *The Myths of Hyginus* (Lawrence: Univ. of Kansas Press, 1933).

9. I have used the Teubner edition, *Mitologiarum libri tres*, in *Opera*, ed. Rudolf Helm (Stuttgart: B. G. Teubner, 1970), 1–80, and the English edition of Fulgentius ed. and trans. Leslie George Whitebread, *Fulgentius the Mythographer* (Columbus: Ohio State Univ. Press, 1971).

10. The psychological structure of the work is seen if we outline the themes that emerge in the three books that make up the *Mythologiae*. The first book is arranged according to a hierarchy of abstractions. It moves from the elemental structure of the universe (Jove, Juno, Neptune, Pluto) to a representation of the psychological forces with which man must contend (Furies, Fates, Harpies). From here it proceeds to relate the principles of generation that affect man (Proserpina, Ceres, Apollo) and the evolution of human knowledge (Muses). It concludes with the presentations of trade and war because it is in man's intercourse with other men that he is most affected by the preceding abstractions. The second book is organized according to the moral struggles that take place in the human soul (Ulysses and the Sirens). The third book depicts the purification of the soul and moves from a portrayal of lust to a desire for truth.

11. For the authorship of the Third Vatican Mythography see Eleanor Rathbone, "Master Alberic of London: 'Mythographus Tertius Vaticanus,'" *Medieval and Renaissance Studies*, I (1941–43), 35–38; and Kathleen O. Elliott and J. P. Elder, "A Critical Edition of the Vatican Mythographers," *Transactions of the American Philological Association*, 78 (1947), 189–207.

12. While the individual entries have received much attention, the work has not been considered from the larger vantage point of structure. For this reason scholars have not noticed the simple historical structure that informs the first half of the work. The *Fabulae* actually begins with Theban material and then proceeds to deal in rough chronological order with material that continues up to the founding of Rome. We may tentatively divide the work up as follows: Early Thebes (fables 1–11), Jason and the voyage to Colchis (fables 12–27), the emergence of the greater leader Hercules (fables 28–36), the story of Theseus and the war between Athens and Crete (fables 37–47), Athens (fables 48–65), later Thebes (fables 66–76), the Trojan War (fables 77–126). After Ulysses' death and an account of the importance of Ulysses' relatives in Italian Roman history (fable 127), the work becomes a random collection of stories and geographical details. In the second half of the work the material seems arranged according to nonhistorical categories. That such historical structure is present in the first half of the work is also suggested by the original title of the work. In the early sixteenth century the renaissance editor Micyllus changed the title of the work from the *Genealogiae* to the *Fabulae*. For the title change see Grant, 1.

13. The glosses which make up the *Narrationes* first appear in extant ninth-century manuscripts of the *Metamorphoses* such as Paris B.N. lat. 12246; mention

of earlier manuscripts is made by Victor Giselinus in his 1566 edition of the *Metamorphoses* and *Narrationes*. The *Narrationes* are attributed to Lactantius in Laurentianus Ms XC 99, a manuscript from the fifteenth century bound with works of Boccaccio. This attribution is repeated in an edition prepared by Venata in 1486, and by Aldina in 1502. See Brooks Otis, "The *Argumenta* of the So-Called Lactantius," *Harvard Studies in Classical Philology*, 47 (1936), 131–63.

14. Reference to Servius in the *Narrationes* indicates the date could be no earlier than the fifth or sixth century. Otis concludes that "the *Argumenta* along with a few scholia existed in some fifth or sixth-century codex." Otis, "The *Argumenta*," 140.

15. D. A. Slater's careful notes to the *Narrationes* emphasize that the author's additions make the work more than a paraphrase; Otis provides detailed lists of the different kinds of additions. He refrains from calling the work a commentary in its present form but concludes that it was "once part of a considerable body of scholiastic material—that is to say the 'commentary hypothesis' is quite correct in the sense that the ensemble (summaries, text, and scholia) constituted a rather elaborately annotated edition." Otis, "The *Argumenta*," 140.

16. D. C. Allen, *Mysteriously Meant*, 163.

17. The use of the *Narrationes* in the Vatican Mythographies is identified by D. A. Slater in the notes to his edition of the *Narrationes*. All references are to this edition. D. A. Slater, *Towards a Text of the Metamorphoses of Ovid* (Oxford: Clarendon Press, 1927). An edition of the *Narrationes* may also be found in Hugo Magnus' edition of the *Metamorphoses* published in 1914 and recently reprinted. *P. Ovidi Nasonis Metamorphoseon libri XV, lactanti placidi qui dicitur narrationes fabularum ovidianarum*, ed. Hugo Magnus (Berlin, 1914; rpt. New York: Arno Press, 1979).

18. Raphael Rhegius' 1493 edition of the *Metamorphoses* and its subsequent reprinting is a good example of a Renaissance edition which includes the *Narrationes*. I have consulted the 1565 edition. *Metamorphoses, Raphaelis regii volaterrani luculentissima explanatio, cum novis Jacobi Micylli . . . additionibus*. (Venice, 1565).The glosses are referred to as *Narrationes* in the earliest extant manuscripts of the *Metamorphoses* from the ninth century. This title continues to be used until renaissance editions begin to refer to the glosses as *Argumenta*.

19. See n. 42 below.

20. See n. 43 below.

21. The *Didascalicon* (III.8) of Hugh of St. Victor contains a helpful account of *expositio*.

> Expositio tria continet: litteram, sensum, sententiam. Littera est congrua ordinatio dictionum, quod etiam constructionem vocamus. sensus est facilis quaedam et aperta significatio, quam littera prima fronte praefert. sententia est profundior intelligentia, quae nisi expositione vel interpretatione non invenitur. in his ordo est, ut prima littera, deinde sensus, deinde sententia inquiratur. quo facto perfecta est expositio.

As cited in Hennig Brinkmann, *Mittelalterliche Hermeneutik* (Tubingen: Max Niemeyer Verlag, 1980), 157.

22. D. A. Slater, *Narrationes*, ff. C2 recto-C2 verso. Unless otherwise indicated all translations are my own.

23. Hyginus refers to Tiresias as the son of Everus in his account of Polynices (68), and of the seer himself (75).

24. D. A. Slater, *Narrationes*, ff. C1 verso, C2 recto, C3 recto.

25. Ovid uses a wide variety of images to convey ideas of love in the story. Liriope is raped (*vim tulit*, 344) youths desire Narcissus (*cupiere*, 353); Echo sees Narcissus and is enflamed (*vidit et incaluit*, 371); Narcissus asks the person who is calling to appear with a word suggestive of sexual union (*huc coeamus*, 386); hiding in a cave Echo's love remains and grows (*haeret amor crescitque dolore*, 395); Narcissus loves hope (*spem amat*, 417); he kindles the love which burns him (*accendit et ardet*, 426); he loves cruelly (*crudelius amavit*, 442); when he recognizes himself self-love is used (*amor sui*, 464); once his love for the image is described with *diligere*, (472) and at the end with *dilectere* (500).

26. See Hans-Jürgen Fuchs, *Entfremdung und Narzißmus: semantische Untersuchungen zur Geschichte der Selbstbezogenheit als Vorgeschichte von französisch 'amour-propre'*. (Stuttgart: J. B. Metzler, 1977). The first chapter which deals with words used to express "love" in classical Greek and Latin is especially relevant. Fuchs distinguishes between *diligere* and *amare* indicating that *diligere*, though also involving emotion, suggests a more guarded, reasoned attitude toward the object than *amare*.

27. Augustine, *The City of God against the Pagans*, 7 vols. trans. Philip Levine (Cambridge: Loeb Classical Library-Harvard Univ. Press, 1966), IV, 404–7.

28. Augustine, *De genesi ad litteram* vol. XLIX in *Oeuvres de Saint Augustin*, ed. Roland-Gosselin et al. (Paris: Descleé de Brouwer, 1941), 258.

29. References to the so-called Vatican Mythographies are from the Bode edition, *Scriptores rerum mythicarum latini tres Romae nuper reperti*, ed. G. H. Bode (Celle: E. H. C. Schulze, 1834). The first mythography includes 234 entries "Liriope et Narcissus" (185) is surrounded by accounts of the following fables: (180) Apollo et Cassandra; (181) Minerva Graecis irata; (182) Picus et Pomona; (183) Astraeus et Aurora; (184) Ganymedes; (185) Narcissus; (186) Sirenes et Proserpina; (187) Latona et Lycii rustici; (188) Medea, Aeson, et nutrices Liberi patris; (189) Deucalion et Pyrrha. The second mythography includes 230 entries "Alciope et Narcissus" (180) is placed among the following fables: (174) Polyphemus; (175) Ceyx; (176) Aesaeus; (177) Cyparissus; (178) Easdem fabula; (179) Priapus; (180) Alciope et Narcissus; (181) Hyacinthus; (182) Amaraeus; (183) Pilumnus.

30. All references are to the edition published by Fausto Ghisalberti in "Arnolfo d'Orleans: un cultore di Ovidio nel secolo XII" in *Memorie del reale istituto lombardo di scienze e lettere*, Classe di lettere, scienze, morali e storiche, 24 (Milan: n.p., 1932), 1–78; the *accessus* appears on 24–25. From here on page references are included in the text. Unless otherwise indicated all translations are my own.

31. Berthe Marti, whose work on Arnulf is indispensable, notes that Arnulf's commentary on Lucan's *Pharsalia* "was written after the death of Thomas Becket (1170), to which he alludes; and before 1211/1212 when a historical novel, the *Faits des Romain*, was published, in which extensive use was made of his glosses on the

Pharsalia." Berthe M. Marti, *Arnulfi Aurelianensis glosule super Lucanum*, Papers and Monographs of the American Academy in Rome, 18 (Rome: n.p., 1958), xxix.

32. Ludwig Traube, *Vorlesungen und Abhandlungen: Einleitung in die Lateinische Philologie das Mittelalters*, 3 vols. ed. P. Lehman, (Munich: C. H. Beck'sche Verlagsbuchhandlung, 1909–20), 2, 113. Although Traube's terms *Aetas ovidiana* is often quoted, it is seldom pointed out that the term originally referred to metrical patterns taken from Ovid.

33. For study of the *accessus* tradition see E. A. Quain, "The Medieval Accessus ad Auctores," *Traditio*, 3 (1945), 215–64; Fausto Ghisalberti, "Medieval Biographies of Ovid," *Journal of the Warburg and Courtauld Institutes*, 9 (1946), 1–110. For collections of early *accessus* see G. Przychocki, ed., *Accessus Ovidiani*, Atti dell'accademia di Cracovia, classe filol. 49 (Crackow: n.p., 1911); *Accessus super Auctores, Bernard D'Utrecht. Conrad D'Hirsau, Dialogus super Auctores*, ed. R. B. C. Huygens (Leiden: E. J. Brill, 1970).

34. "Modo querendum est de titulo, de materia, de utilitate, de intentione, cui parti philosophie supponatur liber iste, de modo tractandi." Ghisalberti, "Arnolfo d'Orleans," 24.

35. "In hoc titulo disignatur materia, de mutacione enim agit tripliciter s. de naturali, de magica, et de spirituali. Naturalis est que fit per contexionem vel retexionem elementorum: per contexionem quando s. elementa coniunguntur ut de spermate fiat puer et de ovo pullus, per retexionem elementorum quando s. retexuntur et dissolvuntur elementa in quelibet corpora vel per ignem vel alio modo in pulverem redigendo. Magica est quando fit per prestigia magicorum, sicut de Licaone et Io qui corpore non animo mutati sunt. Spiritualis que fit circa spiritum ut de insanos fit sanus, vel e contrario ut Agave et Autonoe que spiritu et non corpore mutabantur." Ghisalberti, "Arnolfo d'Orleans," 25.

36. For metaphors of cosmological generation and degeneration see Theodore Silverstein, "The Fabulous Cosmogony of Bernardus Silvestris," *Modern Philology*, 46 (1948–49), 92–116.

37. A work such as the pseudo-Aristotelean *Liber de causis* is a good example of the form in which twelfth-century students were introduced to peripatetic philosophy. It is probably from a text like this that Arnulf's reference to Aristotle is taken. I am indebted to Theodore Silverstein for help in sorting out Arnulf's relation to this pseudo-Aristotelean tradition.

38. "Ethice supponitur quia docet nos ista temporalia, que transitoria et mutabilia, contempnere, quod pertinet ad moralitatem" (25).

39. *Plato's Cosmology*, 47b; 158; see also Chalcidius 47c-d, 57–58.

40. Guillaume de Conches, *Glosae super Platonem*, ed. Edouard Jeauneau, (Paris: Librairie Philosophique J. Vrin, 1965), 254.

41. "Nonne auctorem eundem maximam dixerim partem ydolatriae in Metamorfosion, id est in transformatione substatiarum, ubi obscurata in se ratione, qua ad imaginem et similitudinem dei factus est, de homine lapis et bestia factus et avis, mutatam scribit a diis in bestias diversas naturam creaturae rationalis?" Quoted in *Accessus ad auctores*, ed. R. B. C. Huygens, 114.

42. Macrobius makes a distinction between two kinds of fable: "In the first both

the setting and plot are fictitious, as in the fables of Aesop, famous for his exquisite imagination. The second rests on a solid foundation of truth, which is treated in a fictitious style. This is called the fabulous narrative (*narratio fabulosa*) to distinguish it from the ordinary fable." Macrobius, *Commentary on the Dream of Scipio*, trans. with introd. and notes by William Harris Stahl (New York: Columbia Univ. Press, 1952), 85.

43. Peter Dronke, *Fabula: Explorations in the Uses of Myth in Medieval Platonism*, (Leiden: E. J. Brill, 1974); see esp. 15–32.

44. In general Arnulf follows the same order in his treatment of the fables. He also adopts elements of the earlier work in the summary of each fable which directly precedes the commentary. As a rule the summary is considerably shortened. Indication that Arnulf's commentary has a different bearing than the *Narrationes* is seen in his removal of references to genealogy.

45. "Modo quasdam allegorice, quasdam moraliter exponamus, et quasdam historice." Ghisalberti, "Arnolfo d'Orleans," 45.

46. "Cognita res meritam vati per Achaides urbes/attulerat famam, nomenque erat auguris ingens." *Met*. 3.511–12.

47. For study of fame or glory see Maria Rosa Lida de Malkiel, *L'Idée de la gloire dans la tradition occidentale* (*Antiquité, Moyen-Âge Occidental, Castile*) (Paris: Librairie C. Klincksieck, 1968).

48. Virgil's description begins as follows:

> ille dies primus leti primusque malorum
> causa fuit. neque enim specie famave movetur
> nec iam furtivum Dido meditatur amorem;
> coniugium vocat; hoc praetexit nomine culpam.
> Extemplo Libyae magnas it Fama per urbes,
> Fama, malum qua non aliud velocius ullum. (169–74)

Servius has the following gloss on line 170. "SPECIE FAMAVE MOVETUR species rerum Didonis praesentium est, quod quasi aspictur, fama autem rerum absentium. Hoc ergo dicit: non eam movet nec praesens deformitas, quod non in thalamo, sed in specu concubuerat: sed nec futura mox fama." Servius, *In Vergilii carmina commentarii*, 5 vols., ed. Georg Thilo and Hermann Hagen (1881; rpt. Hildesheim: Georg Olms, 1961), 1, 493.

49. Macrobius, *Commentary*, 216–17.

50. All references are to John of Garland, *Integumenta Ovidii: Poemetto inedito del secolo XIII*, ed. Fausto Ghisalberti, Testi e documenti inediti o rari, 2 (Milan: Casa editrice Giuseppe Principato, 1933). The unpublished edition by Lester Kruger Born has also been helpful. L. K. Born, "The Integumenta on the Metamorphoses of Ovid by John of Garland, Diss. Univ. of Chicago, 1929.

51. The manuscripts which contain both commentaries may be found in the apparatus to Ghisalberti's editions of Arnulf and John. See also Ghisalberti's "Giovanni del Virgilio: espositore delle Metamorfosi," *Giornale Dantesca*, 34, N.S. 4 (1935).

52. Ghisalberti, "Integumenta," 1–2.

53. "It seems as if Dante knew these works throughout his life. Learned by rote

at school, recurring in lectures and in the margins of manuscripts and in scholarly conversation, they must have lurked in the back of the mind of many literate people in the late thirteenth and fourteenth century." C. A. Robson, "Dante's Use in the *Divina commedia* of the Medieval Allegories on Ovid" in *Centenary Essays on Dante* (Oxford: Clarendon Press, 1965), 9.

54. For study of the twelfth-century understanding of *integumentum* see Edouard Jeanueau, "L'usage de la notion d'*Integumentum* à travers les gloses de Guillaume de Conches," in his book of collected studies, *Lectio Philosophorum: Recherches sur l'école de Chartres* (Amsterdam: Adolf M. Hakkert, 1973), 127–92. See also Wetherbee's discussion in *Platonism and Poetry*, 36–48.

55. For a discussion of the evolution of the term *integumentum* see Brian Stock, *Myth and Science in the Twelfth Century: A Study of Bernard Silvestris* (Princeton: Princeton Univ. Press, 1972), 49–55.

56. For the relation between Macrobius and twelfth century applications of *integumentum* see especially Peter Dronke, *Fabula*, 15–32.

57. *The Parisiana Poetria of John of Garland*, ed. with introduction and notes by Traugott Lawler, Yale Studies in English, 182 (New Haven: Yale Univ. Press, 1974), 104–5.

58. For descriptive psychology in the thirteenth century see Murry Wright Bundy, "Mediaeval Descriptive Psychology," Chap. 9 in *The Theory of Imagination in Classical and Medieval Thought* Univ. of Illinois Studies in Language and Literature, 12 (Urbana: Univ. of Illinois Press, 1927), 177–98.

59. The translation of Pentheus' family into a psychological configuration probably stems from the earlier interpretation of Ino, Autonoe, Semele, and Agave as stages in intoxication. See *Fulgentius*, ed. Whitbread, 77. Although Arnulf does not include this psychological reading of Pentheus in his *Allegoriae*, it is included in his *Glosule super Lucanum* (I.577), 71.

60. John's use of *tipice* may be compared to Bede's references to typical interpretation in his work *On Schema and Tropes*. Here Bede relates typical and spiritual interpretation. His simple example of such interpretation is taken from Genesis 49:9: "Judah is a lion's whelp: from the prey, my son, thou art gone up" (KJV) where the lion pertains to the passion and resurrection of Christ. John's "vir factus leo" may also refer to Christ's sacrifice. I am indebted to Philip Rollinson's *Classical Theories of Allegory and Christian Culture* (Pittsburg: Duquesne Univ. Press, 1981) for bringing the Bede passage to my attention. John's passage is noteworthy because it shows a mode of interpretation often thought of as only applying to the Bible being directed at the explication of a pagan text.

61. For a somewhat more general discussion of the figural use of *integumenta* see Winthrop Wetherbee, *Platonism and Poetry*, 36–48.

62. The material on *hyle* or *silva* is extensive. See especially the discussion in Chalcidius 50E–51B and in particular 334–40; 358–64. The most animated use of *hyle* in the twelfth century appears in the *Cosmographia* of Bernard of Silvestris. For a discussion of the concept see Winthrop Wetherbee, *The Cosmographia of Bernardus Silvestris, A Translation with Introduction* (New York: Columbia Univ. Press, 1973). See also Brian Stock, *Myth and Science in the Twelfth Century*, esp. 92.

Other terminology associated with twelfth-century discussions of Platonism also appears in the text. For example John's description of the relation between elements ("Ignis acutus amat subtilis mobilis altum,/Obtusam reddit aera terra gravis," 23–24) repeats vocabulary and distinctions found in Chalcidius: "Si enim vicinum igni elementum quod sit et ex quibus conflatum voluerimus inquirere, sumemus ignis quidem de proximo duas virtutes, subtilitatem et mobilitatem, unam vero terrae, id est obtunsitatem, et invenietur genitura secundi elementi quod est subter ignem, id est aeris," 87. In addition in lines 29–32, John repeats Pythagorean ideas concerning the mathematical basis of creation. For comparison see especially Chalcidius VIII-XXVI, 74–91. See also William of Conches, *Glosae super Platonem*, LXII-LXIII, 133–35.

63. A preliminary examination of how the *Ovide moralisé* makes use of Arnulf and John has been made by Joseph Engels in his *Etudes sur L'Ovide moralisé* (Groningen: J. B. Wolters, 1945), esp. 14–22.

64. All references are to the edition of C. De Boer aided by Matina G. De Boer and Jeannette T. M. Van't Sant, *Verhandelingen der Koninklijke Akademie van Wetenschappen* Afdeeling Letterjunde, N. S. 15 (Amsterdam, 1915).

65. See n. 41 above.

66. The most detailed philological material on the relation between *araisonner* and *adrationare* is found in the *Etymologisches Wörterbuch der französischen Sprache*, ed. Ernst Gemillscheg, f. 9–17 (Heildelberg: Carl Winter, 1968), 746.

67. Pluiseurs i puet on bien trouver
Qui nel lessent, se pour ce non
Qu'il ne vuelent le bon renon
Dou siecle perdre ne le los. (1470–73)

[There you find many who do not leave, if only because they do not want to lose their good reputation and their honor.]

68. D'autre y a, se dire l'os,
Plains de guile et de renardie,
Qui, par fausse pepelardie,
Font en apert le marmiteus,
Si sont si simple et si piteus,
Humble et de bele contenance,
Tant font de biens et d'abstinance,
C'au monde sont li plus avant. (1474–81)

[To tell the truth, there are others full of guile and lies, who by false hypocrisy appear so good, so simple, so pious and humble and of good countenance, who do only good and who abstain from all excess that society puts them on a pedestal.]

69. Si vont le siecle decevant
Par l'ombre de lor faulz renon,
Qu'en ne parole se d'eulz non,
De lor vie et de lor saintise,
Mes il sont si plain de faintise,

Que dessouz fausse couverture
Font il trop de male aventure,
Quant il viennent en recelee,
N'il n'en seront achoisone
Non pas neis soupeconne
Quar lor bons renons coile et coeuvre
Toute lor malisse et lor oeuvre,
Si que ja tant n'avront mesprise,
Qu'il en puissent estre reprise. (1482–96)

[Thus they continue deceiving their peers by the illusion of their falsely earned good reputation so that one talks only about them, about their life and their saintliness but they are so full of falsity that under cover they do much evil in secret but it will never be discovered nor will they be accused or even suspected for their good reputation hides and conceals all their evil and their deeds so that they will never have done so much evil—no matter how much evil they do—that they can be reproached.]

70. Echo fu en pur son muee,
Quar son sans cors est renomee:
Nulz ne puet veoir bon renon,
Quar ce n'est se parole non,
Qui par la gent est puepliee.
L'en l'oit en bois et en valee,
Quar l'en oit ces leux retentir,
Quant l'en i crie: sans mentir,
Il samble c'une vois en isse,
Qui les mos que l'en dist fenisse. (1515–24)

[Echo was transformed into pure sound for she is known as a sound without a body. No one is able to see good reputation for it is only the spoken word disseminated by people. One hears echoes in woods and valleys for in these places sounds return when one calls out. No kidding, it seems as if a voice comes forth from the woods and valleys which finishes the words one says.]

71. De Narcisus, le biau, le gent,
Fu grans la bone renomee,
S'il la vausist avoir amee
Mes il fu tant outrecuidiez
Plains d'orgueil et de sense vuidiez
Qu'il perdi dou siecle la grace. (1504–9)

[The reputation of the beautiful, handsome Narcissus was great, if only he had wanted to love it (renomee) but he was so filled with vanity and pride and so empty of any sense that he lost the good graces of his peers.]

72. Lynn White discusses the rapid developments in the glass industry in the thirteenth century in "The Medieval Roots of Modern Technology and Science," in

Medieval Religion and Technology: Collected Essays (Berkeley: Univ. of California Press, 1978), 75–91; see esp. 87–88.

73. Qui se mirent et qui s'amusent
Aus faulz mireoirs de cest monde,
Qui les plunge et qui les affonde
En folie et en forsenage,
Si les enivre de bevrage
Plain d'amertume, plain d'amer. (1908–13)

[Those who look at themselves and amuse themselves in the deceptive mirrors of the world which plunge and drag them down into folly and madness and inebriate them with a bitter brew.]

74. I have consulted three versions of Bersuire's text: a microfilm of the most authoritative manuscript, Ambros. D66 inf.; the 1515 French edition of the work, *Ovidius moralizatus* (Paris: F. Regnault, 1515); and the Ghisalberti edition, "L'Ovidius Moralizatus di Pierre Bersuire," *Studj Romanzi*, 23 (1933), 5–136. Unless otherwise indicated all references are to the Ghisalberti edition; translations are my own.

75. The text published by Josse Badius Ascensius in 1509 was sent to him by Jean de Voivre, a monk at Clairvaux. Though attributed to Thomas Waleys in the edition, the text has now been identified as the earliest version of the *Ovidius moralizatus* completed by Bersuire in Avignon about 1340. This text is now identified by the signum *A* for Ascensius. When Bersuire reached Paris in 1350 he was shown copies of the French *Ovide moralisé* and John Ridewall's *Fulgentius metaforalis*. Both were used by Bersuire in his final authoritative edition of the *Reductorium* finished in 1359 and are acknowledged in the Proemium to the *Moralizatus*. The signum for this manuscript is *P*. Engels suggests that there may even be another manuscript which he identifies with the signum *Px*. Presumably such a manuscript includes only Bersuire's additions to the *Ovide moralisé*. The reason the *Moralizatus* has been attributed to so many different fourteenth-century scholars (Ridewall, Trivet, Holcot, and Waleys) is that the text, which nowhere refers to Bersuire, was separated from the rest of the *Reductorium* probably already in Avignon. For detailed discussion of the relation between the manuscripts see *De formis figurisque deorum*, ed. Joseph Engels, (Utrecht: Instituut voor Laat Latijn der Rijksuniversiteit, 1966), xx-xxiii. The single best study of these later commentaries in English remains Beryl Smalley, *English Friars and Antiquity in the Early Fourteenth Century* (Oxford: Basil Blackwell, 1960).

76. "Constat enim libros poetrarum transcurrenti quod vix aut nunquam est dare fabulam quin aliquam aut naturalem aut historicam contineat veritatem. Unde et Rabanus, de naturis rerum libro 16 c. 2, dicit quod poete officium est que gesta sunt in aliquas species aliquibus figuralibus cum decore aliquo convertere." Ghisalberti, "Ovidius moralizatus," 87.

77. The best detailed discussion of *De formis* is found in Hans Liebeschütz, ed. *Fulgentius metaforalis: ein Beintrag zur Geschichte der antiken Mythologie im Mittelalter*, Studien der Bibliothek Warburg, 4 (Leipzig-Berlin; n.p., 1926). Erwin Panofsky reviews the history and importance of *De formis* in his *Renaissance and Ren-*

ascences in Western Art (Stockholm, 1960; rpt. New York: Icon-Harper and Row, 1972), 71–81.

78. Although Ghisalberti bases his text on one of the most authoritative manuscripts [Ambros. D 66 inf.], he has not transcribed Bersuire's complete text. I have compared Ghisalberti's text with a microfilm of Ambros. D 66 inf. at the Ambrosiana Microfilm Collection at Notre Dame and have determined that little other than the plot summary has been left out.

79. *Ovidius moralizatus* (1515), f. xxxviii verso.

80. Beryl Smalley, *English Friars and Antiquity*, 261–64.

Chapter Three

1. The bibliography on Ovid and medieval education is extensive. I have found the following works especially helpful: Élisabeth Pellegrin, "Les 'Remedia amoris' d'Ovide, texte scolaire médiéval," *Bibliothèque de l'École des Chartres*, 115 (1957), 172–79; Salvatore Battaglia, "La Tradizione di Ovidio nel medioevo," *Filologia romanza*, 6 (1959), 185–224; Franco Munari, *Ovid im Mittelalter* (Zurich: Artemis, 1960); E. H. Alton and D. E. H. Wormell, "Ovid in the Medieval Schoolroom," Pt. I, *Hermathena*, 94 (1960), 21–38; Pt. II, *Hermathena*, 95 (1961), 67–82; James H. McGregor, "Ovid at School: From the Ninth Century to the Fifteenth Century," *Classical Folia*, 37 (1978), 29–51.

2. The application of Ovidian pedagogy to a fable from Ovid's encyclopedic work points not only to a remarkable invention but shows that Guillaume would subscribe to Alain de Lille's description of Ovid as an *amorigraphus*, one who wrote about love in all its facets. See Alain de Lille, *Summae de arte praedicatoria*, caput 36, *PL* 210:180. I am indebted to Paolo Cherchi for bringing this reference to my attention. Ovid's identity as *amorigraphus* is examined in Jean LeClerc's essay *Monks and Love in Twelfth-Century France* (Oxford: Clarendon Press, 1979).

3. On Guillaume's poem as an *Ars amandi* see Hans Robert Jauss, "Entstehung und Strukturwandel der allegorischen Dichtung," in *Grundriss der romanischen Literaturen des Mittelalters*, (Heidelberg: Carl Winter, 1968), VI, 146–244; see esp. 224–44. The study also appears in Jauss's collected essays, *Alterität und Modernität der Mittelalterlichen Literatur* (Munich: Wilhelm Fink, 1977), 154–218.

4. *The Mirror of Narcissus in the Courtly Love Lyric* (Ithaca: Cornell Univ. Press, 1967).

5. Frank M. Chambers, *Proper Names in the Lyrics of the Troubadours* (Chapel Hill: Univ. of North Carolina Press, 1971), 195.

6. Frank M. Chambers, "The *ensehamen-sirventes* of Bertran de Paris," in *Mélanges de linguistique et de littérature romanes à la mémoire d'Istvan Frank* (n.p.: Universität der Saarlandes, 1957), 129–40. The poem begins "Gordotz, e.us fatz un sol sirventes l'an." Narcissus is referred to in line 16, "Ni co.s perdet Narsisus en la font."

7. All references are to the text and translation in S. C. Aston, *Peirol: Troubadour of Auvergne* (Cambridge: Cambridge Univ. Press, 1953), 92–96.

8. Compare, for example, Peirol's "Narcis, qu'amet l'ombra de se," with Arnulf of Orleans' "Narcissus vero umbram suam dicitur amavisse." See Chap. 2.

9. All references are to the text and translation in *Lyrics of the Troubadours and Trouvères: An Anthology and a History*, ed. and trans. Frederick Goldin (New York: Anchor-Doubleday Books, 1973), 144–49.

10. All references are to the edition by M. M. Pelan and N. C. W. Spence, *Narcisus: Poème du XIIe siècle*, Publications de la faculté des lettres de l'université de Strasbourg, Fasc. 147 (Paris: La Société d'Édition les Belles Lettres, 1964).

11. One day Dané, the "fille au roi de la cité" (128), sees Narcissus, a beautiful "vallé" (113), return from hunting and through the agency of Amors falls in love with him. At night she suffers greatly for her amorous affliction and wonders if her father the king could help her (341–45). Concluding that the king cannot listen to her because he has too much to do (353–54), she resolves to find Narcissus herself and declare her love (366–67).

In the morning she leaves the castle unnoticed and waits for Narcissus in a wood near the town (428–38). When he sees her he thinks she is a goddess or fairy (454); when she sees him she announces her love (466–67) and identifies herself as the king's daughter (474). To Narcissus her actions appear completely mad and he wonders that the daughter of the king would be alone in the wood (497). Love between them is impossible, he argues, because they are still children (498–500). Insistent that her amorous confession is just, she throws off her clothes and stands before him naked (513–14). Narcissus, however, remains unmoved and is described as having a heart harder than any baron, prince, or king (530). In desperation, Dané wonders if she lacks beauty and rejects her identity as daughter of the king and queen (602). At last she seeks aid from Amors (622) who prepares immediately for Dané's revenge.

The remainder of the romance follows Ovid's text closely with the exception that it gives special emphasis to the education Narcissus receives at the fountain. At first his childlike innocence is depicted. When he looks into the fountain he wonders if the image he sees is a water fairy, nymph, or goddess (651, 684–86). As his attraction to the image grows, he declares that he knows nothing about love (739). With great suffering his innocence is outgrown and he acknowledges Amors as his teacher (775–78). At last the lessons he has learned cause him to renounce the villany he has shown Dané (947). Even though he remains fixed to the fountain, Dané once again joins him so they may suffer death together.

12. On the significance the medieval *Piramus* has for the *Lai* see Pelan and Spence, 23–25, and 33–34.

13. It would be wrong to think of Dané as completely separated from Echo. Dané's argumentation with her nurse, with Narcissus, and with herself, can be related to Echo's rhetorical ability. Even her act of disrobing can be regarded as a version of Echo's physical embrace of Narcissus. Her return to the fountain at the end of the poem is obviously modeled after Echo's presence at the end of Ovid's fable.

14. My remarks on composition are indebted to R. R. Bolgar, *The Classical Heritage and Its Beneficiaries* (Cambridge: Cambridge Univ. Press, 1977), 183–201; Edmond Faral, *Les Arts poétiques du XIIe et du XIIIe siècles* (Paris: Librairie an-

cienne Honoré Champion, 1924); Hennig Brinkmann, *Zu Wesen und Form Mittelalterlicher Dichtung* (Halle: Max Niemeyer Verlag, 1928); and James J. Murphy, "Ars poetriae: Preceptive Grammar, or the Rhetoric of Verse-Writing" in his *Rhetoric in the Middle Ages* (Berkeley: Univ. of California Press, 1974), 136–93. On the practice of *amplificatio* see Edmond Faral, "De l'Amplification et de l'Abréviation" in *Les Arts poétiques*, 61–85. See also Michelle A. Freeman, "Problems in Romance Composition: Ovid, Chrétien de Troyes, and the *Romance of the Rose*," *Romance Philology*, 30 (1976), 158–68.

15. All references are to *Le Roman de la Rose*, ed. Félix Lecoy, 3 vols. (Paris: Les Classiques françaises du moyen âge-Librairie Honoré Champion, 1965–70); translations are from *The Romance of the Rose*, trans. Charles Dahlberg (Princeton: Princeton Univ. Press, 1971).

16. See ll. 19, 20, 1555, 2071.

17. The umbrella of branches which protects the garden floor from sunlight (1367–72), the fountains free from animals (1381–82), the luxuriant grass which surrounds the fountain for the nourishment it receives (1389–96)—are all drawn from Ovid's description of the fountain and its setting before it is seen by Narcissus (*Met*. III: 407–12).

18. Ymage/ymages/image: 134, 137, 144, 152, 156, 164, 189, 195, 199, 416, 461. Semblance/semblant/sembloit/sembla/semble: 137, 144, 146, 160, 165, 166, 202, 203, 295, 305, 313, 364, 417, 426, 430.

19. Douglas Kelly makes the following comment about the values in the garden: "Guillaume is concerned with courtly love and courtliness in this world. This is apparent in the noble and courteous personifications that people the garden, and especially in the precise groupings of abstractions without regard for Christian morality. The groupings provide significant clusters of qualities and defects. Such a world will always exist where love is idealized. Jean, on the other hand, is concerned with simpler and more stringent moral values broadly valid for all humanity." See Douglas Kelly, *Medieval Imagination: Rhetoric and the Poetry of Courtly Love* (Madison: Univ. of Wisconsin Press, 1978), 77–78.

20. "Otia si tollas, periere Cupidinis arcus,/Contemptaeque iacent et sine luce faces." ["Take away leisure and Cupid's bow is broken, and his torch lies extinguished and despised," 139–40.] Ovid, *The Art of Love and Other Poems*, ed. and trans. J. H. Mozley (Cambridge: Loeb Classical Library-Harvard Univ. Press, 1969), 186–87.

21. "The Lover's initial encounter in the garden becomes, in short, an encounter with the type of deceptive and phantom female beauty which is his chief goal in the broader field of the poem as a whole." John V. Fleming, *The Roman de la Rose: A Study in Allegory and Iconography* (Princeton: Princeton Univ. Press, 1969), 74. Kelly wonders if it is not possible "to say that Oiseuse represents for Guillaume's aristocratic audience what *otium* did for Cicero's readers . . . ?" *Medieval Imagination*, 79.

22. "In a discussion in the *Republic* about the whirling motion of the heavenly spheres, Plato says that a siren sits upon each of the spheres, thus indicating that by the motions of the spheres divinities were provided with song; for a singing siren is

equivalent to a god in the Greek acceptance of the word." Macrobius, *Commentary on the Dream of Scipio*, 93–94. This reading is included in Alberic of London—the so-called Third Vatican Mythographer: "nam quod Plato in sua Republica quum de sphaerarum caelestium volubilitate tractaret, singulas ait sirenes singulis orbibus insidere, sphaerarum motu harmoniam jucundissimam numinibus significavit exhiberi. Unde sub alia interpretatione siren, inquit Macrobius, *deo canes* graeco intellectu valet." *Scriptores rerum mythicarum*, 234.

23. The negative interpretation of sirens dominates all medieval mythographies. "The sirens are named as deceivers in Greek, for the allure of love is interpreted in three ways, by song or by sight or by habit . . . they are called sirens, because *sirene* is the Greek for betray." *Fulgentius the Mythographer*, ed. Whitbread, 73–74; negative interpretations also appear in the three Vatican mythographies: (I.42 and 186 [Bode, 15, 56–57], II.101 [Bode, 108–9], and III.8–9 [Bode, 233–34]).

24. Alberic of London has the following: "Sirenes igitur corporales illecebras evidenter disignant; unde et nomen congruum meruerunt, quia voluptates corporales ad se mentes quorumlibet *trahunt*. Σείρω namque, ut diximus, *traho* interpretatur." Bode, 233.

25. The most important article on addresses to the reader is Leo Spitzer's "Addresses to the Reader in the *Commedia*," *Italica*, 32 (1955), 143–65. The article is also reprinted in Spitzer's collected articles, *Romanische Literaturstudien 1936–1956* (Tubingen: Max Niemeyer, 1959), 574–95. Eric Auerbach studies the classical background to such addresses in his article, "Dante's Addresses to the Reader," *Romance Philology*, 7 (1954), 268–78. The ways such addresses may be related to the practice of commentary or moral application deserves more attention. While 'casual' addresses to the reader appear in Ovid, as Auerbach observes (268), it is our modern judgment that perceives such addresses as casual. Guillaume de Lorris or Dante may have attributed far greater importance to such internal commentary.

26. The shift is also remarkable because if extended to the entire fable, it causes the male role to become identified with Echo. This has special significance when we remind ourselves that such an identification also transfers Echo's reasonable force to the male, as in the poems by Peirol and Bernart de Ventador. It is tempting to see in this reversal the reasonable form of courtship expected of the male in courtly society. The application of the isolated Narcissus to males may be an example of male assimilation of characteristics actually conceived of in regard to women. The shift alerts us to think of the sociological as well as the epistemological significance of Ovid's fable. See George Duby, "Youth in Aristocratic Society: Northwestern France in the Twelfth Century" in *The Chivalrous Society* (Berkeley: Univ. of California Press, 1977), 113–22.

27. The most comprehensive study of Dante's use of Narcissus is Roger Dragonetti's "Dante et Narcisse ou les faux-monnayeurs de l'image," *Revue des études Italiennes*, 1–3 (1965), 85–146; a more recent survey may be found in Michelangelo Picone's "Dante e il mito di Narciso dal Roman de la Rose alla Commedia," *Romanische Forschungen*, 89 (1977), 382–97.

28. C. S. Lewis first suggested that the crystals are the eyes of the Lady. This position was later argued in detail by Erich Köhler and Jean Frappier and rejected by

D. W. Robertson and John Fleming who have argued that the crystals are the eyes of the Lover and that they affirm his Narcissus-like identity and the consequent folly of his actions. The two positions form the basis for an interpretation of the entire poem. If the crystals are the eyes of a Lady, the Lover can be distinguished from Narcissus. If, on the other hand, the crystals are the eyes of the Lover, he is like Narcissus and the entire nature of his experience is called into question. See C. S. Lewis, *The Allegory of Love: A Study in Medieval Tradition* (London, 1936; rpt. New York: Oxford Univ. Press, 1958), 117, 125, 128, 128n; Erich Köhler, "Narcisse, La Fontaine d'Amors et Guillaume de Lorris," in *L'Humanisme médiéval dans les littératures romanes du XIIe au XIVe siècle*, ed. Anthime Fourrier (Paris: Librairie C. Klincksieck, 1964), 147–64; Jean Frappier, "Variations sur le Thème du Miroir, de Bernard de Ventadour à Maurice Scève," *Cahiers de l'association internationale des études françaises*, 11 (1959), 134–58; D. W. Robertson, Jr., *A Preface to Chaucer: Studies in Medieval Perspectives* (Princeton: Princeton Univ. Press, 1962), 95; John Fleming, *The Roman de la Rose*, 93.

29. Stones are used in Guillaume's personifications to evoke special meanings just as they are in other allegorical poetry of the time. Richesse carries a collection of gems (rubiz, 1095; saphirs, 1095; jagonces, 1095, esmeraudes, 1096; escharbocle, 1098) including stones to protect her from poison (1067–70) and toothache (1075–76). Largesse carries a magnet (1057). See Karl Mieleitner, "Geschichte der Mineralogie im Altertum und Mittelalter," *Fortschritte der Mineralogie, Kristallographie und Petrographie*, 7 (1922), 427–80.

30. I have used the fine recent edition of John M. Riddle, *Marbode of Rennes, De lapidibus*, Sudhoffs Archiv, 20 (Wiesbaden: Franz Steiner Verlag, 1977).

31. The medieval French translations of Marbode's work have been gathered together in *Les Lapidaires françaises du moyen-âge des XIIe, XIIIe, et XIVe siècles*, ed. Léopold Pannier (Paris: F. Vieweg, 1882); see also *Anglo-Norman Lapidaries*, ed. Paul Studer and Joan Evans (Paris: Librairie ancienne Édouard Champion, 1924).

32. *Les Lapidaires français*, 45, l. 313. See also *Anglo-Norman Lapidaries*, 40, l. 313. General application of the stone to love is also found in an early thirteenth-century French prose version of the work. "Ele porte amour entre homme et femme, et fait honorer celi que la porte seur soi." *Anglo-Norman Lapidaries*, 143. It is undoubtedly beryl's relation to vision that is behind its amatory powers. Because the stone could resemble the eye, it could share powers attributed to the human organ. Its association with vision is evident in its ability to aid vision through sympathetic association with water, and in its capacity to magnify images. The connection between beryl and vision becomes more established in the thirteenth century when the invention of spectacles appears directly related to glasses cut from large beryl prisms. The German word for glasses, "die Brille," carries the name of the stone linked with their invention. See Riddle, 49.

33. See Chap. 1.

34. See D. W. Robertson, "The Subject of the 'De Amore' of Andreas Capellanus," *Modern Philology*, 50 (1950–51), 145–61; W. T. H. Jackson, "The *De amore* of Andreas Capellanus and the Practice of Love at Court," *Romanic Review*, 49 (1958), 243–51.

35. André Le Chapelain, *Traité de l'Amours courtois*, trans. with introd. and notes by Claude Buridant (Paris: Klincksieck, 1974), 47.

36. See Buridant, 207–8n.

37. Paolo Cherchi, "Andreas' *De amore*: Its Unity and Polemical Origin" in his book *Andrea Cappellano i trovatori e altri temi romanzi* (Rome: Bulzoni editore, 1979), 83–111. My discussion owes much to Cherchi's inquiry and provides support for his observation that "medical theories on love and their usage by medieval writers have not been sufficiently studied." 89–90n. See also Wilhelm G. Busse, *Courtly Love oder Paramours: Die Liebesauffassungen in der Mittelenglischen Literatur vor dem medizinischen und moraltheologischen Hintergrund der Zeit* (Dusseldorf: Stern Verlag Jansson & Co., 1975).

38. The similarity between the passage from *Cligés* and the *Roman* has been observed by others. See, for example, Paule Demats, "D'Amoenitas à Deduit: André le Chapelain et Guillaume de Lorris," in *Mélanges de langue et de littérature du moyen âge et de la renaissance offerts à Jean Frappier* (Geneva: Droz, 1970), I, 217–33; see esp. 231–32. The most detailed study of the passage is Guido Favati, "Una traccia di cultura neoplatonica in Chrétien de Troyes: Il tema degli occhi come specchio" in *Studi in onore di Carlo Pellegrini* (Turin: Biblioteca di studi francesi-Società editrice internazionale, 1963), 3–13.

39. Chrétien de Troyes, *Arthurian Romances*, trans. W. W. Comfort (1914; rpt. London: Everyman's Library-Dent, 1977), 100–1. The French text reads as follows:

> Se li darz parmi l'vel i antre,
> Li cuers por coi s'an dialt el vantre,
> Que li ialz ausi ne s'an dialt,
> Qui le premier cop an requialt?
> De ce sai ge bien reison randre:
> Li ialz n'a soin de rien antandre,
> Ne rien ne puet feire a nul fuer,
> Mes c'est li mereors au cuer,
> Et par ce mireor trespasse,
> Si qu'il ne blesce ne ne quasse,
> Le san don li cuers est espris.
> Donc est li cuers el vantre mis,
> Ausi com la chandoile esprise
> Est dedanz la lenterne mise,
> Se la chandoile an departez,
> Ja n'an istra nule clartez;
> Mes tant con la chandoile dure,
> Ne est pas la lanterne oscure,
> Et la flame qui dedanz luist
> Ne l'anpire ne ne li nuist.
> Autresi est de la verrine:
> Ja n'iert si forz ne anterine
> Que li rais del soloil n'i past,

Sanz ce que de rien ne la quast;
Ne ja li voirres si clers n'iert,
Se autre clartez ne s'i fiert,
Que par le suen voie l'an mialz.
Ce meismes sachiez des ialz,
Et del voirre et de la lanterne:
Car es ialz fiert la luiserne
Ou li cuers se remire, et voit
L'uevre de fors, quex qu'ele soit;
Si voit maintes oevres diverses,
Les unes verz, les autres perses,
L'une vermoille, et l'autre bloe
L'une blasme, et l'autre loe,
L'un tient vil, et l'autre chiere.
Mes tiex li mostre bele chiere,
El mireor, quant il l'esgarde,
Qui le traist, s'il ne s'i garde.
Moi et les miens m'ont deceu
Car an lui a mes cuers veu
Un rai don je sui anconbrez
Qui dedanz lui s'est anombrez
Et por lui m'est mes cuers failliz.

Chrétiens de Troyes, *Cligés*, ed. Alexandre Micha (Paris: Les Classiques françaises du moyen âge-Librairie ancienne Honoré Champion, 1957), 697–741.

40. Aristotle, *De sensu* (437b–38a), trans. J. I Beare, Vol. 3, *The Works of Aristotle*, ed. W. D. Ross et. al. (Oxford: Clarendon Press, 1931). For knowledge of the *Parva naturalia* in the twelfth century see Fernand van Steenberghen, *Aristotle in the West*, 2nd ed. (Louvain: Nauwelaerts Publishing House, 1970), 62–66.

41. "The Platonic theory of vision (received largelý through Chalcidius' translation, early in the fourth century, of the first half of Plato's *Timaeus*) dominated until the thirteenth century. Plato's stress on the visual fire emanating from the observer's eye (coupled, of course, with external illumination and light or fire from the observed object) was reinforced by St. Augustine, who also taught an extramission theory." David C. Lindberg, "The Science of Optics," in *Science in the Middle Ages*, ed. David C. Lindberg (Chicago: Univ. of Chicago Press, 1978), 338–68; 349.

42. "Whatever is visible is colour and colour is what lies upon what is in its own nature visible; 'in its own nature' here means not that visibility is involved in the definition of what thus underlies colour, but that that substratum contains in itself the cause of visibility. Every colour has in it the power to set in movement what is actually transparent; that power constitutes its very nature. That is why it is not visible except with the help of light; it is only in light that the colour of a thing is seen." Aristotle, *De anima*, (418b). Great importance was given to the relation between light and color in contemporary discussions. See, for example, the inquiry in Albertus Magnus' "De visu" in *Summae de creaturis* (seconda pars, quaestiones

XIX-XXII) in *B. Alberti Magni opera omnia*, 38 vols., ed. Auguste Borgnet (Paris: Ludwig Vives, 1896), XXXV, 164–228.

43. My discussion of Hunain is indebted to the discussion and extensive bibliography in Lindberg, *Theories of Vision*; for Hunain see esp. 33–42.

44. All references to the Latin text are to the *Liber de oculis*, ed. Pierre Pansier in *Collectio ophtalmologica veterum auctorum*, 7 fasc. (Paris: Libraire J. B. Baillière et fils, 1903–33), fasc. 7, 163–210. Translations are my own. Meyerhof's translations are at times too free to be useful. See Hunain ibn Ishaq, *The Book of the Ten Treatises on the Eye*, ed. and trans. Max Meyerhof (Cairo: n.p., 1928). Preliminary study of seven other twelfth and thirteenth-century ophthalmological manuals published by Pansier indicates that knowledge of the crystalline humor was very common. See in addition Avicenna, *Liber canonis* (Venice, 1507; rpt. Hildesheim: Georg Olms, 1964), f. 203 verso. The *Liber canonis* was translated into Latin in the twelfth century by Gerard of Cremona; see Lindberg, *Theories of Vision*, 43–52, and 237 n. 116. References to the crystalline humor also appear in Albertus Magnus' discussion of vision in his *Summae de creaturis*, and in optical works by Robert Grosseteste and Roger Bacon.

45. "Les hommes du moyen âge sont-ils réellement sérieux lorsqu'ils se réfèrent a Ovide à propos des questions scientifiques? Certes, le contexte dans lequel se situe une telle utilisation exerce ici une influence déterminante. Encyclopédistes, spécialistes et poètes scientifiques participent à une tendance générale. Ovide, aux XIIe et XIIIe siècles, est cité ou imité par eux en même temps qu'il est commenté par les grammairiens, exploité par les poètes de l'amour, par les romanciers, voire par les théologiens ou la légende populaire. Mais nous avons vu qu'il y avait autre chose qu'une coïncidence entre l'*aetas ovidiana* et la renaissance scientifique du XIIe siècles. Notre poète—qui doit une place de choix, bien avant Lucrece ou Lucain, à ses préoccupations néophythagoriciennes et surtout encyclopédiques—se situe dans la second catégorie des *auctores* auxquels on se fie pour présenter un exposé complet sur l'oeuvre de Dieu dans son ensemble." *La Survie d'Ovide*, 158.

46. Guillaume de Conches, *Dramaticon sive de substantiis physicis*, ed. Gratarolus (Strasbourg, 1567; rpt. Frankfort am Main: Minerva, 1967), 295.

47. Alexander Neckam, *De naturis rerum*, ed. Thomas Wright in *Rerum Britanicarum medii aevi scriptores or, Chronicles and Memorials of Great Britain and Ireland during the Middle Ages* (1857; rpt. Neudeln: Kraus, 1967), 239–40.

48. See, for example, Hunain's discussion of the brain, "De naturis cerebri," in *Liber de oculis*, 171–73.

49. See, for example, Guillaume de Conches, *De philosophia mundi*, *PL*: 95–96; John of Salisbury, *De septem septenis*, *PL*: 953–54.

50. Jean's use of fable is indebted to the use of fable in twelfth-century philosophy, as Wetherbee and others have shown. But at the same time that Jean's methodology looks back to fabulous systems at least two generations before his own, there is particularly in his synthetic use of fable, an element that anticipates what Giordano Bruno in the Renaissance referred to as "thinking in pictures." See Jean Seznec, *The Survival of the Pagan Gods*, 273n; see too Ernst Cassirer, *The Individual and the*

Cosmos in Renaissance Philosophy (1927; Philadelphia: Univ. of Pennsylvania Press, 1963), 74.

51. The first study to consider the scholastic background of Jean's work was Ernest Langlois, *Origines et sources du Roman de la Rose*, Bibliothèque des écoles françaises d'Athènes et de Rome, fasc. 58 (Paris: n.p. 1891): This preliminary work was continued in two studies by Gérard Paré, *Le Roman de la Rose et la scolastique courtoise* (Paris: Librairie Philosophique J. Vrin, 1941) and *Les Idées et les lettres au XIIIe siècle: Le Roman de la Rose*, Université de Montréal, Bibliothèque de Philosophie, (Montréal: Édition le centre de psychologie et de pédagogie, 1947). The best recent study is Patricia J. Eberle, "The Lover's Glass: Nature's Discourse on Optics and the Optical Design of the Romance of the Rose," *Univ. of Toronto Quarterly*, 46 (1977), 241–62.

52. Both works provide a remarkable collection of common physical phenomena which are carefully explained so that the student may recall the reasons for such conditions. What we find is an encyclopedic treatise on physics with experiments and demonstrations. Many of the physical exempla are introduced with *per experimentum* or *per demonstrationem*, expressions indicative of Albert's interest in the objective nature of the phenomena he collected. See "De visu," in *Summae de creaturis* (seconda pars, quaestiones XIX-XXII), 164–228; and *De anima*, vol. 7, pt. 1 in *Opera omnia* (Aschendorff: Monasterii Westfalorum, 1968).

53. Albertus Magnus, "De visu," 225.

54. See Harry Austryn Wolfson, "The Internal Senses in Latin, Arabic, and Hebrew Philosophic Texts," *Harvard Theological Review*, 28 (1935), 69–133.

55. See, for example, Albert's discussion of *phantasia* in his commentary on *De anima*. He is careful to emphasize the danger of fantasy but also notes that it can translate abstractions into metaphors and can make ideas more accessible.

> Ista etiam vis est quae plurimum impedit intellectum, eo quod nimis occupat animam compositione et divisione imaginationum et intentionum, quarum magna copia est apud eam, quia non tantum potest componere recepta a sensibus, sed etima fingere his similia. Et quia intellectus conceptiones ut frequenter non sunt similes imaginibus et finctionibus phantasiae, ideo quando vistit concepta imaginibus et intentionibus, plerumque generat deceptionem et errorem, maxime autem, quando aliquid de caelestibus et divinis intellectui imprimitur. Hae est causa, quod somnia, quae sunt prophetiae futurorum, plerumque applicata ad imagines, fiunt illusiones et deceptiones. Sed quando applicat conceptibus intellectus imagines et intentiones congruas, tunc adhuc indigent interpretatione compositiones imaginum et intentionum, eo quod non conveniunt conceptibus divinis et caelestibus imagines et intentiones sensibilium nisi secundum metaphoram (169).

56. Unfortunately the only Latin version of Alhazen's treatise remains the renaissance edition published in 1572. All references are to Alhazen, *Opticae thesaurus* (Basel, 1572). For the assimilation of visual imagery by the internal senses, see especially Bk. III, 75–102.

57. An exception to this is Hans Bauer, "Die Psychologie Alhazens" in *Beiträge zur Geschichte der Philosophie des Mittelalters*, 10, pt. 5 (Munster: Aschendorffsche Verlag, 1911), 1–73.

58. Alhazen, *Opticae thesaurus*, 31–32.

59. Nature's demonstration is an example of the growing use of optical phenomena for lessons in morals and questions of faith. See, for example, the interesting treatise, *De oculo morali* by Peter of Limoges, which urges the use of optical imagery in sermons. Peter was dean of the Faculty of Medicine in Paris in 1267 and 1270. The treatise still exists in 100 MSS. and was printed three times in the fifteenth century (1476, 1477, and 1497). See David L. Clark, "Optics for Preachers: the *De oculo morali* by Peter of Limoges," *Michigan Academician: Papers of the Michigan Academy of Science, Arts, and Letters*, 9 (1977), 329–43. A good example of optical imagery in homiletic literature may be found in a sermon preached by Giordano of Pisa at Santa Maria Novella in Florence on Wednesday morning, 23 February 1305. The sermon includes the first known reference to spectacles. For eyeglasses see Edward Rosen, "The Invention of Eye Glasses," *Journal of The History of Medicine and Allied Sciences*, 11 (1956), 13–46; 183–218. Another example, though somewhat later, is Nicholas of Cusa's use of optical phenomena to demonstrate the omnipresence of God in *De visione dei* (1453).

60. An association between Vulcan's net and fabulous narrative is not as abstract as may at first appear. Vulcan's identity as an artist was well known from the *Aeneid* (8: 379–453), and the extension of his craftsmanship to poetry appears in Ovid's *Amores* (II.17.17–22).

CONCLUSION

1. For a discussion of Academic skepticism in the Augustan period, particularly as it relates to poetry see Michael Murrin's *The Allegorical Epic: Essays in its Rise and Decline* (Chicago: Univ. of Chicago Press, 1980), 27–50; For general discussion of Ovid and skepticism see Harold Skulsky, "Ovid's Epic: Metamorphosis as Metaphysical Doubt," in his *Metamorphosis: The Mind in Exile* (Cambridge: Harvard Univ. Press, 1981), 24–61. For bibliographies of skepticism see Richard H. Popkin, *The History of Scepticism From Erasmus to Spinoza* (Berkeley: Univ. of California Press, 1979), and Charles B. Schmitt, *Cicero Scepticus: A Study of the Influence of the 'Academica' in the Renaissance* (The Hague: Martinus Nijhoff, 1972).

2. Here I am especially thinking of Freud's "On Narcissism: An Introduction," included in Sigmund Freud, *General Psychological Theory* (New York: Collier Books, 1963), 56–82; and Heinz Kohut, *The Analysis of the Self*.

APPENDIX

1. All references are to Matteo Maria Boiardo, *Orlando Innamorato*, 4 vols., ed. Luigi Garbato (Milan: Marzorati editore, 1970).

2. From an unpublished translation of Boiardo's epic by Charles S. Ross, Department of English, Purdue University.

3. All references are to Edmund Spenser, *The Faerie Queene*, 2 vols. (London: Everyman's Library-Dent, 1966).

4. All references are to John Milton, *Complete Poems and Major Prose*, ed. Merritt Hughes (New York: Odyssey Press, 1957).

Selected Bibliography

Primary Sources

Accessus ad Auctores: Bernard D'Utrecht. Conrad d'Hirsau, Dialogus super Auctores. Ed. R. B. C. Huygens. Leiden: E. J. Brill, 1970.

Accessus Ovidiani. Ed. G. Przychocki. Atti dell'Accademia di Cracovia, classe filol. 49. Crackow: n.p., 1911.

Alain de Lille. *Summae de arte praedicatoria*. *PL* 210:109–98.

Albertus Magnus. *Summae de creaturis*. Vol. XXXV of *B. Alberti Magni opera omnia*. 38 vols. Ed. Auguste Borgnet. Paris: Ludwig Vives. 1896.

———. *De anima*. Vol. VII, pt. 1 of *Opera omnia*. Ed. Bernard Geyer. Aschendorff: Monasterii Westfalorum, 1968.

Alhazen. *Opticae thesaurus*. Basel, 1572.

André le Chapelain. *Traité de L'Amours courtois*. Trans. with introd. and notes by Claude Buridant. Paris: Klincksieck, 1974.

Anglo-Norman Lapidaries. Ed. Paul Studer and Joan Evans. Paris: Librairie ancienne Edouard Champion, 1924.

Apollodorus. *The Library*. 2 vols. Trans. James G. Frazer. Cambridge: Loeb Classical Library-Harvard University Press, 1921.

Aristotle. *De anima*. Trans. J. A. Smith. Vol. III of *The Works of Aristotle*. Ed. W. D. Ross et al. Oxford: Clarendon Press, 1931.

———. *De sensu*. Trans. J. I. Beare. Vol. III of *The Works of Aristotle*. Ed. W. D. Ross et al. Oxford: Clarendon Press, 1931.

Arnulf of Orleans. *Allegoriae super Metamorphosin*. Ed. Fausto Ghisalberti. In "Arnolfo d'Orleans: un cultore di Ovidio nel secolo XII." *Memorie del reale istituto lombardo di scienze e lettere*. Classe di lettere, scienze, morali e storiche, 24 (Milan: n.p., 1932), 194–229.

———. *Glosule super Lucanum*. Ed. Berthe Marti. Papers and Monographs of the American Academy in Rome, 18. Rome: n.p., 1958.

Augustine. *The City of God against the Pagans*. 7 vols. Trans. Philip Levine. Cambridge: Loeb Classical Library-Harvard Univ. Press, 1966.

———. *De genesi ad litteram*. Vol XLIX of *Oeuvres de Saint Augustin*. Ed. Roland-Gosselin et al. Paris: Desclé de Brouwer, 1941.

Avicenna. *Liber canonis*. 1507; rpt. Hildesheim: Georg Olms, 1964.

Bernardus Silvestris. *The Cosmographia*. Ed. Winthrop Wetherbee. *The Cosmographia of Bernardus Silvestris: A Translation with Introduction and Notes*. New York: Columbia Univ. Press, 1973.

Bersuire, Pierre. *De formis figurisque deorum*. Ed. Joseph Engels. Utrecht: Instituut voor Laat Latijn der Rijksuniversiteit, 1966.

———. *Ovidius Moralizatus*. 1509; rpt. Paris: F. Regnault, 1515.

———. *Ovidius Moralizatus*. Ed. Fausto Ghisalberti, "L'Ovidius Moralizatus di Pierre Bersuire." *Studj Romanzi*, 23 (1933), 5–136.

Boiardo, Matteo Maria. *Orlando innamorato*. 4 vols. Ed. Luigi Garbato. Milan: Marzorati editore, 1970.

———. *Orlando innamorato*. Unpublished translation by Charles S. Ross. Purdue University, Department of English.

Chalcidius. *Platonis timaeus interprete chalcidio cum eiusdem commentario*. Ed. J. Wrobel. Leipzig: B. G. Teubner, 1876.

Chrétien de Troyes. *Arthurian Romances*. Trans. W. W. Comfort. 1914; rpt. London: Everyman's Library-Dent, 1977.

———. *Cligés*. Ed. Alexandre Micha. Paris: Les Classiques françaises du moyen âge-Librairie ancienne Honoré Champion, 1957.

Cicero. *De inventione*. In *De optimo genere oratorum. Topica*. Trans. H. M. Hubbell. Cambridge: Loeb Classical Library-Harvard Univ. Press, 1949. 1–346.

Cintio, Giraldi. *Discorsi intorno al comporre dei romanzi*. Ferrara, 1554.

Clement of Alexandria. *The Instructor*. In Vol. 4 of *The Ante- Nicene Christian Library*. Ed. Alexander Roberts and James Donaldson. Edinburgh: T. and T. Clark, 1871. 111–342.

Collectio ophtalmologica veterum auctorum. 7 fasc. Ed. Pierre Pansier. Paris: Libraire J. B. Baillière et fils, 1903–33.

Fulgentius. *Mitologiarum libri tres*. In *Opera*. Ed. Rudolf Helm. Stuttgart: B. G. Teubner, 1970. 1–80.

———. *Mythologies*. Ed. and trans. Leslie George Whitbread. In *Fulgentius the Mythographer*. Columbus: Ohio State Univ., 1971. 13–102.

Fulgentius metaforalis. Ed. Hans Liebeschütz. *Fulgentius metaforalis: ein Beitrag zur Geschichte der antiken Mythologie im Mittelalter*. Studien der Bibliothek Warburg, 4. Leipzig-Berlin: n.p., 1926.

Giovanni del Virgilio. *Allegorie librorum Ovidii Metamorphoseos*. Ed. Fausto Ghisalberti. *Giovanni del Virgilio: espositore delle Metamorfosi*. Florence: Leo S. Olschki Editore, 1933.

Guillaume de Conches. *Dramaticon sive de substantiis physicis*. Ed. Grataroius. Strasbourg, 1567; rpt. Frankfort am Main: Minerva, 1967.

———. *Glosae in Iuvenalem*. Ed. Bradford Wilson. Textes Philosophiques du Moyen Âge, 18. Paris: Librairie Philosophique J. Vrin, 1980.

———. *Glosae super Platonem*. Ed. Edouard Jeauneau. Paris: Librairie Philosophique J. Vrin, 1965.

———. *De philosophia mundi*. *PL* 172:39–102.

Guillaume de Lorris, Jean de Meun. *Le Roman de la Rose*. 3 vols. Ed. Félix Lecoy. Paris: Les classiques français du moyen- âge-Librairie Honoré Champion, 1965–70.

———. *The Romance of the Rose*. Trans. Charles Dahlberg. Princeton: Princeton Univ. Press, 1971.

Hunain ibn Ishaq. *The Book of the Ten Treatises on the Eye*. Ed. and trans. Max Meyerhof. Cairo: n.p., 1928.

Hyginus. *Fabulae*. Ed. H. I. Rose. Leyden: A. W. Sythoff, 1933.

———. *The Myths of Hyginus*. Trans. and ed. Mary Grant. Lawrence: Univ. of Kansas Press, 1960.

John of Garland. *Integumenta Ovidii*. Ed. Fausto Ghisalberti. *Integumenta Ovidii: Poemetto inedito del secolo XIII*. Testi e documenti inediti o rari, 2. Milan: Casa editrice Giuseppe Principato, 1933.

———. *The Parisiana Poetria of John of Garland*. Ed. with introd. and notes by Traugott Lawler. Yale Studikes in English, 182. New Haven: Yale Univ. Press, 1974.

John of Salisbury. *De septem septenis*. *PL* 199:945–64.

Les Lapidaires françaises du moyen âge des XIIe, XIIIe, et XIVe siècles. Ed. Léopold Pannier. Paris: F. Vieweg, 1882.

Lucretius. *De rerum natura*. Ed. Cyril Bailey. 2nd ed. Oxford: Oxford Classical Texts-Clarendon Press, 1922.

Lyrics of the Troubadours and Trouvères: An Anthology and a History. Ed. and trans. Frederick Goldin. New York: Anchor-Doubleday Books, 1973.

Macrobius. *Commentary on the Dream of Scipio*. Trans. with introd. and notes by William Harris Stahl. New York: Columbia Univ. Press, 1952.

Marbode of Rennes. *De lapidibus*. Ed. John M. Riddle. Sudhoffs Archiv, 20. Wiesbaden: Franz Steiner Verlag, 1977.

Milton, John. *Complete Poems and Major Prose*. Ed. Merritt Hughes. New York: Odyssey Press, 1957.

Narcisus: Poème du XII siècle. Ed. M. M. Pelan and N. C. W. Spence. Publications de la Faculté des lettres de l'université de Strasbourg, Fasc. 147. Paris: La Société d'Edition les Belles Lettres, 1964.

Narrationes. Ed. D. A. Slater. In *Towards a Text of the Metamorphoses of Ovid*. Oxford: Clarendon Press, 1927.

Neckam, Alexander. *De naturis rerum*. Ed. Thomas Wright. In *Rerum Britanicarum medii aevii scriptores or, Chronicles and Memorials of Great Britain and Ireland during the Middle Ages*. 1857; rpt. Neudeln: Kraus, 1967.

Nonnos. *Dionysiaca*. 3 vols. Trans. W. H. D. Rouse. Cambridge: Loeb Classical Library-Harvard Univ. Press, 1940.

Ovid. *The Art of Love and Other Poems*. Ed. and trans. J. H. Mozley. Cambridge: Loeb Classical Library-Harvard Univ. Press, 1969.

———. *Fasti*. Trans. James G. Frazer. Cambridge: Loeb Classical Library-Harvard Univ. Press, 1976.

———. *Metamorphoses*. Ed. William S. Anderson. Leipzig: B. G. Teubner Verlagsgesellschaft, 1982.

———. *Metamorphoseon libri XV, Lactanti Placidi qui dicitur narrationes fabularum ovidianarum*. Ed. Hugo Magnus. Berlin, 1914; rpt. New York: Arno Press, 1979.

———. *Metamorphoses, Raphaelis regii volaterrani luculentissima explanatio, cum novis Jacobi Micylli . . . additionibus*. Venice, 1565.

———. *The Metamorphoses*. 2 vols. 3rd ed. Trans. Frank Justus Miller. Cambridge: Loeb Classical Library-Harvard Univ. Press, 1977.

Ovide moralis;œ. Ed. C. De Boer, aided by Matina G. De Boer and Jeannette T. M. Van't Sant. *Verhandelingen der Koninklijke Akademie van Wetenschappen*. Afdeeling Letterjunde, N.S. 15 (1915), 21 (1920), 30 (1931), 37 (1936), and 42 (1938).

Pausanius. *Description of Greece*. 6 vols. Trans. W. H. S. Jones. Cambridge: Loeb Classical Library-Harvard Univ. Press, 1961, 4.

Peter of Limoges. *De oculo morali*. Augsburg, 1476.

Philostratus. *Imagines and Callistratus Descriptions*. Trans. Arthur Fairbanks. New York: Loeb Classical Library-G. P. Putnam, 1931.

Pigna, Giovanni. *I romanzi*. Venice, 1554.

Plato. *Plato's Cosmology*. Trans. F. M. Cornford. London, 1937; rpt. Indianapolis: Bobbs-Merrill Co., 1975.

———. *The Phaedrus*. Trans. R. Hackforth. In *The Collected Dialogues*. Ed. Edith Hamilton and Huntington Cairns. New York: Pantheon Books, 1961. 475–525.

Pliny. *Natural History*. 10 vols. Loeb Classical Library- Harvard Univ. Press, 1951. VI.

Plotinus. *The First Ennead*. Vol. I of *The Complete Works of Plotinus*. Ed. and trans. Kenneth S. Guthrie. London: George Bell and Sons, 1918.

Scriptores rerum mythicarum latini tres Romae nuper reperti. Ed. G. H. Bode. Celle: E. H. C. Schulze, 1834.

Servius. *In Vergilii bucolica et georgica commentarii*. Ed. Georg Thilo. 1887; rpt. Hildesheim: Georg Olms, 1961.

———. *In Vergilii carmina commentarii*. 5 vols. Ed. Georg Thilo and Herman Hagen. 1881; rpt. Hildesheim: Georg Olms, 1961.

Sophocles. *Oedipus at Colonus*. Trans. Robert Fitzgerald. In *Greek Tragedies*. 3 vols. Ed. David Grene and Richard Lattimore. Chicago: Univ. of Chicago Press, 1960. III, 107–87.

Spenser, Edmund. *The Faerie Queene*. 2 vols. London: Everyman's Library-Dent, 1966.

Strabo. *The Geography of Strabo*. 8 vols. Trans. Horace Leonard Jones. New York: Loeb Classical Library-G. P. Putnam's Sons, 1927.

Toscanella, Orazio. *Bellezze del Furioso di M. Lodovico Ariosto*. Venice, 1574.

Virgil. *Eclogues*. Trans. H. Rushton Fairclough. In *Virgil*. 2 vols. Rev. ed. Cambridge: Loeb Classical Library-Harvard Univ. Press, 1935. I, 2–77.

Secondary Sources

Allen, Don Cameron. *Mysteriously Meant: The Rediscovery of Pagan Symbolism and Allegorical Interpretation in the Renaissance*. Baltimore: Johns Hopkins Press, 1970.

Allen, Judson B. *The Ethical Poetic of the Later Middle Ages*. Toronto: Univ. of Toronto Press, 1982.

———. *The Friar as Critic: Literary Attitudes in the Later Middle Ages*. Nashville: Vanderbilt Univ. Press, 1971.

Alpers, Paul. *The Singer of the Eclogues: A Study of Virgilian Pastoral*. Berkeley: Univ. of California Press, 1971.

Alton, E. H. and D. E. H. Wormell. "Ovid in the Medieval Schoolroom." Pt. I, *Hermathena*, 94 (1960), 21–38; Pt. II, *Hermathena*, 95 (1961), 67–82.

Armstrong, A. H. *Plotinus*. London: George Allen & Unwin, 1953.

Aston, S. C. *Peirol: Troubadour of Auvergne*. Cambridge: Cambridge Univ. Press, 1953.

Auerbach, Eric. "Dante's Addresses to the Reader." *Romance Philology*, 7 (1954), 268–78.

Badel, Pierre-Yvre. *Le Roman de la Rose au XIVe siècle: étude de la réception de l'oeuvre*. Geneva: Droz, 1980.

Barsby, John. *Ovid*. New Surveys in the Classics, 12. Oxford: Clarendon Press, 1978.

Battaglia, Salvatore. "La Tradizione di Ovidio nel medioevo." *Filologia romanza*, 6 (1959), 185–224.

Bauer, Hans. "Die Psychologie Alhazens." In *Beiträge zur Geschichte der Philosophie des Mittelalters*. Munster: Aschendorffsche Verlag, 1911. X, pt. 5, 1–73.

Boillat, Michel. *Les Métamorphoses d'Ovide: Thèmes majeures et problèmes de composition*. Publications Universitaires Européennes. Bern: Herbert Lang, 1976.

Bolgar, R. R. *The Classical Heritage and Its Beneficiaries*. Cambridge: Cambridge Univ. Press, 1977.

Bömer, Franz. *Metamorphosen: Ein Kommentar*. Heidelberg: Carl Winter, 1969. I.

Born, Lester Kruger. "The Integumenta on the Metamorphoses of Ovid by John of Garland." Diss. Univ. of Chicago, 1929.

———. "Ovid and Allegory." *Speculum*, 9 (1934), 362–79.

Brenkman, John. "Narcissus in the Text." *Georgia Review*, 30 (1976), 293–327.

Brinkmann, Hennig. *Mittelalterliche Hermeneutik*. Tübingen: Max Niemeyer Verlag, 1980.

———. *Zu Wesen und Form Mittelalterlicher Dichtung*. Halle: Max Niemeyer Verlag, 1928.

Bundy, Murry Wright. *The Theory of Imagination in Classical and Medieval Thought*. Univ. of Illinois Studies in Language and Literature, 12. Urbana: Univ. of Illinois Press, 1927.

Busse, Wilhelm G. *Courtly Love oder Paramours: Die Liebesauffassungen in der*

Mittelenglischen Literatur vor dem medizinischen und moraltheologischen Hintergrund der Zeit. Dusseldorf: Stern Verlag Jansen & Co., 1975.

Cassirer, Ernst. *The Individual and the Cosmos in Renaissance Philosophy.* 1927; rpt. Philadelphia: Univ. of Pennsylvania Press, 1963.

Chambers, Frank M. "The ensehamen-sirventes of Bertran de Paris." In *Mélanges de linguistique et de littérature romanes à la mémoire d'Istvan Frank.* n.p.: Universität des Saarlandes, 1957. 129–40.

———. *Proper Names in the Lyrics of the Troubadours.* Chapel Hill: Univ. of North Carolina Press, 1971.

Cherchi, Paolo. *Andrea Cappellano i trovatori e altri temi romanzi.* Rome: Bulzoni editore, 1979.

Clark, David L. "Optics for Preachers: The *De oculo morali* by Peter of Limgoes." *Michigan Academician: Papers of the Michican Academy of Science, Arts, and Letters*, 9 (1977), 329–43.

Coleman, Robert. "Structure and Intention in the Metamorphoses." *Classical Quarterly*, N.S. 21 (1971), 461–77.

Cormier, Raymond J. *One Heart One Mind: The Rebirth of Virgil's Hero in Medieval French Romance.* Romance Monographs. University, Miss.: n.p., 1973.

Corte, Francesco della. "L'idea della preistoria Varrone." In *Atti del Congresso Internazionale di Studi Varroniani.* Rieti: Centro di Studi Varroniani, 1976, 111–36.

Demats, Paule. "D'Amoenitas à Deduit: André le Chapelain et Guillaume de Lorris." In *Mélanges de Langue et de littérature du moyen âge et de la renaissance offerts à Jean Frappier.* 2 vols. Geneva: Droz, 1970. I, 217–33.

———. *Fabula: Trois études de mythographie antique et médiévale.* Geneva: Droz, 1973.

Doran, Madeleine. "Some Renaissance Ovids." In *Literature and Society.* Ed. Bernice Slote. Lincoln: Univ. of Nebraska Press, 1964. 44–61.

Dörrie, Heinrich. "Echo und Narzissus (Ovid, Met. III:341- 510) Psychologische Fiktion in Spiel und Ernst." *Der Altsprachliche Unterricht*, 10 (1967), 54–75.

Dragonetti, Roger. "Dante et Narcisse ou les faux-monnayeurs de l'image." *Revue des études Italiennes*, 1–3 (1965), 5–146.

Dronke, Peter. *Fabula: Explorations in the Uses of Myth in Medieval Platonism.* Leiden: E. J. Brill, 1974.

———. *Poetic Individuality in the Middle Ages: New Departures in Poetry 1000–1150.* Oxford: Clarendon Press, 1970.

———. *Medieval Latin and the Rise of European Love-Lyric.* 2 vols. Oxford: Clarendon Press, 1968.

Duby, George. *The Chivalrous Society.* Berkeley: Univ. of California Press, 1977.

Durling, Robert M. *The Figure of the Poet.* Cambridge: Harvard Univ. Press, 1965.

Eberle, Patricia J. "The Lover's Glass: Nature's Discourse on Optics and the Optical Design of the Romance of the Rose." *Univ. of Toronto Quarterly*, 46 (1977), 241–62.

Elliott, Kathleen O. and J. P. Elder. "A Critical Edition of the Vatican Mythographers." *Transactions of the American Philological Association*, 78 (1947), 189–207.

Engels, Joseph. *Études sur L'Ovide moralisé*. Groningen: J. B. Wolters, 1945.

Etymologisches Wörterbuch der französischen Sprache. Ed. Ernst Gemillscheg. Heidelberg: Carl Winter, 1968.

Faral, Edmond. *Les Arts Poétiques du XIIe et du XIIIe siècles*. Paris: Librairie Ancienne Honoré Champion, 1924.

Favati, Guido. "Una traccia di cultura neoplatonica in Chrétien de Troyes: Il tema degli occhi come specchio." In *Studi in onore di Carlo Pellegrini*. Turin: Biblioteca de studi francesi-Società editrice internazionale, 1963. 3–13.

Fleming, John V. *The Roman de la Rose: A Study in Allegory and Iconography*. Princeton: Princeton Univ. Press, 1969.

Fränkel, Herman. *Ovid: A Poet between Two Worlds*. Berkeley: Univ. of California Press, 1945.

Frappier, Jean. "Variations sur le Thème du Miroir, de Bernard de Ventadour à Maurice Scève." *Cahier de l'association internationale des études françaises*, 11 (1959), 134–58.

Freeman, Michelle A. "Problems in Romance Composition: Ovid, Chrétien de Troyes, and the *Romance of the Rose*." *Romance Philology*, 30 (1976), 118–68.

Freud, Sigmund. *General Psychological Theory*. New York: Collier Books, 1963.

Fuchs, Hans-Jürgen. *Entfremdung und Narzißmus: Semantische Untersuchungen zur Geschichte der Selbstbezogenheit als Vorgeschichte von französisch 'amour-propre,'*. Stuttgart: J. B. Metzler, 1977.

Fyler, John M. *Chaucer and Ovid*. New Haven: Yale Univ. Press, 1979.

Galinsky, Karl G. *Ovid's Metamorphoses: An Introduction to the Basic Aspects*. Berkeley: Univ. of California Press, 1975.

Ghisalberti, Fausto. "Medieval Biographies of Ovid." *Journal of the Warburg and Courtauld Institutes*, 9 (1946), 1–110.

Goldin, Frederick. *The Mirror of Narcissus in the Courtly Love Lyric*. Ithaca: Cornell Univ. Press, 1967.

Greene, Thomas M. *The Descent from Heaven: A Study in Epic Continuity*. New Haven: Yale Univ. Press, 1963.

Gunn, Alan M. *The Mirror of Love: A Reinterpretation of the Romance of the Rose*. Lubbock: Texas Tech, 1952.

Harlaub, Friedrich. *Zauber des Spiegels: Geschichte und Bedeutung des Spiegels in der Kunst*. Munich: R. Piper & Co., 1951.

Hill, Thomas D. "Narcissus, Pygmalion, and the Castration of Saturn: Two Mythographical Themes in the Roman de la Rose." *Studies in Philology*, 71 (1974), 404–26.

Homans, Peter. *Jung in Context: Modernity and the Making of a Psychology*. Chicago: Univ. of Chicago Press, 1979.

Jackson, W. T. H. "The *De amore* of Andreas Capellanus and the Practice of Love at Court." *Romanic Review*, 49 (1958), 243–51.

Jacobson, Howard. *Ovid's Heroides*. Princeton: Princeton Univ. Press, 1974.

Jauss, Hans Robert. *Alterität under Modernität der Mittelalterlichen Literatur*. Munich: Wilhelm Fink, 1977.

———. "Entstehung und Strukturwandel der allegorischen Dichtung." In *Grundriss der romanischen Literaturen des Mittelalters*. Heidelberg: Carl Winter, 1968. VI, 146–244.

Jeauneau, Edouard. *Lectio Philosophorum: Recherches sur l'école de Chartes*. Amsterdam: Adolf M. Hakkert, 1973.

Kayser, Wolfgang, *Das Sprachliche Kunstwerk*. 2nd ed. Bern: Francke Verlag, 1967.

Kelly, Douglas. *Medieval Imagination: Rhetoric and the Poetry of Courtly Love*. Madison: Univ. of Wisconsin Press, 1978.

Kenney, E. J. "The Style of the Metamorphoses." In *Ovid*. Ed. J. W. Binns. London: Routledge & Kegan Paul, 1973. 116–53.

Kirk, G. S. *The Nature of Greek Myths*. Harmondsworth: Penguin Books, 1974.

Kohut, Heinz. *The Analysis of the Self: A Systematic Approach to the Psychoanalytic Treatment of Narcissistic Personality Disorders*. The Psychoanalytic Study of the Child, 4. New York: Universities Press, 1971.

Köhler, Erich. "Narcisse, La Fontaine d'Amors et Guillaume de Lorris." In *L'Humanisme médiévale dans les littératures romanes du XIIe au XIVe siècle*. Ed. Anthime Fourrier. Paris: Librairie Klincksieck, 1964. 147–64.

Lafaye, Georges. *Les Métamorphoses d'Ovide et leur modèles grecs*. Paris, 1904; rpt. Hildesheim: Georg Olms, 1971.

Langlois, Ernest. *Origines et sources du Roman de la Rose*. Bibliothèque es écoles françaises d'Athènes et de Rome, fasc. 58. Paris: n.p., 1891.

LeClerc, Jean. *Monks and Love in Twelfth-Century France*. Oxford: Clarendon Press, 1979.

Leach, Eleanor Winsor. *Virgil's Eclogues: Landscapes of Experience*. Ithaca: Cornell Univ. Press, 1974.

Lehmann-Hartleben, Karl. "The 'Imagines' of the Elder Philostratus." *The Art Bulletin*, 23 (1941), 16–44.

Lida de Makiel, Maria Rosa. *L'Idée de la gloire dans la tradition occidentale* (*Antiquité, Moyen-Âge occidentale, Castile*). Paris: Librairie C. Klincksieck, 1968.

Lewis, C. S. *The Allegory of Love: A Study in Medieval Tradition*. London, 1936; rpt. New York: Oxford Univ. Press, 1958.

Lindberg, David C. "The Science of Optics." In *Science in the Middle Ages*. Ed. David C. Lindberg. Chicago: Univ. of Chicago Press, 1978. 338–68.

———. *Theories of Vision from Al-Kindi to Kepler*. Chicago: Univ. of Chicago Press, 1976.

Ludwig, Walter. *Struktur und Einheit der Metamorphosen Ovids*. Berlin: W. de Gruyter, 1965.

McGregor, James H. "Ovid at School: From the Ninth Century to the Fifteenth Century." *Classical Folia*, 37 (1978), 29–51.

Manitius, Max. "Beiträge zur Geschichte des Ovidius und andrer römischer Schriftsteller im Mittelalter." *Philologus* (Supplement Band), 7 (1899), 721–68.

Martini, Edgar. *Einleitung zu Ovid*. Darmstadt: Wissenschaftliche Buchgesellschaft, 1970.

Menzione, Antonio. *Ovidio: Le Metamorfosi*. Turin: Biblioteca della revesta di studi classici, 1964.

Mieleitner, Karl. "Geschichte der Mineralogie im Altertum und Mittelalter." *Fortschritte der Mineralogie, Kristallographie, und Petrographie*, 7 (1922), 427–80.

Momigliano, Arnaldo. "Time in Ancient Historiography." In *Essays in Ancient and Modern Historiography*. Middletown: Wesleyan Univ. Press, 1977. 179–204.

Munari, Franco. *Ovid im Mittelalter*. Zurich: Artemis, 1960.

Murphy, James J. *Rhetoric in the Middle Ages*. Berkeley: Univ. of California Press, 1974.

Murrin, Michael. *The Allegorical Epic: Essays in Its Rise and Decline*. Chicago: Univ. of Chicago Press, 1980.

———. *The Veil of Allegory: Some Notes Toward a Theory of Allegorical Rhetoric in the English Renaissance*. Chicago: Univ. of Chicago Press, 1969.

Otis, Brooks. "The *Argumenta* of the So-Called Lactantius." *Harvard Studies in Classical Philology*, 47 (1936), 131–63.

———. *Ovid as an Epic Poet*. 2nd rev. ed. Cambridge: Cambridge Univ. Press, 1970.

Panofsky, Erwin. *Renaissance and Renascences in Western Art*. Stockholm, 1960; rpt. New York: Icon-Harper and Row, 1972.

Paré, Gérard. *Les Idées et les lettres au XIIIe siècle: Le Roman de la Rose*. Université de Montréal Bibliothèque de Philosophie, 1. Montréal: Edition le centre de psychologie et de pédogie, 1947.

———. *Le Roman de la Rose et la Scolastique Courtoise*. Paris: Librairie Philosophique J. Vrin, 1941.

Parry, Hugh. "Ovid's Metamorphoses: Violence in a Pastoral Landscape." *Transactions and Proceedings of the American Philological Society*, 95 (1964), 268–82.

Pellegrin, Élisabeth. "Les 'Remedia amoris' d'Ovide, texte scolaire médiévale." *Bibliothèque de l'école des Chartres*, 115 (1957), 172–79.

Pépin, Jean. *Mythe et Allégorie: les origines grecques et les contestations judéo-chrétiennes*. 2nd rev. ed. Paris: Etudes Augustiniennes, 1976.

Picone, Michelangelo. "Dante e il mito di Narciso del Roman de la Rose alla Commedia." *Romanische Forschungen*, 89 (1977), 382- 97.

Poirion, Daniel. "Narcisse et Pygmalion dans le Roman de la Rose." In *Essays in Honor of Louis Francis Solano*. Ed. Raymond J. Cormier and Urban T. Holmes. Chapel Hill: Univ. of North Carolina Press, 1970. 153–65.

Popkin, Richard H. *The History of Scepticism from Erasmus to Spinoza*. Berkeley: Univ. of California Press, 1979.

Putnam, Michael C. J. *Virgil's Poem of the Earth: Studies in the Georgics*. Princeton: Princeton Univ. Press, 1979.

Quain, E. A. "The Medieval Accessus ad Auctores." *Traditio*, 3 (1945), 215–64.

Rathbone, Eleanor. "Master Alberic of London: 'Mythographus Tertius Vaticanus.'" *Medieval and Renaissance Studies*, 1 (1941- 43), 35–38.
Rand, E. K. *Ovid and His Influence*. Boston: Longmans, Green and Co., 1928.
Robertson, D. W., Jr. *A Preface to Chaucer: Studies in Medieval Perspectives*. Princeton: Princeton Univ. Press, 1962.
———. "The Subject of the 'De Amore' of Andreas Capellanus." *Modern Philology*, 50 (1950–51), 145–61.
Robson, C. A. "Dante's Use in the *Divina commedia* of the Medieval Allegories on Ovid." In *Centenary Essays on Dante*. Oxford: Clarendon Press, 1965. 1–38.
Rollinson, Philip. *Classical Theories of Allegory and Christian Culture*. Pittsburgh: Duquesnes Univ. Press, 1981.
Rosen, Edward. "The Invention of Eye Glasses." *Journal of The History of Medicine and Allied Sciences*, 11 (1956), 13–46; 183–218.
Santini, Lea Ritter. "La Favola di Echo: Langue et parole." In *Retorica e critica letteraria*. Ed. Lea Ritter Santini and Ezio Raimondi. Bologna: Società editrice il Mulino, 1978, 151–78.
Schmitt, Charles B. *Cicero Scepticus: A Study of the Influence of the 'Academica' in the Renaissance*. The Hague: Martinus Nijhoff, 1972.
Segal, Charles. *Landscape in Ovid's Metamorphoses: A Study in the Transformation of a Literary Symbol. Hermes Zeitschrift für klassische Philologie*, 23. Wiesbaden: Franz Steiner Verlag, 1969.
Schevill, Rudolph. *Ovid and the Renaissance in Spain*. Univ. of California Publications in Modern Philology, 4. 1913; rpt. New York: Georg Olms, 1971.
Schickel, Joachim. "Narziss: Zu Versen von Ovid." *Antaios*, 3 (1962), 486–96.
Seznec, Jean. *The Survival of the Pagan Gods*. Trans. Barbara Sessions. Princeton: Princeton Univ. Press, 1953.
Silverstein, Theodore. "The Fabulous Cosmogony of Bernardus Silvestris." *Modern Philology*, 46 (1948–49), 92–116.
Skulsky, Harold. *Metamorphoses: The Mind in Exile*. Cambridge: Harvard Univ. Press, 1981.
Smalley, Beryl. *English Friars and Antiquity in the Early Fourteenth Century*. Oxford: Basil Blackwell, 1960.
Snell, Bruno. "The Discovery of a Spritual Landscape." In *Virgil: A Collection of Critical Essays*. Ed. Steele Commanger. Engelwood Cliffs, N.J.: Prentice-Hall, 1966, 14–27.
Spitzer, Leo. "Addresses to the Reader in the *Commedia*." *Italica*, 32 (1955), 143–65.
———. *Romanische Literaturstudien 1936–56*. Tübingen: Max Niemeyer Verlag, 1959.
Spotnitz, Hyman and Phillip Resnikoff. "The Myths of Narcissus." *Psychoanalytic Review*, 41 (1954), 173–81.
Steen, Otto Due. *Changing Forms: Studies in the Metamorphoses of Ovid*. Copenhagen: Gyldendal, 1974.
Steenberghen, Fernand van. *Aristotle in the West*. 2nd ed. Lowvain: Nauwelaerts Publishing House, 1970.

Stock, Brian. *Myth and Science in the Twelfth Century: A Study of Bernard Silvestris*. Princeton: Princeton Univ. Press, 1972.

Sugerman, Shirley. *Sin and Madness: Studies in Narcissism*. Philadelphia: Westminster Press, 1976.

Traube, Ludwig. *Vorlesungen und Abhandlungen: Einleitung in die lateinische Philologie des Mittelalters*. 3 vols. Ed. P. Lehman. Munich: C. H. Beck'sche Verlagsbuchhandlung, 1909–20.

Viarre. Simone. *Ovide: Essai de Lecture Poétique*. Collection d'Etudes Latines, fasc. 33. Paris: Société d'Edition les Belles Lettres, 1976.

———. *La Survie d'Ovide dans la littérature scientifique des XIIe et XIIIe siècles*. Publications du centre d'études supérieures de civilisation médiévale, IV. Poitiers: Université de Poitiers, 1966.

Vinge, Louise. *The Narcissus Theme in Western Literature up to the Early 19th Century*. Lund: Gleerups, 1967.

Weinberg, Bernard. *A History of Literary Criticism in the Italian Renaissance*. 2 vols. Chicago: Univ. of Chicago Press, 1961.

Weisstein, Ulrich. *Comparative Literature and Literary Theory*. Bloomington: Univ. of Indiana Press, 1973.

Wetherbee, Winthrop. "The Literal and the Allegorical: Jean de Meun and the 'de Planctu Naturae.'" *Medieval Studies*, 33 (1971), 264–91.

———. *Platonism and Poetry in the Twelfth Century: The Literary Influence of the School of Chartres*. Princeton: Princeton Univ. Press, 1972.

White, Lynn. "The Medieval Roots of Modern Technology and Science." In *Medieval Religion and Technology: Collected Essays*. Berkeley: Univ. of California Press, 1978. 75–91.

Wieseler, Friedrich. *Narkissos: Eine kunstmythologische Abhandlung nebst einem Anhang über den Narcissen und ihre Bezeihung im Leben, Mythos und Cultus der Griechen*. Göttingen: Dietrich'schen Buchhandlung, 1856.

———. *Die Nymphe Echo: Eine kunstmythologische Abhandlung*. Göttingen: Dietrich'schen Buchhandlung, 1844.

Wilkinson, L. P. *The Georgics of Virgil: A Critical Survey*. Cambridge: Cambridge Univ. Press, 1969.

———. *Ovid Recalled*. Cambridge: Cambridge Univ. Press, 1955.

———. "The World of the *Metamorphoses*." In *Ovidiana: Recherches sur Ovide*. Ed. N. I. Herescu. Paris: Société d'Editions les Belles Lettres, 1958. 231–44.

Wolfson, Harry Austryn. "The Internal Senses in Latin, Arabic, and Hebrew Philosophic Texts." *Harvard Theological Review*, 28 (1935), 69–133.

Name Index